LITERARY AND RELIGIOUS PRACTICES IN MEDIEVAL AND EARLY MODERN INDIA

Literary and Religious Practices in Medieval and Early Modern India

Edited by

RAZIUDDIN AQUIL

DAVID L. CURLEY

MANOHAR

2026

First published 2016

Reprinted 2026

ISBN 978-93-5098-136-8

Published by
Ajay Kumar Jain *for*
Manohar Publishers & Distributors
4753/23 Ansari Road, Daryaganj,
New Delhi 110 002

Typeset by
Ravi Shanker
Delhi 110 095

Printed at
Replika Press Pvt. Ltd.

Contents

Preface

Covering the history of medieval and early modern India, from the eighth to the eighteenth centuries, this volume is part of a new series of collections of essays publishing current research on all aspects of polity, society, economy, religion and culture. The thematically organized volumes will particularly serve as a platform for younger scholars to showcase their new research and, thus, reflect current thrusts in the study of the period. Established experts in their specialized fields are also being invited to share their work and provide perspectives. The geographical limits will be historic India, roughly corresponding to modern South Asia and the adjoining regions.

This series of essay collections will, thus, provide a forum where some of the best researches on medieval and early modern India can be published at regular intervals. Mr Ramesh Jain and his able staff at Manohar Publishers & Distributors, are bringing out these volumes. Two collections currently being planned include a volume on Sufism, bringing together contributions on Sufi sources, historiographical analysis of existing research, and fresh study of themes relating to Sufism in the Indian Subcontinent. Another volume on religion and political culture, focuses on critical connections between religion and politics, significance of the intermeshing of religious and political ideas in statecraft, religious justifications not only of political conquests, but also of governance, roles of men of religion (*ulama*, Sufis, *yogis*, *gurus*, Brahmins) as power-brokers or legitimizers of political authority as well as violent claims to authority between political and spiritual power-holders, significance of religious shrines as political symbols, medieval rulers' inability to disentangle the interconnections between the affairs of the 'church' and the state, etc.

As part of this project, chapters in the current volume cover a wide variety of connected themes of crucial importance to the understanding of literary and historical traditions, religious practices and encounters as well as intermingling of religion and politics over a long period in Indian history. The contributors to the volume comprise some fine historians of the present generation working in institutions across South Asia, Europe and the United States. It is also a matter of great pleasure to have a veteran scholar of literary and religious texts, Professor David Curley, as co-editor of the volume, who besides providing valuable guidance, has also contributed a chapter on local and popular historical memories as significant material for the history of the eastern Bengal region in the eighteenth century.

RAZIUDDIN AQUIL

Introduction

Literary and Religious Practices

RAZIUDDIN AQUIL AND DAVID L. CURLEY

Some Historiographical Concerns

The essays in this volume comprise histories that use religious or literary texts. The authors explore a variety of practices that made it possible for the texts to be created, to circulate, and to shape beliefs, sentiments, and institutions. Religious and literary texts often were received as 'documents' and 'histories' in their own contexts. They preserved authoritative stories about the past, and retold them to comment on the present.

Of course, religious beliefs and texts that justify them have been central to all societies across the centuries of medieval and early modern history. In the field of medieval and early modern history of South Asia, however, to take religious and literary texts seriously represents a departure from some usual practices of history as a social science. We have in mind the preference for causal explanations over explanations that relate parts to a larger whole, the preference therefore for documents that can be thought to record objective facts, the distrust of 'subjective' and 'fictive' aspects of narrative history, and the preference especially for causal explanations based on demographic, economic, or ecological systems and relations (White 1987, compare Braudel 1980).

When academic historians discuss contentious religious issues in medieval and early modern times, the sentiments and perspectives of current issues and debates tend to frame their discussions and are imposed upon the past, so that remarkable differences of the past from the present are elided. In particular, strongly held beliefs about the 'naturalness' of religious conflict in medieval South Asia shape what is popularly accepted now as 'true' and 'factual' history. Based on strict standards of evidence accepted by their profession, academic historians can label much in popular discourse about South Asian religion in the past as 'myth', 'legend', or 'fiction'. Should academic historians attempt to intervene politically? When they have intervened to correct popular history, however, they often have been accused of being partisan against religion. Is it possible for historians to be unbiased in their approach to history-writing about religion, even when dealing with contentious issues about which religious communities feel sensitive?

While popularly accepted 'myths' and 'legends' about medieval South Asia often have been ignored or dismissed by academic historians, the space so vacated has been enthusiastically occupied by 'popular' historians, religious leaders, and politicians. One task of academic history should be to analyse the history of changing beliefs, including both religious and those about the past, and to consider them in relation to changing contexts.

Outside of history departments, in the fields of literary studies and history of religion, many fine studies have been produced on both religious and secular literature in medieval and early modern South Asia. These studies have treated texts from classical and vernacular languages of South Asia, and they have treated texts belonging to each of the major religious traditions, as well as texts claimed by several religions at once, texts that maintained a strict independence from all accepted orthodoxies, and secular texts claimed by no religion (for an introduction to languages and texts, see Pollock 2003). Perhaps what historians can best contribute to the discussion of literary texts is rigorous criticism of the situations in which they were produced, careful comparison of texts whose contextual relations have escaped notice, and careful attention to changing rules for the production, reception, and institutionalization of genres over time.

For example, in a study that ranges from the sixteenth century to the present, Ramya Sreenivasan (2007) has written about changing traditions of the legend of Padmini. Her legend was first composed both as a Sufi allegory about love for God, and as a heroic romance related to pre-Mughal politics in north India. Emphasizing Rajput heroism, quite different versions of the Padmini legend subsequently were produced at Jain and Rajput courts, and even in faraway Arakan. In the nineteenth-century, Rajput 'histories' in turn were synthesized by James Todd, who gave new emotional colour to the final 'tragic' act of self-immolation by Padmini and other Rajput women. For modern Hindu nationalists Padmini thus came to be both a 'real' historical woman, and 'a perfect model of ideal Indian womanhood' because she fought against an evil Muslim king.

Another very interesting approach has been to compare public spaces and 'historical memories' created by literary and oral histories, and their changing interactions. Using this approach Prachi Deshpande (2007) and Chitralekha Zutshi (2014) have written about the profound changes in history writing in Maharashtra and Kashmir respectively. Deshpande is concerned with historical traditions that have come to be used to project Hindus and Muslims as natural enemies. On the other hand, Zutshi argues that in Kashmir, local Persian histories and traditions of oral story-telling continued to tell legends of the origin of Kashmir first told in Sanskrit. Through most of the nineteenth-century alternative versions of familiar 'legends' explained the creation of Kashmir as a sacred place, and circulated it in the public which included both Muslims and Hindus. But in the twentieth-century historians redefined the Sanskrit *Rajatarangini* as a classical Hindu Indian history text, and not a Kashmiri history, while the Dogra dynasty withdrew its patronage of Persian language and literature, thus severing a centuries long bridge between Sanskrit and Persian histories, and between them and oral story-telling in Kashmiri.

Much good research on literary texts and their histories is happening in North America and Europe, but new subjects, methods, and discoveries are often ignored in Indian researches and teaching, except in the field of research on popular and vernacular histories, both precolonial and colonial (for the latter see also: Ali 1999; Rao, Shulman, and Subrahmanyam 2003; Aquil and Chatterjee 2008; Chatterjee 2009). The problem is not merely a concern for historians of pre-colonial India. Can South Asian literature, in many different languages and genres, be brought within the ambit of historical research in colonial and modern history? How well are scholars of colonial and modern history linguistically equipped to delimit and understand cultural transformations in the nineteenth century from the period immediately preceding it?

Popular myths about Indian history, especially on questions of religion and identity, attract harsh criticism, but professional historians also need some soul searching. Despite more than sixty years of investment in history as a discipline in independent India, the general public remains historically uneducated. One may also like to ask what exactly historians are doing that has international importance in terms of knowledge production? Where does Indian history exist in relation to global standards of historical research? Experts on medieval India need to reflect on the state of their historiography even in relation to other fields within Indian history. How often do we peddle the same old stuff and block fresh thinking by younger scholars, with the result that a civilized and rational discussion of new thinking becomes impossible? Much as the upsurge of right-wing censorship in education and in scholarly publication is justifiably lamented, censorship of the same kind unfortunately happens even within liberal academia.

A great deal that was written about medieval India in the late nineteenth and early twentieth century has turned out to be inaccurate, incomplete and even downright false and misleading. We now understand that to justify British rule, colonial historians made broad and untenable generalizations about the lawless tyranny of Brahmins and Indian states over the weak, and about habits of servile submission, inveterate dishonesty, and moral and cultural decadence in 'pre-colonial' India. Is it not also possible that many current assumptions about Indian history are stereotypes relevant only to the politics of the present? Fifty years from now, in new contexts, historians may laugh at the irrationalities of our time. Opinions contrary to those now dominant may turn out to be more accurate or more insightful than our own.

Adherents of contemporary political ideologies, to say nothing of political propagandists committed to party interests, presume that only their own understanding of history is true, 'factual' history, and that their opponents' versions are imaginary 'fictions'. They try to establish their understanding of the truth through a variety of strategies, including illogical arguments, personal attacks, and straightforward and obvious forms of academic suppression, as philosopher Akeel Bilgrami (2014) has recently delineated in his exposition on liberalism and the academy. Rather than attempting to establish an absolute truth, Chitralekha Zutshi has recently suggested that we frankly admit the existence of 'mutually contested historical narratives with no possibility of ultimate resolution or verifiability' (2014: 314). What happens to standards of truth in history if we allow that a variety of approaches and perspectives to history can be valid? Is it too much to expect from historians that we attempt to provide an approximate representation of the human past in all its dimensions, sources permitting, even if dominant politics of the time dictate otherwise? Academic historians can and usually do begin by insisting on careful and skeptical criticism of the provenance of our sources, before going on to the work of deciding which questions we can and should ask, and how we can generalize about them, and connect our sources to larger issues.

One problem in writing history pertains to the connection between ideology and how historians configure historical evidence. Religious and political ideologies deeply affect the questions historians ask, and how we write historical essays and narratives. Competing ideologies, such as imperialism and nationalism in the colonial period, and Marxism, secular liberalism, and religious nationalism in more recent times, have produced alternative 'schools' of historiography. Schools of historiography in turn seek to denigrate and thwart each other, both rhetorically and in practice. On the other hand, the rhetoric of a politically neutral and strictly empirical approach to history, representing itself as nothing beyond what the evidence suggests, often masked the dominant ideology of the colonial state. Anti-colonial historians produced in turn a counter-rhetoric that sought to unmask hidden interests served by historical empiricism, and to assert evidence for 'emotional truths' knowable only by historians who belong to the nation, religion, or social group about which they write (Chatterjee, in Aquil and Chatterjee 2008: 1-24). Perhaps writing history has always been a weapon in political struggles.

Some of the debates in medieval Indian history that have been shaped by ideological struggles or identity politics include the level of rents extracted by medieval and early modern states, the incidence of violence against non-Muslims in states ruled by Muslims, the incidence and significance of desecration of temples, and other non-Muslim sites of worship and study, and the role of Sufis in conversion of non-Muslims to Islam, versus the role of Sufis in the inclusion of non-Muslims at Sufi shrines, and in making a 'pluralistic' society. Thus, the study of history is not only about what probably happened in the past, but it is also about competing claims for counter-factual alternatives: what might have happened, or what should have happened.

Political pressures and political appointments will also continue. After all, conquerors have always written histories on the bodies of those they have vanquished. The UPA/NDA governments determining and sponsoring divergent kinds of politically-motivated histories, not only at the level of school textbooks but also by controlling academic institutions, is now a matter of routine, seriously affecting the autonomy of the discipline of history.

Furthermore, more crucial and disappointing is factional politics within academia, often of a very petty kind: the use of power experienced in struggles over the topics of PhD theses, research grants and fellowships, over control of journals and publishing houses, over appointments, syllabus revisions, and reading lists, and in arbitrary decisions about course allotments and requirements for promotion. For those at the receiving end of academic power relations, there can be a long period of frustration; and once senior dons retire, the next generation takes over and repeats the same pattern.

Languages, Literatures, and Permeable Boundaries

In medieval India, some of the masterpieces of classical Hindi literature are written by Muslim writers on themes related to Islam and Muslim cultural practices. Medieval Islamic association with Arabic and Persian languages has justifiably been recognized in literary and intellectual histories, but the emergence of a vast and fascinating corpus of Indic vernacular literature and its association with Islam in medieval India has not been adequately appreciated. Of a variety of Indian languages, in which a whole range of literary compositions emerged by fifteenth and sixteenth centuries, Hindvi, or Hindi, was not only understood and spoken in large parts of the subcontinent, but it was also the language used in many complex literary productions.

Though Islamic theoretical and political discussions could still be accessed in Arabic and Persian, Sufis and other Muslim holy men were being heard, already in the thirteenth and fourteenth centuries, speaking languages such as Punjabi and Bengali, besides what is now identified as Hindi/Urdu. Of particular significance is the composition of a huge body of Sufi poetry of love (*premakhyan*), in Awadhi dialect of medieval Hindi. Beginning with Mulla Daud's *Chandayan* as early as fourteenth century and reaching its climax with Malik Muhammad Jaisi's *Padmavat* in the sixteenth century, with a large number of other scintillating examples in-between and later, this literature could captivate Muslims and non-Muslims alike. Jaisi's voluminous text also appropriated almost the entire Awadhi *Ram-Katha* then very popular with the public.

Thirty years later, this was indeed the inspiration for Tulsidas to garner all the glories with his Awadhi text par excellence, *Ramcharitamanas*. Smarting under their own pedantry of classical Sanskrit, the *pundits* of Banaras must have scoffed at Tulsidas for what they thought was a perversion of sorts, but the latter had the satisfaction not only of seeing its wide circulation amongst a large public of Ram-*bhakts*, but also had patrons in powerful Mughal quasi-officials, or *mansabdars*. Tulsidas and his work could easily fit the cultural taste of stalwarts like Todarmal and Man Singh. The biggest patron of Awadhi and Braj corpus of Hindi, both *bhakti* (devotional) and *riti* (erotic courtly) variety, was Abdur Rahim Khan-i-Khanan, a multilingual polyglot, with considerable political clout as a foster son of Emperor Akbar.

Hindi was, indeed, the *lingua franca* of Mughal India. The Mughal court being located at the centre of Braj Mandal, the dialect of the region, Braj, came to occupy an important place as the language of the court. Modern historians of Mughal India have conventionally portrayed Persian as the language of power and dominance, but, as literary historian Allison Busch (2011) has put it, Hindi is hidden in plain view of those who are obsessed with Persian in medieval India, as they are with English in modern times. It is naïve to imagine that influential Mughal nobles and cultural personalities such as Todarmal, Birbal, Man Singh, Tansen, and Surdas transacted their private and public businesses only in Persian.

Much as a certain degree of Persianization happened in many fields over five-six centuries, it will be absurd to assume that people in the bazaars of Jaunpur, or even in Agra and Delhi, would speak Persian—the status of the language was somewhat like English today, a language of the power-elite and international discursive engagements. One doubts very much, however, whether even someone like Akbar would speak to the visiting foreign dignitaries in Persian (the official language of the empire) or in Turkish (his mother tongue). While Abul Fazl, his brother Faizi, and Abdur Rahim could engage with the visitors in their own languages, Akbar himself could be comfortable in Hindustani—whether in quiet contemplation or when emotionally overwhelmed.

Before the nineteenth-century colonial divide, it was possible for leading Muslim intellectuals and theologians in Delhi to call their language 'Hindi' and even translate the Holy Koran in that language. At that time, the Persianized language of poetry was called Rekhta, or mixed language, and the more deeply rooted (*theth*) language of prose was referred to as Hindi. The imposition of Sanskritized Hindi in Devanagari script for Hindus and Persianized-Arabicized Urdu in Persian script for Muslims had not come about yet. Still, when a history of Hindi literature is written, even the most prejudiced authors are unable to completely bypass the Awadhi *premakhyan* or altogether ignore the seminal Mughal contribution to the growth of Braj corpus. On the other hand, the Urdu field, now identified with Muslims alone, is still learning to come to terms with a tradition torn asunder (for more on the history of these difficulties, see Orsini 2010).

Earlier, led by reformers from lower sections of society, several strands of medieval Bhakti movements condemned religious rituals, criticized caste or *jati*-based hierarchies and discrimination and advocated the need to discover Ram, the formless God inside one's heart. Some traditions of *bhakti* are also identified as Hindu religious movements, revolving around Sri Ram of Ayodhya as an epitome of virtues, and juxtaposed with forms of popular Islamic spirituality identified as Sufism. Though saint-poets such as Kabir and Guru Nanak transcended contentious political boundaries of Islam and Hinduism, religious fields were often marred by violent formations of communities. The *gurus* were involved in a competitive spirituality of sorts and often fed off each other, in terms of appropriating ideas and attracting followers, not necessarily to organize them as sparring communities.

In many cases, however, the followers completely transformed the original teachings of their spiritual *gurus*, and communities (*panths* and *sampradays*) that formed around them often sought to use political power to demean and subdue each other. Memories of terrible struggles between Muslim and non-Muslim followers of Kabir and Nanak over their dead bodies are a case in point. These saintly figures, who challenged religious boundary-markers and hypocrisies, were to be buried or cremated depending upon which group dominated the funeral proceedings. It was in the fitness of things that the bodies disappeared, by miracle or design, so that these fine souls could not be easily trapped into the politics of religious identities (for some of the details of these contestations, see Aquil 2009).

One of the most respected scholars of Bhakti movements, David Lorenzen (2010) has recently explored the question of religious identities (Hindu, Muslim, Yogi and Sant) in the teachings of Gorakhnath and Kabir. Though much of the lives and teachings of both Gorakhnath and Kabir remain shrouded in legends, it is possible to cull out some of the essence of their teachings through compositions attributed to them since medieval times. Gorakhnath may have lived in the period between eleventh-twelfth centuries and some of his religious ideas, subsequently compiled in *Gorakhbani*, are significant in the current context of the politics of Hindutva.

As an accomplished *yogi*, Gorakhnath distinguished himself from formal and ritualistic Hindu traditions and considered himself closer to Sufi-oriented Islam. He says: he originated as a Hindu, matured as *yogi* and was a Muslim by intellect (*utpati hindu jaranam yogi akli pari musalmanin*). Paying tribute to Muslim intellect might seem a contradiction in terms in these times of all-round deterioration, but Gorakhnath lived in an age when Muslims were still setting standards of excellence in many fields of expertise. Though Gorakhnath, like Kabir subsequently, could notice how the ignorant guardians of Islam (*mullas* and *qazis*) were unable to follow the correct path (*raah*), he recognized that through established spiritual practices and deep contemplation the Sufi *dervishes* were able to discover the door to the house of the Lord (*darwesh soi jo dar ki janain*) and, therefore, they belonged to the caste of Allah (*so darwesh alah ki jati*). Several other verses strongly reject Muslim and Hindu rituals and highlight the virtues of a separate and superior yogic tradition.

Anticipating Kabir's iconoclasm, Gorakhnath strongly proclaimed: Hindus worship in temples and Muslims go to mosques, but the *yogis* spend time in meditation in the presence of the omnipotent, where there is neither a temple nor a mosque (*hindu dhyawai dehura musalman masit, yogi dhyawai parmad jahan dehura na masit*). Further distancing himself from both Hindu and Muslim traditions which were based on particular readings of scriptures such as Vedas and Koran, Gorakhnath pointed out that the verses on the secrets of the Supreme Being are understood only by the *yogis*, whereas the rest of the world is lost in this-worldly illusions and enterprise (*te pad janan birla yogi aur duni sab dhandhe laayi*).

Gorakhnath's compositions clearly bring out three distinct religious positions — the dominating and formal Islamic and Hindu traditions as well as the mystical world of the *yogis*, which was confident enough to recognize the value of the mystic path of the Sufis. Preaching in the latter half of the fifteenth and early decades of the sixteenth century, Kabir went a step further. Locating himself right at the centre of the marketplace (*Kabira Khara Bajaar Mein*), the latter sharply criticized not only Hindu and Muslim religious leaders, but also found faults with self-styled Sufis and *yogis*. Kabir criticized the ritual of animal sacrifice among Hindus, but he reserved his choicest language for condemnation of slaughter of animals by Muslims (*bakri murgi kinh phurmaya kiske kahe tum chhuri chalaya . . . din ko roja rahat hai raat hanat hai gai*). For *yogis*, Kabir's advice was that spiritual practices like *pranayama* and other forms of meditations are of no use until the heart of the person concerned is cleansed and Ram is discovered within (all the statements attributed above to Gorakhnath and Kabir are derived from Lorenzen, 2010).

Fresh Insights

The essays in this volume deal with the composition and reception of symbolic representations, and with social practices in literature and religion. In them we have many opportunities to think about writing practices and literary genres in relation to religious boundaries and identities, whether multiple, dual or exclusive (see also Leiberman, 2013). Some of the genres that will be explored are letters, hagiographies, translations or transcreations of sacred texts, and ballads. All of them depended on an archive of other texts and memories, and all tried to maintain and reshape public memories. All of them used configurative devices—symbols and dreams, story, plot and character, parables, and affective and memorable verses, for example—to construct ideas and sentiments that defined religious identities and supported action in their defence.

We also will have many occasions to think particularly about genres of vernacular and academic history in relation to religion. Domains of religion and literature frequently overlapped in the practice of writing vernacular histories of South Asia. Vernacular genres of history perhaps can be placed on a scale that ranges from the factual to the artfully configured, as Rao, Shulman, and Subrahmanyam have suggested (2001: 1-23). However, prosaic genres of history also employ the literary devices of scene, character, and plot, together with more or less 'factuality', to imitate human actions and their consequences in time, while they also depend upon and reinforce an archive of public memories attached to local sites and prominent people of a shared past. Public memories were shared in oral performances as well as in written literature. Religious as well as secular purposes shaped the formation of archives of memory and the choice of vernacular genres, and secular histories as well as religious ones used literary devices to configure narratives and to shape affective responses in their audiences.

Scott Kugle's chapter attempts to explore Sufi attitudes toward homosexuality, by means of Sufi literature about the propriety and spiritual value of the homoerotic devotional practice of 'playing the witness', gazing at a good-looking young boy as a way of seeking union with God, the ultimate beloved. The texts examined are records of discussions between a Chishti shaykh and his disciples, discussions that in turn drew upon a variety of stories and parables, and one public letter of instruction to Sufis at large, a letter that used personal experience, logic, and the authoritative warnings of other Sufis. Kugle finds that these Chishti texts did not employ the many technical legal terms aimed to control social behaviour and define sexual acts as licit or illicit in Islamic jurisprudence. Instead they appear to be more concerned with questions of inner disposition: intention, the presence or absence of lust, and the spiritual condition of the practitioner. These texts exist alongside and in obvious contrast to others that do use the legal terms that define specific acts as lawful or not.

Engagement with love poetry and music in some Sufi hospices relied on an underlying current of eroticism that in the social context of Sufi hospices can be considered homoerotic. Both texts and practices are related to homoerotic sociability and to sexuality in general in pre-modern Sufi hospices, and in South Asian society more broadly. Conflicting texts reveal attitudes and beliefs about both homoerotic sociability and sexuality, especially in relation to Sufi spiritual disciplines. Kugle concludes that homoerotic feelings apparently were accepted as normal by many Chishti saints. Discourse about sexuality was flexible with regard to homosexuality, homoeroticism was accepted, and homosexual acts were not seen as a matter to refer to forensic investigation and legal adjudication. Most Chishti discourse about homoerotic devotional practices was not legalistic or condemnatory, but discourse that supports 'playing the witness' was reticent (or discrete) about homosexual acts. Although homoerotic feelings and relations were not condemned in this relatively sympathetic discourse, they are placed in a moral and spiritual hierarchy that valued sublimation and discipline of sexuality as part of the path to God. Chishti Sufis valued love, but condemned the attitudes of selfishness, possession and domination that were part of a socially constructed experience of sexuality in their society.

Indeed, it seems to be difficult to try to answer questions about 'homosexuality' in pre-modern Islamic societies, as homosexuality is conceived in current discourses. In particular the current discourse about equal rights has been tied closely to a 'natural' homosexual orientation, formed at, or soon after birth as a component of homosexual identity. Pre-modern discourses seem to recognize homoerotic attractions, both as normal in general and as more strongly present in some men than others, especially in the early stages of their spiritual path. Still, homosexual orientation as a fact of birth or as a deep personality trait was not discussed in these pre-modern texts, and it is difficult to see how to retrieve its discussion from them.

Exploring Dashanami ascetics, and especially their military *naga* associates, Matthew Clark's chapter interrogates processes of religious change that involved borrowing from a 'common pool' of practices, a pool to which Sufis and especially their militant and antinomian *qalandar* lineages had contributed. At the same time, change was disguised by projecting borrowed practices back in time to Shankara as the founder of the Dashanami order, and by projecting his authority forward in time to include all new groups who traced a *guru*-disciple relationship back to him. Clark raises questions about the elasticity of religious identities and the permeability of religious boundaries, by examining who defines and what constitutes borrowing from the outside ('syncretism' in the author's terminology), versus what constitutes 'internal' change. Perhaps more important historically is the process of boundary maintenance that allowed for dramatic expansions of Dashanamis to include the roving bands of warrior ascetics. With regard to the contemporary historiography, Clark's essay raises difficult questions about what constitutes adequate evidence for demonstrating influence in historical change. Even though we may not have specific acknowledgements of borrowing by those who made the change, how smaller group identities were subsumed into a larger religious order remains an important issue.

Mridula Jha focuses on a single author, Dara Shikuh, and not on the reception of texts he authored. In his writing career, Dara attempted to preserve the authority of Muslim saints who taught the concept and meditative practices of *wahdat-ul-wujud* (unity of being), and to defend them against their critics. By tracing his rhetoric, Jha explores religious identity in the context of intense controversy concerning the concept of *wahdat-ul-wujud*, and the Sufi practices of meditation related to it. Jha refers to an 'outpouring' in Dara's writing of a 'deluge of sentiments' for his teachers and their lineage. Their characters had all the virtues in balance: they were 'compassionate, magnanimous, independent, learned, perfect and erudite, and yet at the same time practical, humble, polite and heroic'. Sentiments of love, honour and loyalty attached to the lineage, its great men, and their virtues, and sentiments of self-respect and courage in one's own role in maintaining the lineage in the face of opposition probably were some of the supports for the religious identity of those who belonged to the lineage, though more discussion of such sentiments in hagiographies would help. At the end of his life Dara Shikuh also attempted to include among authoritative scriptures, Hindu sacred texts that he thought taught the same concept and practices of *wahdat-ul-wujud*. He translated the principle Upanishads, believing that they also were expressions of 'unity of being' and would help illuminate the esoteric messages in the Koran. And finally he attempted to produce a comparative lexicon of Muslim and Hindu terms based on the idea that all religions teach the same fundamental truths. In Dara's case, as in general, religious identities and boundaries were contested by gaining access to political power, against others who also had access to political power, and Dara eventually lost his life as a result.

Sandhya Sharma's study of the 'Hinduization' of *ketab* (sacred 'books' revealed to prophets) in the Prannath Sampraday is made possible by a two-step statement of equivalence: that *avatar* equals true *guru*, and that *avatar/guru* equals true Prophet. Prannath also taught two, related soteriological ideas, that true *gurus* are reborn, and that the Mahdi, Jesus and the Prophet reborn, will come again before the Day of Judgement to provide salvation to the faithful. In time Prannath claimed to be the Mahdi. We see a context of writing, as Prannath travelled from Gujarat to Sindh, to the Persian Gulf, and on to Iraq, and frequent written communications passed between him and his foremost disciples. Prannath finally returned to Delhi and Rajasthan. There we also see a social gulf that separated him and his followers from the Mughal court, in language, dress, and diet, and in the very idea that Prannath was the Mahdi. Without correctly understanding their relations, Prannath attempted to play Rajput rulers against Aurangzeb. Prannath's claims to divinity, and to reveal (again) a renewed, true and universal religion, as the *gurus* and prophets had done, were the fundamental issues dividing him from orthodox Sunni Muslims. He and his disciples sought to establish these claims through new, revealed scriptures that have 'descended' and are preserved in writing (modelled on the scriptures of Judaism, Christianity and Islam), and by oral preaching and recitations to ordinary people based on scriptures.

The basic source for this chapter is the *Bijak*, a hagiography of Prannath written by Laldas. It is a record of how Prannath won adherents from ordinary people across the country but how he sought and failed to get political support of the rulers for his movement. The *Bijak* seems to be surprisingly unconfigured by retrospective plot; instead we get a detailed chronicle, and, at peak moments of interest in the negotiations with Aurangzeb, almost a day-to-day record. Considered as a chronicle, Laldas' text was possible because of the role and prestige of written communications within the *sampraday*: everything was both communicated and recorded in writing, and copies seem to have been kept. Laldas apparently had access to a rich archive of written communications, and to have followed that archive in his composition. The chronicle-like entries from *Bijak* are very different from miracle stories and parables that we encounter, for example, in hagiographies of Sufi saints in the chapters by Kugle and Jha.

Therefore, we might think of at least three levels of texts: letters, 'translations', and hagiography. If this idea is correct, we might say that in the case of the *Bijak*, writing history based on documents was a religious practice for Laldas, and his hagiography would occupy a position on the 'factual' pole of a genre of texts that usually lie toward a much more configurative pole, to use the terms proposed by Rao, Shulman and Subrahmanyam.

Moving into the 'permeable' littoral zones of eastern Bengal, David Curley notices religious frontiers there were vague or non-existent; rather, the whole sub-region was a 'space of interaction' characterized by ethnic, religious and cultural diversity. Curley discusses the relatively oral genres of romantic and historical ballads in relation to two purposes, maintaining public memories, and representing and negotiating social boundaries. Socially transgressive marriages were chosen as subjects for romantic ballads because they helped audiences negotiate contested social boundaries. They encouraged audiences to balance sentiments in favour of personal independence and romantic love on the one hand, and family and social bonds, and patriarchal and religious authority on the other hand.

Ballads drew on archives of public memories attached to local sites and prominent people of the past, but they also relied upon public amnesia to allow for stereotypical characters and satisfying plots that met the expectations of their audiences. Two versions of the ballad of *Rangamala Sundari* illustrate the general purpose of negotiating social boundaries, while they support opposite sides of the divide between rich and powerful zamindars and their lowly subjects. The two versions also show how public memories changed over time, thereby allowing renewed ballads to be performed in the changed contexts. In order to explore the social boundary of caste, nineteenth century versions of the *Rangamala Sundari* ballad almost forgot a local zamindar's participation in a widespread rebellion against the East India Company in the 1760s.

At the beginning of the twentieth century many ballads were written about marriages across the Hindu-Muslim divide, but in general they did not negotiate this boundary. Instead they validated one religious community only. When members of the other religion were erased by death, marriage, or conversion, ballads symbolically constructed a radically simplified new community. In a changing relation to print culture, such ballads were often printed and read, perhaps as well as being performed, and they also drew upon local histories and genealogies that were distributed in locally printed books.

The literary practice considered in Sudeshna Purkaystha's chapter is history, and especially relations between academic history and prosaic and poetic genres of vernacular history. Her essay is not concerned with religious practices, except to the extent that religious myths and sentiments entered into moral discourse in modern, nationalist and popular works of Assam's history. Her method is that of 'mnemo-history': i.e., tracing representations of a single person, event, or theme in different historical works and genres produced at different times, in order to reveal their joint construction of a public memory. The present study has selected three different narratives on Jaymati. Their common, basic plot is that Jaymati was tortured and killed because she would not reveal the location of her noble husband to his enemies. The three narratives are Harakanta Sharma Barua's story of Jaymati included in his *Assam Buranji*, Kripanath Phukan's literary ballad about Jaymati, and a verse narrative on Jaymati composed by the rationalist and professional historian, Surya Kumar Bhuyan. Figurative devices were essential to the writings of all three historians, whether they used prose or traditional emotive verse forms. For instance, Surya Kumar Bhuyan's metaphors that describe Jaymati by referring to the myths of Sati, Savitri and Damayanti were designed to assert the cultural affinity of Assam with India's classical past, and to assimilate Assamese nationalism to Indian nationalism. These iconic figures were chosen to legitimize the popular notion of the good woman who can sustain the community and be the symbol of the Assamese nation (*jati*).

Purkayastha's chapter argues against the modern Western assumption that prose is a necessary medium for 'factuality in history', because 'poetry ingrains emotion and imagination which inhibits the true representation of facts'. Instead she writes:

> The past as constituted by its existing traces is always appropriated textually through the sedimented layers of previous interpretations and through the reading habits and categories developed by previous or current methodological practices. The present study argues that the truth in history may transgress the contours of factuality.

Questions about the relation between 'factuality' and 'truth' are relevant to concerns in this and other chapters about public memory and its necessary and dialectical relation to public amnesia.

In the concluding chapter, Mikko Viitamäki offers a fine reading of *Nizami Bansuri*, a creative retelling of medieval history for twentieth-century readers. The work was authored in 1941 by a Sufi shaykh and prolific author, Khwaja Hasan Nizami, and it narrates the life story of the celebrated Sultanate Sufi, Khwaja Nizam-ud-Din Auliya (died 1325). Khwaja Hasan Nizami was an influential twentieth-century figure: a versatile author, an activist who campaigned against the Arya Samaj, an outspoken supporter of the Sufi practices that were condemned by Muslim reformists, and a spiritual guide to numerous disciples. A prolific author (it is claimed that he wrote over 200 books), he also translated the Koran into Urdu and Hindi, and wrote diaries to document the events of his life in India, and his journeys to Afghanistan and the Middle East. His best-known works are his autobiography, and 12 historical volumes describing the events and aftermath of the 1857 uprising.

The peculiar title of Khwaja Hasan Nizami's book, *Nizami Bansuri* (The Bamboo Flute of Nizam [-ud-Din] or The Nizami [Brotherhood of the] Bamboo Flute), alludes to the Sufi master Nizam-ud-Din Auliya and to the flute-playing god Krishna. Both figures have a role in a mystical experience of the book's protagonist, Prince Hardev. *Nizami Bansuri* is a reworked Urdu translation of a Persian text called *Chihal Roza* (Forty Days) that is supposed to be a fourteenth-century diary of Hindu prince Hardev, describing his experiences with Nizam-ud-Din in Delhi. Thus Nizami's book is based on the allegedly contemporary diary made by Nizam-ud-Din's Hindu disciple, Prince Hardev. It has been impossible, however, to trace the origins of Hardev's diary; moreover, Hardev's diary is fully amalgamated with Khwaja Hasan Nizami's footnotes, insertions and appendices, so that his *Nizami Bansuri* is essentially a new literary work, not a mere translation. For this reason Viitamäki argues that it should be read both as a twentieth-century handbook of a Sufi disciple, and as an effort to shape the present through a dialogue with the past.

The narrative revolves around Hardev's meetings with Nizam-ud-Din and his disciples. Nizam-ud-Din was a paragon of human virtue: truthful, and free from scheming and false pretensions. He was a person who saw everyone as equal regardless of his background. Moreover, he was also a spiritual stalwart capable of performing miracles (*karamat, kharq-i adat*). The miracles are essential to the narrative, since they feed Hardev's fascination and pull him closer to Nizam-ud-Din. Formal conversion was not necessary for Hardev to associate with the shaykh; he believed that God is One, and that Muhammad is his last prophet, and he therefore would refrain from worshipping idols.

Hasan Nizami filled in the gaps concerning Nizam-ud-Din's life in Hardev's diary with material derived from the three collections of the master's discussions, and from the comprehensive biography *Siyar-ul-Auliya*, as well as from the works of the Sultanate historians. In addition to these literary sources, the author seems to have drawn from the oral tradition connected with the shrine of Nizam-ud-Din. The main body of the text is further augmented with copious notes in which Nizami discusses some historical discrepancies, and comments on the contemporary relevance of the events described. In addition to the annotated narrative running to 363 pages, *Nizami Bansuri* includes a 200-page appendix that covers the lives of the important disciples of Nizam-ud-Din as well as the history of the shrine where he is entombed.

Keeping his own contemporary context in mind, Nizami enters into a dialogue with the past, and succeeds in making the medieval events highly relevant to twentieth-century Sufi disciples. Nizam-ud-Din's Sufi practices that had been contested by religious scholars in the fourteenth century also became a subject of criticism by modern reformists who called for purification of Islam, including the Deobandis, Tablighi Jamaat, and Ahl-i Hadis, beginning in the late nineteenth century. Nizami's description of a warm welcome of Hardev into the circle of Nizam-ud-Din challenged the idea of clearly defined religious boundaries that had gained currency in twentieth-century India. Nizam-ud-Din is portrayed as a spiritual teacher who appeals to people across religious boundaries, but is simultaneously an exemplary Muslim different from Hindu ascetics. Nizami's work includes arguments that a twentieth century disciple could utilize when he encountered the reformists' criticism of Sufi practices like music (*sama'*) and prostration before the shaykh. By means of Hardev's narrative, the text prescribes the proper etiquette towards Hindu disciples, some of whom may convert like Hardev, while others remain Hindus like Hardev's parents. Hardev's story in *Nizami Bansuri* is not a bid to ease the integration of Muslims into the Hindu nation's space, but a legitimation of continued incorporation of Hindu disciples into a Muslim Sufi brotherhood in an era of rising communal tensions.

Khwaja Hasan Nizami's careful assembly of multiple sources, and his work's abundant notes and appendices seem designed to present a work of history, if we consider the various genres of vernacular South Asian history, traditional and contemporary. One might think of it both as a work of history considerably weighted towards factuality, and as a work of devotion. The central miracle in the narrative, by which Hardev saw Krishna in a mystical experience, and its configuring power for the narrative as a whole, might not have to be seen as fictional as opposed to historical.

Thus, several chapters in this volume discuss writing practices in the context of religious identities and boundaries: Prannath and his followers tried to identify themselves as Muslim; the use of religious history in boundary maintenance and identity defence while encouraging Hindu disciples by a twentieth-century Indian Sufi teacher; boundary maintenance and redefinition across a wide variety of genres from hagiographies to translation and construction of a shared lexicon by Dara Shikuh; defence and criticism of Sufis and the Sufi practice of 'playing the witness', again in a variety of rhetorical modes: story and parable, appeals to personal experience, logical argument, and citation of religious authorities. Criticism was directed at homoerotic meditative and devotional practices.

Several chapters discuss vernacular genres with a religious dimension, and their use as sources for contemporary history: how Assamese historians used affective and configurative resources of vernacular religious genres to rewrite the bare account in chronicles of a heroic woman's suffering, placing the story in a wider context of Indian myths, as well as in the context of the familiar sentiments of Assamese Vaishnavism; how Eastern Bengal ballads changed when they portrayed religious identities in stories about marriages across the Hindu-Muslim divide in a period of intense political competition and religious nationalism; and how an account of a Hindu disciple of a medieval Sufi saint was rewritten in a factual but religiously configured history to provide instruction for twentieth-century followers of Sufi-oriented Islam.

References

Ali, Daud (ed.). 1999. *Invoking the Past: The Uses of History in South Asia*. Oxford and New York: Oxford University Press.

Aquil, Raziuddin. 2009. *In the Name of Allah: Understanding Islam and Indian History*. New Delhi: Penguin-Viking.

Aquil, Raziuddin and Partha Chatterjee (eds.). 2008. *History in the Vernacular*. Ranikhet: Permanent Black.

Bilgrami, Akeel. 2014. *Secularism, Identity and Enchantment*. Ranikhet: Permanent Black.

Braudel, Fernand. 1980. *On History*, tr. Sarah Matthews. Chicago: University of Chicago Press.

Busch, Allison. 2011. *Poetry of Kings: The Classical Hindi Literature of Mughal India*. New York: Oxford University Press.

Chatterjee, Kumkum. 2009. *The Cultures of History in Early Modern India: Persianization and Mughal Culture in Bengal*. New Delhi: Oxford University Press.

Chatterjee, Partha. 2008. 'Introduction: History in the Vernacular', in Raziuddin Aquil and Partha Chatterjee (eds.), *History in the Vernacular*. Ranikhet: Permanent Black.

Deshpande, Prachi. 2007. *Creative Pasts: Historical Memory and Identity in Western India, 1700-1960*. New Delhi: Permanent Black.

Lieberman, Benjamin. 2013. *Remaking Identities: God, Nation, and Race in World History*. Lanham: Rowman & Littlefield.

Lorenzen, David N. 2010. *Nirguna Santon ke Swapna*, Hindi translation by Dhirendra Bahadur Singh. New Delhi: Raj Kamal.

Orsini, Francesca (ed.). 2010. *Before the Divide: Hindi and Urdu Literary Culture*. New Delhi: Orient Blackswan.

Pollock, Sheldon (ed.). 2003. *Literary Cultures in History: Reconstructions from South Asia*. Berkeley and Los Angeles: University of California Press.

Rao, Velcheru Narayana, David Shulman and Sanjay Subrahmanyam. 2001. *Textures of Time: Writing History in South India, 1600-1800*. New Delhi: Permanent Black.

Sreenivasan, Ramya. 2007. *The Many Lives of a Rajput Princess: Heroic Pasts in India, c. 1500-v1900*. New Delhi: Permanent Black.

White, Hayden. 1987. *The Content of the Form: Narrative Discourse and Historical Representation*. Baltimore and London: The Johns Hopkins University Press.

Zutshi, Chitralekha. 2014. *Kashmir's Contested Pasts: Narratives, Sacred Geographies, and the Historical Imaginations*. New Delhi: Oxford University Press.

1

Sufi Attitudes toward Homosexuality

Chishti Perspectives from South Asia

SCOTT KUGLE

Gender Studies have opened new approaches to research in the field of Islamic Studies including the study of Sufism. The scholarship that is emerging makes the previous generation of works on Sufism—like those of Annemarie Schimmel or Sachiko Murata—seem stiff and Victorian.[1] Gender and sexuality were once considered 'off-limits' and déclassé, but now are legitimate and urgently important topics. Today there is a body of insightful studies of the experiences of Sufi women, the role of masculinity in Sufi authority, and Sufi attitudes towards marriage, sex and the body.[2] Even so, the subject of homoerotic imagery or homosexual desires in Sufi communities remains understudied.

How should scholars of Sufism approach questions of sexuality in general and homosexuality in particular? What methodology should they adopt and what evidence should they explore? Recent studies use Sufi-authored poetry as evidence of social attitudes toward sexuality and homosexuality.[3] Some scholars of Sufism have missed opportunities to address homosexuality while studying Sufi poetry.[4] Others hit the mark, and scholarship is moving from addressing questions of sexuality as a sideline to translating Sufi poetry as a means to address questions of sexuality.[5]

This chapter will move the investigative lens away from Sufi poetry and look at how Sufis engaged in more prosaic discourses about sexuality and homosexuality, discourses rooted in social mores and communal life. It focuses on Chishti Sufis because they are known for producing prose that clothed spiritual insights in the garb of quotidian questions-and-answers, parables and stories, or moral advice. They created records of their spiritual masters' oral discourses (*malfuzat*), left voluminous collections of letters of spiritual guidance (*maktubat*), composed epistles of moral exhortation (*nasihat*), and wrote spiritual biographies (*tazkirat*) as examples to be admired and imitated. This prose literature contains responses, parables, narratives and debates about male homosexuality that are rooted in social practices of medieval and early modern South Asia.

This chapter addresses homoerotic attraction through two examples of this literature spanning the fourteenth to the seventeenth centuries. Of initial interest are seldom-interpreted passages from the most famous Chishti text, the *malfuzat* of Nizam-ud-Din Auliya (d. 1325 CE at Delhi) entitled *Fawa'id-ul-Fu'ad* or 'Morals for the Heart'. Then there follows a translation of an almost unknown and partly lost text, a moral exhortation by Muhammad ibn Fazlullah (d. 1619-20 CE at Burhanpur). Focusing on these texts allows us to illustrate how Chishti Sufis debated amongst themselves about homosexuality without using that word. In their discussions, they did not revert to technical terms from the Islamic legal tradition, legal discourse aimed to control social behaviour and define sex acts as licit or illicit.[6] The Chishtis tended to not engage in that discourse. Instead, they appear more concerned with questions of inner disposition than with outer action; and the terms that become pivotal for them are intention (*niyyat*), lust (*shahwa*) and spiritual condition (*hal*).

Homosexuality and Homoeroticism

Chishti discussions of homosexuality appear to a contemporary reader to be rather indirect. They neither address the phenomenon head-on nor do they use a technical term in Persian for 'homosexuality' or 'homosexual'. In that sense, the subject of their discussions is more properly 'homoeroticism' rather than homosexuality. Since the two phenomena are closely related, let us try to grasp the theoretical complexity of their convergence before moving to analyse Sufi discourses that are the subject of this essay.

Homosexuality as understood in modern times is a complex phenomenon. It includes the elements of identity, sexual orientation, gendered behaviour, social relationships and sex acts. Male homosexuality and female homosexuality may manifest quite differently in patriarchal societies like Islamic societies, and the Chishti Sufi discussions that this chapter analyses are limited to male homosexuality so this chapter is similarly limited. The easiest element to label is sex acts, and Islamic law addresses primarily sex acts between males. Homosexual acts are sex acts between two males, simply stated (though which acts constitute 'sex' is ambiguous and legal discussions define this activity in contradictory ways). On a subtler plane than sex acts, there are attitudes and relationships; this is the realm of homoeroticism. Homoeroticism can be defined as cultivating love between two males, with the term *eros* understood to mean love that includes emotional bonding, passionate feeling, and urgent longing (*'ishq*). Whether homoerotic relationships lead to sex acts or whether their participants remain chaste (*pak-baz* or 'playing clean' in the Persian used by Chishti authors) is debatable.

For men who experience homoerotic love, the question arises about suitable partners. This is where gendered behaviour comes into play: behaviours, cues, and social scripts may exist between men to signal openness to homoerotic bonding or rejection of it. If these behaviours become organized, then one can speak of homoerotic sub-cultures; they form when some males come to recognize others who also seek homoerotic bonding; such sub-cultures may offer clearly defined social roles for the lover and the beloved, and they will be organized around other social markers of belonging (such as age, ethnicity, social class, religious affiliation). The question every modern observer asks is: when and how does such homoerotic bonding lead to homosexual acts? But that is a modern question. It is hard to determine its answer in pre-modern Islamic societies. In general, we can say that homoerotic bonding seems to be ubiquitous while legal punishment for homosexual acts only rarely appears.

Homoerotic bonding may be casual or it may be causal. 'Casual' means that for some homoerotic bonding might be merely social—more akin to passionate friendship. 'Causal' means that for others homoerotic bonding might become urgently important; it might cause a person to foresake marriage, question patriarchal norms or reject routine house-holding expectations. Whether a person acts upon such feelings or not depends upon personal courage, family constraints, social pressures, and fortuitous timing or their lack. In pre-modern times, few individuals rejected social pressure and led autonomous lives, though the history of Sufism does offer us some rare examples of individuals who did reject social conformity for the sake of homoerotic relationships. What might drive a man to reject the routine gendered and sexual life of a privileged householder who is empowered in a patriarchal society? It could be misogyny—the perception that females are degraded and polluting—that pushes some men to create loving relationships with other males. It could be masculine asceticism—the perception that women symbolize worldly attachment and ambition—that causes some men to debase relationships with wives or women and to seek edifying relationships only with other males. It could be aesthetics—the perception that the masculine physique epitomizes beauty—that leads some men to devalue women and raise other males as the objects of passionate love. Or it could be sexual orientation—the psychic and largely irrational feeling of sexual attraction toward a gendered person—that leads some men to focus their intimate relationships and emotional investment with other males rather than with females.

Those who feel the urge to make homoerotic relations the centre of their emotional life (whether they do so or are constrained from doing so) point to the subtlest element of homosexuality, the element of identity. Within homoerotic feelings and practices may reside the kernel of personal identity. This is the case with men who feel sexual orientation towards other males and who therefore engage in homoerotic practices. This is less clearly the case for men who do so for reasons of misogyny, asceticism or aesthetics. These are social values that are learned, but sexual orientation is a psychic feeling that is not learned (according to contemporary theories of sexuality in which orientation is inherent in a person from childhood at least, or perhaps infancy due to uterine environment or genetic predisposition). Contemporary theories of sexuality assert a dichotomy between identity and acts: one is homosexual by inward disposition and sexual orientation, whether or not one engages in sexual acts with someone of the same gender or not, and conversely one could engage in sex acts in certain situations (for example youthful experimentation, prison deprivation, or military regimentation) without those actions making a person homosexual in orientation. The distinction advanced here between identity and performance is crucial. Contemporary theory of sexuality places primary emphasis on individual identity and only secondarily considers sex acts. Most theorists take for granted intimate friendship, passionate love and emotional attachment that belong to the realm of homoeroticism.[7]

Medieval Islamic societies had only rudimentary elements of a theory of sexual orientation, linked mainly to medicine and astronomy. The concept of sexual orientation was not highly developed, so medieval discussions of homosexuality do not accord with contemporary notions of homosexuality. Rather, most Chishti Sufi discussions, such as those detailed below, focus on homoeroticism rather than homosexuality *per se*. They deal with intimacy between males, intimacy that could be loving and passionate but is not clearly marked as involving sex acts or exclusive relationships akin to marriage. In this sense, the following analysis discusses mainly homoeroticism which is but one element of homosexuality as currently understood; it is important to stress that it does not specify whether or not sex acts are involved. The Chishti case shows us how the range of reflection within one community of pre-modern Muslims: they discussed homoeroticism openly and thereby indirectly addressed homosexuality without privileging the discourse of Islamic law.

Discussing Sexuality and Homoeroticism in Delhi

The attitudes of Chishti Sufi masters toward sexuality and homosexuality were subtle and complex. Apart from their intrinsic interest, they provide a useful model for modern Muslims who tend to approach the subject bluntly or sometimes brutally.[8] In the fourteenth-century record of Nizam-ud-Din Auliya's conversations and discourses, we find that the subject came up occasionally. He did not shy away from addressing it and one of his oldest disciples and later successor in the Deccan, Burhan-ud-Din Gharib (d. 1344 at Daulatabad), was an avid conversation partner on this topic. Their basic position was that sexual activity was not sinful in itself, but that it often became the conduit for sinful attitudes—like possessiveness, craving, lust, selfishness and domination. To the extent that sexuality was an obstacle toward spiritual growth and refinement, it was not because of the physical acts involved but because of the psychic attitudes behind them. Nizam-ud-Din Auliya and Burhan-ud-Din Gharib both renounced sexual acts and took upon themselves chastity as a spiritual practice, but they did not make this a required condition for others in their order.[9] One could rise to high levels in the Chishti order without renouncing sexual acts or marriage. But the example of Nizam-ud-Din Auliya certainly did mean that Chishti Sufis had an alternative discourse on what constituted 'masculinity'. They contrasted routine understanding of masculinity—which equated it with physical virility, sexual potency and aggressive dominance—with their own understanding of masculinity as the power to uphold spiritual virtues and to transform others for the better.

Their attitudes toward masculinity are expressed in Nizam-ud-Din's discourses, *Morals for the Heart* as recorded by Amir Hasan Sijzi (d. 1336 in Daulatabad). Amir Hasan recorded that Nizam-ud-Din once spoke about the Sufi masters Jalal-ud-Din Tabrizi and Hamid-ud-Din Nagauri.[10] Burhan-ud-Din Gharib asked him why they had few disciples and whether this meant that their sainthood was not so potent. Nizam-ud-Din answered, 'Try to understand it with an example: Suppose there are two persons whose virility is beyond doubt. But one of them has got progeny and the other has no sons and daughters; yet it cannot be said that this other person is not potent or there is some deficiency in his virility'.[11]

The early Chishti masters taught that masculinity is the spiritual quality of having the highest aspiration: to love God and to provide effective attention to others and their needs. Mistaken, in their view, was the routine social understanding of masculinity—to be sexually potent, sire offspring, and provide them with wealth and power. They taught this persistently, even against the assumptions of their followers like Amir Hasan (who asks the question and records the answer). Sexual acts and sexuality do not make or unmake a man, in their view. A man is masculine only by his moral acts and the spiritual attitudes that underlie them. In this sense, Sufis often speak of female mystics as 'men' because they partake in these moral acts and spiritual aspirations on par with male mystics, without being prevented by their reproductive anatomy, their female gender or their feminine socialization.[12]

If real masculinity means spiritual potency and this is decoupled from social manifestations of masculine potency as manifested through sexual acts, then there is room for alternative social expressions of sexuality. Most importantly for the early Chishtis, there was room for non-sexuality like abstinence (refraining from sexual acts), chastity (restraining sexual attraction) or asexuality (not having sexual desires). But there might also be room for homoerotic behaviour or even homosexual orientation. The early Chishtis discussed these controversial matters because the religious tradition they inherited from Iran and Khurasan had homoerotic episodes in it.

The Chishti lineage is very close to the Suhrawardi lineage, which was seen to include the much revered figures of Ahmad Ghazali (d. 1120-1 in Qazvin) and 'Ayn al-Quzat (d. 1131 in Hamadan). Both hailed from Iranian highlands and were deeply immersed in its 'Khurasani' tradition of love mysticism while engaging intellectually with the *madrasa* system from Baghdad. The stories of these two luminaries are linked in the Chishti discussions of homosexuality.

Ahmad Ghazali is a primary exemplar in the Suhrawardi community and a great crafter of Persian mystical love poetry. He was the younger brother of the famous theologian, Abu Hamid Ghazali. Chishti Sufis saw the younger brother as a more powerful figure who gave new depth to love poetry and was also adept at Sufi music.[13] 'Ayn al-Quzat was a brilliant intellectual and gifted writer of Persian prose who was reputed to be Ahmad Ghazali's disciple in Sufism.[14] His many books launch a philosophical assault on dry reason and scholastic theology despite the fact that he was executed at a young age. His prose inspired many later Chishti Sufis along with Ahmad Ghazali's poetry.[15] Both figures were beloved but also controversial.

Ahmad Ghazali used to practice 'playing the witness' (*shahid-bazi*) both in Sufi musical gatherings and outside its ritual space. It is said that the young 'Ayn al-Quzat served as a 'witness' for Ahmad

Ghazali, who contemplated his beauty in such an intense way that 'Ayn al-Quzat's father, a theologically trained judge, tried to keep him away. This context shaped the discussion of Nizam-ud-Din Auliya. Amir Hasan records that once, Nizam al-Din brought up the danger of criticizing others' negative personality traits, with reference to 'Ayn al-Quzat's writings.

[Khwaja Nizam-ud-Din] told us that 'Ayn al-Quzat had written that his father was a *qazi* [judge], accepted bribes and lived on forbidden earnings. He had written a number of things like that. I [Amir Hasan] submitted as to what was his purpose in giving such details about his father. The Khwaja said that he had also written that his father was an inspired person. Once in a gathering of *sama'* where darweshes and their friends had assembled, 'Ayn al-Quzat's father, who was also there, claimed that he had seen Shaykh Ahmad Ghazali (God's mercy be upon him) in the assembly. People could not believe him as the place where he lived was at a great distance from the place of the *sama'*. But on investigation his statement turned out to be correct. The purpose of 'Ayn al-Quzat narrating the anecdote was, according to the Khwaja, to let it be known that divine blessings were not contingent upon prayers, litanies and good deeds. Whomever God willed to favor, he could be inspired and perform miraculous deeds.[16]

This story reveals how Nizam-ud-Din Auliya taught that even a flawed person could become the channel through which God's mercy flowed. The judge ('Ayn al-Quzat's father) may have been caught up in worldly affairs, used his knowledge of religion for profit, or accepted bribes. But to criticize him is to assert that 'I am better than him' which is Satan's pronouncement against Adam's creation which led to his expulsion and Adam's fall from grace (as told in the Koran 2:34 and 15:33). Rather, Nizam-ud-Din pointed out that, despite these flaws the judge could still be the conduit for miracles, such as his experience of seeing Ahmad Ghazali participate in a *sama'* gathering which he could not attend.

Withhold judgement, teaches Nizam-ud-Din, rein in your own ego; acknowledge your own faults rather than seeking faults in others. This is the moral framework through which he will address questions of homosexuality and propriety, which were raised in his company upon the mention of Ahmad Ghazali. Again from *Morals for the Heart:*

This was followed by the Khwaja's remark that Shaykh Ahmad [Ghazali] was arraigned (for his liking for young boys); and this was why 'Ayn al-Quzat's parents had kept him hidden [when Shaykh Ahmad once came to his house asking to see the boy, and the parents insisted that he had died, which the Shaykh protested was untrue]. Maulana Burhan-ud-Din Gharib who was present, submitted that Shaykh Ahmad was known as one affected (with an unnatural propensity).[17]

What the translator describes as 'an unnatural propensity' means homosexuality—if not an identity based on sexual orientation then at least a homoerotic bonding with younger males that is often described as 'platonic love'. It is crucial to note that the term 'unnatural' is a commentary by the translator; it is not a direct translation of any word used in Persian by the speakers in this discussion. Bruce Lawrence translates this as 'crazed with an affection for young boys' and 'cavorting with young boys' which more aptly reflects medieval Persian.[18] Seeing homosexuality as 'unnatural' is a modern description not based in pre-modern discourses; such discourses describe it as a kind of activity expressing affection, attraction and passion. Whether the attitudes associated with homosexuality were sinful or not, and whether acting upon them were legal or not, were questions that medieval Muslim jurists and Sufis discussed; but the terms of these discussions were not defined by whether homosexuality was natural or unnatural. Ahmad Ghazali was known to choose younger males as his 'beloved' who would act as his 'witness' through whom he could contemplate the beauty of God's creation. The question is whether this attitude constituted a character flaw and whether this action involved sinful sexual acts.

As if he had not heard the moral lesson offered, Burhan-ud-Din Gharib commented critically that Ahmad Ghazali was affected by homosexuality. Nizam-ud-Din Auliya reprimanded him, countering that Shaykh Ahmad acted in this way only because he wanted to court the public's blame (*malam*), 'otherwise he was a pious man of purity and abstinence.' To illustrate his good qualities, Nizam-ud-Din narrated a story:

Shaykh Ahmad was accused of having developed an unnatural liking for [or as translated by Lawrence 'was accused of cavorting with'] the son of a butcher who, having been informed of that, started a campaign of detracting the Shaykh publicly. One night the son of the butcher was with the Shaykh in his chamber. His father reached there to find out the truth and secretly posted himself at a place adjacent to the chamber. He peeped into it through a hole and saw the Shaykh standing in prayer, and when the prayer was over, he saw him giving a sermon of good conduct to the boy, which he repeated after every two *rak'at* of prayer. This he did throughout the night. In the morning the butcher entered the chamber, fell at the feet of the Shaykh and he and his son both became his *murids* [disciples].[19]

Typical of his teaching style, Nizam-ud-Din Auliya refrained from giving an injunction. His intention was to distract his listeners from their egoistic preoccupations and prejudices and to draw them into the story. Through the story, his listeners can interact with the moral question in a fresh way and realize its relevance for them at a deeper level.

In the narrative that Nizam-ud-Din told, Shaykh Ahmad Ghazali played with the disjunction between what others observed and his inner intention. He was observed keeping the company of young boys, admiring their beauty, and living with them; this roused the suspicion that he was engaging in sexual acts out of lust. But at the end it is revealed that his inner spiritual self was pure and thus his actions violated no norms. Nizam-ud-Din Auliya concluded, 'The powerful spirituality as possessed by Shaykh Ahmad was not a common thing and could be the characteristic of only a pious man of perfect abstinence'.[20]

Reflecting on Homoerotic Mysticism in Khurasan

Nizam-ud-Din Auliya drew this story from a wide variety of anecdotes told about Ahmad Ghazali and his practice of 'playing the witness'. In modern terms, we would call this a 'homoerotic devotional practice' in which sensual and aesthetic enjoyment of human beauty is transmuted into spiritual contemplation of God's presence in and through created beings, especially handsome young men. Through it, erotic forces were sublimated and transformed into spiritual insights. The question of whether this homoerotic devotional practice led to sexual relations between the males involved cannot be resolved by the evidence at hand. Still more difficult is the question of whether practitioners of 'playing the witness' were homosexual in identity. The narratives told about them do not answer these questions. Rather, the narratives assert that they were pure in their practice (*pak-baz*) and not engaged in lustful activity, and they highlight the spiritual insights generated from this practice.

The scholar of Persian literature, Nasrollah Pourjavady, has analysed these narratives about Ahmad Ghazali. He mentioned several other 'witnesses' whose beauty Ahmad Ghazali used to gaze upon in contemplation. The story of the son of the Turkish Atabeg or chief is most similar to that narrated in *Fawa'id-ul-Fu'ad* about a suspicious father spying on Ahmad Ghazali. From the perspective of oral narrative and folklore studies, we can say that these are two versions of the same story; even if their details differ, the underlying narrative structure and moral of the story are the same. Nizam-ud-Din Auliya was trying to teach his audience morals rather than to convey textual details.

As Pourjavady explains, narratives about Ahmad Ghazali's love for a younger male abound in Persian Sufi hagiographies. One important source of stories about Ahmad Ghazali 'playing the witness' is the *maqalat* or discourses attributed to Shams-i Tabrizi (the friend and teacher of Maulana Rumi, and possibly also his lover). Shams writes that Ahmad Ghazali was an exponent of 'contemplating through gazing at an exemplary beauty (*nazar-baz*) and loved a young man (*shahid-dost*)'.[21] Shams does not find fault with Ahmad Ghazali's personality and justifies his practices, but still shows discomfort discussing it. As Pourjavady explains, 'Despite the fact that Ahmad Ghazali's passionate love for his chosen male lover was platonic and chaste, the common people saw it as a kind of bodily lust'. There were even some Sufis who did not consider 'playing the witness' by gazing at a beautiful youth, loving him, sitting in the company of a handsome young man or beardless youth to be a virtuous practice or one allowed by religious law. . . . Still, Shams-i Tabrizi was careful to mention that the gazing of Ahmad Ghazali upon the beautiful faces was not lustful. 'If you opened up his heart you could not find any trace of lust inside him.' This special kind of gazing the early Sufis called *nazar-i 'ibrat*, or 'a gaze of transcendental contemplation' as did Ahmad Ghazali himself.[22]

Shams tells a story about Ahmad Ghazali spending time alone with a male beloved in the public bath; the youth's father spies on them from a window but in the end is convinced of the Sufi's purity of heart and absence of lust.[23] The structure of this story is the same as the anecdote told by Nizam-ud-Din Auliya, though in this second version, the young male beloved is 'Ayn al-Quzat himself and the one who tries to keep them apart is his father, the local judge. Nizam-ud-Din Auliya reflects a long tradition that depicts Ahmad Ghazali enjoying a loving relationship with the young 'Ayn al-Quzat.[24]

Drawing Spiritual Lessons from Nizam-ud-Din's Discourses

What can we conclude from this discussion of sexuality in the conversations of early Chishti masters? The teachings of Nizam-ud-Din Auliya are subtle: he saw sexuality as intimately related to spirituality, for both flow from the wellsprings of human life and are expressions of its power. His concern was to direct this power from crude physical dimensions, away from socially competitive dimensions and toward spiritually refined dimensions. When issues of sexuality arose in his discussions, Nizam-ud-Din Auliya did not condemn sexual activity in legalistic ways but encouraged considering what attitudes gave rise to it and how it affected human relationships. He resisted the urge, so common in his patriarchal society, to use the sexuality of others as an opportunity to condemn them. Rather, he taught that one should always restrain one's egoistic urge to criticize others and see negative qualities in them, especially with issues as visceral as sex.

This is how Nizam-ud-Din Auliya linked the two stories told above about Ahmad Ghazali and 'Ayn al-Quzat. 'Ayn al-Quzat criticized his own father for moral lapses and political machinations, but Nizam-ud-Din countered that his father also had good qualities; and it is through people's good qualities undeterred by their flaws, faults or sins, that God worked miracles in the world.

Likewise Ahmad Ghazali was persecuted for his loving attachment to other males and was accused of homosexual activity. But Nizam-ud-Din Auliya points out that this accusation was misguided, for it was caused by others' egoistic obsessions with sex rather than Ahmad Ghazali's own attitudes or actions.

Nizam-ud-Din Auliya does not say that homosexuality is legal or illegal for that is not his concern; his concern is spirituality and he leaves it to judges and politicians to argue about legal rules. He does not say whether homosexuality is natural or unnatural; the translator of his discourses raises that issue, though we can infer from Nizam-ud-Din's language that he saw nothing unnatural about erotic attraction between men, as it was a common theme in the stories and poetry of many esteemed Muslim literati, scholars and Sufis. Nizam-ud-Din's concern was not homosexual orientation which he viewed with no more alarm than he viewed heterosexual orientation. His concern was rather about sexual activity of any kind, which he saw as leading to obsessive attachment to worldly ambitions and sensual pleasures. His personal example is that sexual desire should be sublimated—not denied through bodily austerities but redirected toward spiritual discipline.

In these early Chishti conversations, the alarm is voiced by Burhan-ud-Din Gharib. When Nizam-ud-Din commented that Ahmad Ghazali had been accused of loving young men he stressed the 'accusation' as the problem. But Burhan-ud-Din suggested that Ahmad Ghazali's 'homosexuality' (as orientation or attraction) was the problem. Nizam-ud-Din Auliya gently corrected Burhan-ud-Din and responded with a story addressing accusations of impropriety that underestimated the spiritual reality of Ahmad Ghazali. From the conversation, we cannot gauge whether Burhan-ud-Din Gharib learned his lesson. His attitudes are important because Burhan-ud-Din was one of the chief exemplars of Chishti Sufism in the Deccan region of South-Central India. He may have carried his alarm about whether homoerotic attachments could lead to sexual activity with him to the Deccan. In any case, he acknowledged that heated engagement with love poetry and ritual music relied on an underlying current of erotic force that, in his social context, was homoerotic. Burhan-ud-Din Gharib was concerned that it might give license to homosexual behaviour. Despite this concern, he remained a staunch advocate of music, poetry and dance in a ritual context.

'Playing the Witness' in the Deccan

Despite Burhan-ud-Din's concerns, there is evidence that homoerotic bonding was common in *sama'* sessions as they were practised by his followers in the Deccan. Inspired by Burhan-ud-Din Gharib's teachings, Shah Bajan (d. 1507 in Burhanpur) led a local flowering of the Chishti community in Burhanpur, a capital city of the Deccan region. In Shah Bajan's circle, the practice of 'playing the witness' was common.[25] A few generations later, we find a moral critique written by Muhammad ibn Fazlullah Burhanpuri. He is a Chishti Sufi most famous for writing the *al-Tuhfa al-Mursala ila al-Nabi al-Mukhtar* [Gift Addressed to the Spirit of the Prophet], a text that was influential in South Asia, Arabia and Southeast Asia. He wrote a commentary on his own text (sparking a long series of commentaries in many languages) to argue that existential philosophy was compatible with *shari'a*-minded piety.[26] This Chishti master was deeply influenced by Ibn 'Arabi's monistic thought. He was a scholar as well, who had studied *hadis* with luminaries like Shaykh 'Ali Muttaqi (who was born in Burhanpur but lived in Mecca) and Shaykh Wajih-ud-Din 'Alavi (in Ahmedabad).[27]

Muhammad ibn Fazlullah lived in Burhanpur in the era when the Shattari Sufi order was ascendant. There is evidence of competition between the Chishti and Shattari Sufis. The Shattaris adopted many elements from the Chishti repertoire (like musical *sama* and love poetry) and took them to vivid extremes, causing some *shari'a*-minded scholars from the Chishti order to react conservatively.[28] Muhammad ibn Fazlullah wrote his text of moral critique in this environment and alleged that Sufis in his city were engaging in 'gazing at beautiful young males' as a form of worship. He feared this would become heresy if taken to the extreme where they claimed God manifested in the bodily form of youths.[29]

From what we know of homoerotic contemplative practices

through the writings and stories of Ahmad Ghazali and others in his circle, Muhammad ibn Fazlullah's accusation seems exaggerated. He may have been provoked by competition against Shattari Sufis who appear to have cultivated homoerotic contemplation; this hypothesis will be detailed below after presenting the text. The text is translated here since it is a rare manuscript and gives a glimpse into the debate stirred by homoerotic contemplation; sadly the unique copy of this manuscript is fragile, eaten by insects and repaired in ways that obscure the writing (such that lacunae are marked here by editorial ellipses [...]).

In the name of God, the compassionate and caring. All praise be to God, the lord of all worlds, for the good end comes to those who are free from desiring both worlds. Blessings and peace be upon the most complete manifestation, Muhammad, and upon his family members and companions, each and every one.

This sinful man, Shaykh Muhammad ibn Fazlullah, who is in dire need of the intercession of the Prophet Muhammad—may peace and blessings be upon him—says the following. This is just a short discourse I composed merely by the grace of God. I dedicate any spiritual reward that might accrue to me because of it to the spirit of the Prophet—may peace and blessings be upon him. I have entitled it 'Warning to Spiritual Seekers against Gazing at Young Men as a Way to Reach God' for some pretenders have claimed that the surest way to reach intimate union with God is to gaze lovingly upon young men. I ask God to increase any merit for this to the account of the Prophet—may peace and blessings be upon him—for indeed God is capable of all things and is quick to answer all requests.

Know this, my brothers—may God ease your way and also mine—that the practice of gazing at young men (*ru'iyat al-amrud*) has spread widely in our land of Burhanpur. It has spread to such an extent that some pretenders claim that the surest way to reach union with God is gazing at young men. So God inspired me by divine grace to warn sincere spiritual seekers against this gazing practice. I refute by spiritual experience (*hal*), traditional teaching (*naql*) and rational logic (*'aql*) those who make this claim.

Let us begin with spiritual experience. I threw myself headlong into this practice three times with such great intensity that I cannot express it with words. But I swear by God, I did not find anything in it except a hidden [. . .] and dissipation of the presence of God. By petitioning God with prayer and humility and turning to God often, I was extracted by

God from this practice by divine grace. All praise and thanks be to God for that!

Oh beloved of hearts who have none but you
Long I've been longing just to be with you
Oh my love, oh my desire, oh my only goal
My heart lies if it tries to love anyone but you

So much for my personal experience; now let us then consider argument by reason.

If anyone claims, 'I look at young men only for the purpose of seeing God (*al-haqq*) through them', I would answer him thus. I would say, 'Just as God manifests and appears to sages in the form of young men, God also manifests and appears to sages in other things and in all phenomena. So why do you insist on this special role [for young men]'? One might give an answer, 'The reason for this special role is that God manifests in a man with God's attributes and qualities in a way that is much more than in other things. So I witness in young men these qualities in a pure way and I see divine beauty most perfected in them more than in any other thing or phenomenon'. Then I would answer, '[. . .] if one witnesses divine qualities they may derive from God, but they are not God's essence, for they have emanated from the highest level of divinity to the lowest level of phenomenality. So in your claim that you witness in them God's qualities, I counter that God manifests in the saints the sum total of divine qualities. Saints exist in every land, for the cosmos exists based upon their existence; all people see them but common people do not recognize them as saints. And God also manifests in the sun and moon and flowers with a predominance of God's beautiful qualities. Yet you expend so much energy in gazing upon young men in which some of God's qualities of beauty are manifest and you ignore gazing at the sun or moon or flowers in which God also manifests in many beautiful divine qualities. That is a horrible fact that requires your claim to be called a lie. It is false that God manifests in young men with divine qualities of beauty in a way that exceeds God's manifestation in all other things by being an absolute expression of God's beauty and perfection. [. . .] So it is proved that you only gaze at young men because of their human beauty that is limited and phenomenal (*husn muqayyad*). You desire and bear witness to only that phenomenal beauty and not to the absolute beauty related to God's essence or God's divine qualities'.

Witnessing human beauty is never free of lustful desire (*shahwa*), whether expressed outwardly or hidden inwardly. This is true because the soul (*nafs*), due to its very nature (*tab'*), longs and craves for physically sensing another person's beauty as long as one is witnessing it. Now if a spiritually realized sage (*'arif wasil*) is witnessing the limited and phenomenal beauty, then his psyche does not crave or long for the person to sense the beauty because the sage has departed from his earthly disposition and its desires. He has even departed from egoistic desires of the heart, and even from the sensing of all things including feelings of the self. So the sage does not see phenomenal beauty at all, but rather sees in all things only the presence of God. [For a sage, God's presence is] unconditioned by any specification or limitation in one thing rather than another.

Let us pause for a while in presenting this text. The author, Muhammad ibn Fazlullah, has considered arguments based on his own personal spiritual experience and on rational logic. He then turns to traditional teachings as found in Persian and Arabic books much esteemed by Sufis in South Asia, and quotes their authors describing the dangers of gazing at young men. He quotes Ibn 'Arabi, 'As for him who witnesses phenomenal things, that is among the worst humiliations and the most intense kinds of corruption'.[30] He also quotes al-Qushayri, 'Among the hardest afflictions in this path is keeping company with young men. All the Sufi masters agree that if God has tried anyone with this in some form, then he has been brought low by God and has been disgraced, or rather that God has distracted him with his own self'.[31] He also extracts such warnings from the writings of Abu Hamid al-Ghazali and also from *'Ayn al-'Ilm*, the South Asian abridgment of al-Ghazali's masterwork on Sufism, *Ihya' 'Ulum al-Din*.

Muhammad ibn Fazlullah also cites authorities closer to South Asia. He cites the classic handbook on Sufi ethics, *'Awarif al-Ma'arif* by Shihab-ud-Din 'Umar Suhrawardi (d. 1234 in Baghdad) which was used by Chishti Sufis as a training manual. Then he cites Chishti authors like Muhammad Husayni Gisudaraz (d. 1422 at Gulbarga), the Sufi scholar of the Deccan who points out that there is no report of the earliest generations of Muslims engaging in this practice and claims that witnessing the presence of God in a phenomenon is *shirk* or associating something or someone with God.[32] The author also cites Mas'ud Bakk (d. *c.* 1380 at Delhi), an ecstatic Chishti author through whom Shah Bajan and many Chishtis of Burhanpur traced their spiritual lineage.[33] To close this list of quotes, he recites a couplet by 'Abd al-Rahman Jami (d. *c.* 1492 at Herat) whose Persian love poems were a favourite in Chishti sessions of *sama'*: 'From every side, the absolute beauty of the divine is beaming // Oh fool, to catch a human beauty why're you scheming?'[34]

After marshalling these quotations from books of Sufi learning, Muhammad ibn Fazlullah addresses the fundamental point about interpreting them. His text continues:

> All of this is related in traditional learning and Sufi books. Now one might make objections that some Sufis teach that 'The metaphorical is a bridge to the real (*al-majaz qantara li'l-haqiqa*),' and that contradicts what you have related above. I would answer this saying, 'I accept that it might be that some scholars say this proverb. If they say it, it might be that they might have meant looking with love at young men, and if it were love pure of outward lust and free of hidden desire, then this might be beneficial to the one looking. [. . .] but it separates his heart from [. . .] upon his spiritual guide. If it makes his heart separate from his spiritual guide [. . .] in this one single place, then it distracts him with God such that it lets him achieve connection with God, then it is true that the metaphorical is a bridge to the real, in this context alone. This does not in fact contradict what I have related above. Since the metaphorical love is devoid of any damage from lustful desire [. . .] benefit, if it was before he set foot on this Sufi path of spiritual training. But after entering this path of God, it has no benefit at all. Rather, it harms him with terrible damage, such that he will never reach the desired goal except by one of two means. Either God will shelter him in divine mercy, or God will take him out of it and make him repent to the divine essence.

At this point the text ends at the bottom of a page, with the edges of the paper badly damaged which prevents a clear reading. The text probably continued further for another page at least. But the rest of the text is sadly lost.[35]

Muhammad ibn Fazlullah was reaching the end of his exposition but the full conclusion is absent. He was explaining how a Sufi who was accustomed to practising this gazing at young men might get rid of it through concentrating on his spiritual guide and turning toward God with repentance and prayer. Clearly, Muhammad ibn Fazlullah felt that many Sufis of Burhanpur in the late sixteenth century were in need of repentance. He was critical of Shattari

Sufis (though he wrote his critique in a general fashion and may also have been addressing his fellows in the Chishti order). In particular, he was embroiled in rivalry with the pre-eminent Shattari of Burhanpur in that generation, Shaykh 'Issa Jundullah Shattari.

Competition with the Shattari Order pertaining to Homoeroticism

The Shattari order has a colourful history and one of its most vivid advocates is Shaykh 'Issa Jundullah (d. 1622 in Burhanpur). He was a contemporary of Muhammad ibn Fazlullah but one biographer writes that 'the conduct of these two great saints was complete opposite. The gatherings of Shaykh 'Issa would openly discuss existential realities (*haqa'iq*) and spiritual subtleties (*ma'rifat*) without observing in proper order and etiquette (*hifz-i maratib*). For this reason, the Shaykh [Muhammad ibn Fazlullah] was unhappy with him.'[36] 'Issa Jundullah practised homoerotic contemplation. In his autobiographical statements, he explains that when young he had taken initiation with his spiritual guide, Shaykh Lashkar Muhammad 'Arif Shattari (d. 1585 in Burhanpur).[37] At that time, he experienced a life-transforming episode of ecstatic love:

In those days, my heart became imprinted with the form and figure of a beautiful man (*sahib-i husn*). In every moment, was transfixed by imagining his form. Eventually, the beauty of his appearance overwhelmed my senses such that a state of ecstasy (*mahwiyat*) overtook me. It became so strong that while studying, each letter on the page appeared in his form and in my sight each leaf on every tree manifested his beauty. Even at the time of performing my prayers, his form was ever before my gaze! I lost the feeling of all my five senses because other than the form of his beauty I could perceive no other thing. . . . When this state persisted and began to lead to behavior that was seen to be against the *shari'a*, I thought of trying to get rid of it and so went to consult my spiritual guide. When I explained to him how I had gone astray, he said 'The metaphorical is a bridge to the real', so leave this lowly affliction and through it reach to God.[38] He then recounts how his Shattari Sufi guide taught him a *zikr* or meditation practice that replaced his obsession with this beautiful man. He learned to sublimate his feelings of love and longing, such that he expressed them during sessions of musical meditation.[39]

An interesting point in this narrative is that it depicts 'Issa Jundullah hearing the very same advice—'The metaphorical is a bridge to the real' (*al-majaz qantara li'l-haqiqa*)—that Muhammad ibn Fazlullah quotes in his critical text. He wrote that those who object to his criticism might say this and then refuted their objection. Another ambiguous point is the identity of the person whose appearance fascinated 'Issa Jundullah. The text implies that he is male but does not name him. Skeptics might question whether the object of his affection was male or female, since terms like *sahib-i husn* (one possessing beauty), though gendered male as they were derived from Arabic, could be applied to women as well when used in Persian.

Examining the biographies of other Shattari Sufis of this era helps to clarify this doubt. The lesser-known Shaykh Makhu (d. 1601-2 AH in Burhanpur) was slightly older than 'Issa Jundullah. He was from Gujarat and took initiation from Muhammad Ghaus (d. 1563 in Gwalior), much like the father and uncle of 'Issa Jundullah did; and like 'Issa Jundullah, he was ardent in his practice of musical meditation (*sama'*). Shaykh Makhu sponsored so many *qawwali* sessions that he earned the title *Daya-yi Darweshan* or 'Wet-nurse of the Renunciants'. He used to 'nourish' the Sufis with music (known in Chishti and Shattari circles as 'food for the soul' or *ghaza-yi ruh*) enriched by his own spiritual state, just as a wet-nurse breastfeeds infants.

This title hints at some gender ambiguity in the personality of Shaykh Makhu. He never married, which is not so unusual for Sufi masters. However, Shaykh Makhu fell in love with a man.

> At age 40, he was seduced by a handsome man named Hansu and fell in love. But this man, because of the blessing of the attention of the Shaykh and his spiritual striving, was transformed from within. He joined the group of Sufis and began to serve his lover with heart and soul. Eventually, because of the Shaykh's guidance and advice, this beloved chose the path of spiritual purity.[40]

In this narrative, the gender of the beloved is not ambiguous. He is male but is also Hindu. The narrative suggests that he joined the circle of Shattari Sufis (who were apparently open to participation by Hindus, used Hindi poetry freely, and made allusions to Hindu mythology without scruples).[41] Then later, he became a Muslim after spending time in this community and enjoying a love relationship with Shaykh Makhu. The narrative harbours anxiety about the beloved being Hindu but displays no tension about his being male.

We cannot conclusively say Shaykh Makhu's relationship was sexual or not, but it was a publicly-known homoerotic love affair that perhaps lasted a long time and coincided with his refusing conventional marriage. Shaykh Makhu suffered no stigma from it. The ruler of Burhanpur, 'Ali 'Adil Shah Faruqi, appreciated his 'pleasant disposition' and his 'melodious voice' and appointed him as preacher and prayer-leader for the congregational mosque at Zaynabad (the twin city of Burhanpur, named after Zayn-ud-Din Shirazi the successor to Burhan-ud-Din Gharib).[42] There are other examples of South Asian Sufis who were apparently homosexual and had public love affairs but suffered little stigma if they could demonstrate a noble spiritual calling.[43]

In conclusion, it appears that this text of Muhammad ibn Fazlullah is exceptional rather than typical. It voices skepticism about homoerotic contemplation that was a common practice in his environment. It is uncommon for a Chishti Sufi to write down such a critique in philosophical terms. Muhammad ibn Fazlullah was apparently provoked by the rise of the Shattari Sufis in Burhanpur who competed with the Chishtis with much success. The fact that Muhammad ibn Fazlullah wrote a text called *Mi'raj-Nama*, an account of the Prophet Muhammad's ascension into heaven, hints that he felt threatened by the Shattari followers of Muhammad Ghaus Gwaliori; he claimed to have experienced a similar ascension and wrote a popular account of it which fueled the rapid popularity of his order. Muhammad ibn Fazlullah's contemporary, 'Ali Muttaqi (who was also his teacher in *hadis* studies in Mecca), took Muhammad Ghaus to task for this, writing tracts against him and sparking a persecution campaign. Muhammad ibn Fazlullah might have gotten caught up in this controversy if he, too, began to write *hadis*-based accounts of the *mi'raj* in order to counter Shattari claims.[44]

In this context, Muhammad ibn Fazlullah's competition with the Shattaris, based mainly on theological and spiritual points of difference, seems to have spilled over into debate about homoerotic practices. Even more than the Chishti Sufis, the Shattaris of this era seem to have embraced homoerotic contemplation and musical meditation. The Shattari order provides several examples of homoerotic relationships and hints that several of its leading figures may have had a homosexual orientation irrespective of whether they acted upon it or not.

Conclusion

Chishti Sufis discussed sexuality and homosexuality in a long tradition stretching from the fourteenth century when they began to write books until the eighteenth century cusp of modernity. This article assesses two Chishti discussions—of homosexuality and more specifically homoeroticism. The first is in the earliest Chishti book, *Morals for the Heart*, recording discourses of Nizam-ud-Din Auliya. The second is an obscure epistle by Muhammad ibn Fazlullah of sixteenth-century Burhanpur. Other textual evidence from Aurangabad in the eighteenth century shows the persistence of this tradition.[45] Chishti discussions of homoerotic longing and homosexuality were not just theoretical debates but were rooted in social reality.

Chishti Sufis had alternative discourses about sexuality and homosexuality that did not, in general, make reference to Islamic laws. Spiritual values were their reference point, and though Chishti Sufis rhetorically upheld the *shari'a* they did not generally limit their discussion of sexuality to legal rulings or norms from the *fiqh* tradition. An exception to this generality is one teacher who lived just after the great Chishti masters, namely Muhammad Husayni Gisudaraz; he does make direct reference to the story of Lut (the Prophet Lot) and to Islamic legal punishments for homosexual acts in his oral discourses (*malfuzat*).[46] His reversion to legalistic thinking is probably due to his emigrating to the new Bahmani kingdom in the Deccan when Timur sacked Delhi. In the Deccan, he was placed in a position of intense competition with other Sufi orders for the position of patron saint with political authority. This was a completely novel situation for a Chishti Sufi master, as prior Chishti leaders had scrupulously avoided political authority and carefully contained rivalry with other orders.[47] The position taken by Gisudaraz was unusual in comparison to other Chishti Sufis both before him and after him. However, his legalistic position became more the norm for modern Sufis under the impact of reformist Islam.

In the pre-modern period, the Chishti Sufis did not generally resort to legal discourses (*fiqh*) to discuss homoeroticism. We must now turn to the alternative discourse that they constructed. It was based on four basic principles recurrent throughout the above instances, drawn from the evidence of their foremost writings. The first principle is 'love'. Love is the highest kind of devotion and worship, such that all kinds of 'metaphorical love' can be refined to more closely approach 'real love' of God. The second principle is 'spiritual growth'. Not physical but spiritual growth is the essential element to human life, such that spiritual growth from wherever a person starts is more important than conformity to legal rules or social norms. The third principle is restraint. Sexual urges are a force to be sublimated for good rather than repressed as evil. And finally, intimately related to the third principle is a fourth: vigilance. Sexual desire is an obstacle to spiritual growth, and it must be continuously, daily monitored. There is no proper sexuality on the spiritual growth curve. Neither is homosexuality in itself condemnable nor is heterosexuality in itself laudable.

This chapter does not demonstrate the change that came over Chishti Sufi discourse about sexuality in the modern period. Nor does it make a comprehensive comparison to the discourse of other Sufi orders in the pre-modern period or throughout the South Asian region. Any distinctiveness of the Chishti Sufi discourse is due to their strong emphasis on love as the highest value, superseding and transforming all other values and virtues. This chapter only illustrates a pattern in Chishti discourse about sexuality to highlight its flexibility with regard to homosexuality, especially in so far as homoeroticism is accepted and homosexual acts are not seen as a matter of serious concern.

Does this stand as a contrast to other kinds of Islamic discourses in the modern era? Yes, since most of the Islamic discourses (like that of other religions) condemn homosexual acts and admit little ambiguity. There has always been a Sufi difference, however, in pursuit of divine love. The Chishti accent to this difference can now be appreciated for the subtlety and sensitivity it brings to this notion of human potential for self-expression.

Notes

1. Schimmel, 2003.
2. See for example on Sufi women Cornell, 1999 and Pemberton, 2010; on Sufi attitudes toward marriage see Shaikh, 2012; on sex and the body see Bashir, 2011 and Kugle, 2007.
3. Andrews and Kalpakli, 2005 and El-Rouayheb, 2005.
4. Chittick and Lamborn Wilson, 1982.
5. Tourage, 2007; see also Weisher and Lamborn Wilson, 1978.
6. Such terms include sodomy (*liwat*), adultery (*zina'*), transgression (*fahisha*) or abomination (*kabira*); see Ali, 2006.
7. Kugle, 2010 gives detailed references.
8. The bluntness and brutality of contemporary Neo-traditionalist Islamic discourse on homosexuality is the subject of and article by Kugle and Hunt, 2012: 254-79.
9. Ernst and Lawrence, 2002: 75.
10. Hamid-ud-Din Nagauri was an early Chishti master who died in 1274 in Rajasthan. Jalal-ud-Din Tabrezi was a master of the Suhrawardi lineage who died *c.* 1225 in Bengal. This discussion of masculinity began with the mention of Jalal-ud-Din Tabrezi who, while residing in Delhi, was falsely accused of sexual intimacy with a Turkish male slave as well as adultery with a female Indian dancer; see N. Hanif, 2000: 376-82.
11. Faruqi, 1996: 117-18 (Part 1, Majlis 30).
12. Chishti Sufis admire Bibi Zulaykha (mother of Nizam-ud-Din Auliya) and Bibi Fatima Sam (holy woman of Delhi who was adopted as a sister by Farid-ud-Din Ganj-i Shakar, Nizam-ud-Din's spiritual guide). In reference to the latter's spiritual power, Nizam-ud-Din used to teach, 'When a lion comes out of the forest, nobody bothers to ask if it is male or female'—see Lawrence, 1994: 149-61.
13. Ahmad Ghazali authored a treatise defending the practice of listening to music as devotion, *Bawariq al-Ilma'*, which was read avidly by Chishti Sufis; see Papan-Matin, 2010: chapter six; see also Ernst and Lawrence, 2002: 36-44.
14. Nizam-ud-Din Auliya addresses the question of whether 'Ayn

al-Quzat was a disciple of Ahmad Ghazali or some other Sufi master, in *Fawa'id al-Fu 'ad*, Part II, Majlis 33.

15. 'Ayn al-Quzat's *Tamhidat* was required reading in Chishti circles (and was the first text to be translated into Dakhani Urdu as that language developed into a literary idiom); see Safi, 2006: 169, and Papan-Matin, 2009: 112-32.
16. Faruqi, 1996: 194-5 (Part 2, Majlis 33) with phrases in ( ) by the translator and phrases in [ ] by the author of this article.
17. Ibid.: 195 (Part II, Majlis 33).
18. Lawrence, 1992: 177.
19. Faruqi, 1996: 196 and Lawrence, 1992: 177.
20. Ibid.: 196 (Part II, Majlis 33). Chishti Sufis held Ahmad Ghazali and 'Ayn al-Quzat in high esteem, and one scholar is investigating whether the Chishti lineage might have direct initiatic links to these Iranian masters; see Papin-Matin, 2009: 112-27.
21. Pourjawady, 2005: 203.
22. Ibid.: 204. In contemplation, one transcended the physical beauty of the object of gazing.
23. Ibid.: 204-5. In versions told by Shams-i Tabrizi, the beloved youth lived in Tabriz and his father was the governor (Atabeg).
24. Safi, 2006: 159-81 discusses 'Ayn al-Quzat and his father, and reproduces a miniature painting of Ahmad Ghazali and a young male beloved, possibly 'Ayn al-Quzat.
25. On Shah Bajan, see Bawa and Kugle, forthcoming; see also Kugle, 2009.
26. Green, 2012: 168; see also Feener and Sevea, 2009: 56. Muhammad ibn Fazlullah's most famous text has been published in Johns, 1965.
27. Kugle, 2007: chapter 3 tells of Shaykh Ali Muttaqi's contribution to Sufi-oriented *hadis* studies and his opposition to some Shattari leaders.
28. Khan, 1997: vol. 1, 361-71 gives details of his life, teachings and writings which include *al-Tuhfa al-Mursala* (mentioned above), *Hadiya al-Mursala ila al-Nabi* (a commentary on the famous prayer called 'Du'a Sayfi'), *Sharh al-Lawa'ih* (commentary on Jami's work about Ibn 'Arabi's thought), *Wasila ila Shifa'at al-Nabi* (on intercession by the Prophet Muhammad), *Mi'raj-Nama*, and *Risala Ahkam Umur* (a collection of treatises about *shari'a* rulings on various matters; the small text translated here is not listed among his major written works but might be part of this final volume of collected works).
29. Muhammad ibn Fazlullah Burhanpuri. *Tahzir al-Talibin 'an Ru'iyat al-Amrad li'l-Wusul ila Allah*, manuscript.

30. Ibid., folio 115a. The text quoted is Ibn Arabi's *al-Amr al-Muhkam.*
31. Ibid., folio 115a. The text quoted is *Risala Qushayriyya fi al-Tasawwuf.*
32. Ibid., folio 115b. The text quoted is *Asmar al-Asrar*, 'Oh men of heart, oh men who play at gazing, Muhammad Husayni Gesudaraz says . . . that gazing at handsome young men can never be free of hidden desire.'
33. Ibid., folio 116a. The text quoted is Mas'ud Bakk's *Mir'at al-'Arifin.*
34. Ibid., folio 116v. The text quoted is Jami's *Lawa'ih*,
35. No other copy is known by which we might fill in the gaps in this manuscript. There are marginal notes throughout the text, which explain vocabulary or phrases in the text, but they are not profound and do not aid the translator. This translation presents the full extent of the text, except for the quotations from other books that were abridged.
36. Khan, 1997: 367.
37. Ibid.: 255. Shaykh 'Issa Jundullah was from Gujarat where he took initiation first in the Chishti order then later in the Shattari order from Muhammad Ghaus, after which he moved to Burhanpur.
38. Ibid.: 380 recounts autobiographical statements from *Kashf al-Haqa'iq*, a *malfuzat* text recording the oral teachings of Shaykh 'Issa Jundullah.
39. Ibid.: 401-2.
40. Ibid.: 341.
41. Manjhan, 2000: introduction.
42. Khan, 1997: 341.
43. Shah Hussain of sixteenth-century Lahore provides the most cogent example; see Kugle, 2007: 181-220.
44. Without having located and read Muhammad ibn Fazlullah's *Mi'raj-Nama*, the argument remains hypothetical, but it is suggested by the title of his text, its being written in Arabic, and his cooperative relationship through *hadis* studies with 'Ali Muttaqi.
45. The Chishti master and poet Siraj (d. 1763 in Aurangabad) wrote a *masnavi* about his love affair with a young man; see Kugle, 2007b: 571-610. Naqshbandi *malfuzat* from Aurangabad in the same period recounts several incidents of homoerotic attraction or relationships, see Digby, 2001.
46. His *malfuzat* is entitled *Jawami' al-Kalim* (The Most Comprehensive Discourse).
47. Several factors lead Gisudaraz to his unusual opinion. First, he had juridical training and was competing with other more senior Chishtis

who did not have such training for the position of successor after the death of Nasir-ud-Din Chiragh-i Dehli. Second, he allied with rulers who expected him to uphold social order rather than merely promote spiritual growth. Third, he rivalled the Junaidi Sufis—who were more attuned to *shari'a*-minded jurisprudence—for the position of advisor to the king; see Siddiqi, forthcoming.

References

Ali, Kecia. 2006. *Sexual Ethics and Islam: Feminist Reflections on Qur'an, Hadith and Jurisprudence*. Oxford: Oneworld Publications.

Andrews, Walter and Mehmet Kalpakli. 2005. *The Age of Beloveds: Love and the Beloved in Early-Modern Ottoman and European Culture and Society*. Durham: Duke University Press.

Bashir, Shahzad. 2011. *Sufi Bodies*. New York: Columbia University Press.

Bawa, Oudesh Rani and Scott Kugle. Forthcoming. 'Shah Bajan's Contribution to Sufism in the Deccan', in *Proceedings from the National Seminar on Religion and Society in Peninsular India, Pondicherry University on 24-26 February, 2011*. Puducherry: Pondicherry University Press.

Burhanpuri, Muhammad ibn Fazlullah. *Tahzir al-Talibin 'an Ru'iyat al-Amrad li'l-Wusul ila Allah*. Manuscript housed at Hyderabad: Salar Jung Museum Library, 29 Arabic Tasawwuf, folios 112b-117b.

Chittick, William and Peter Lamborn Wilson. 1982. *Fakhruddin Iraqi: Divine Flashes*. Mawa, Paulist Press.

Cornell, Rkia Laroui. 1999. *Early Sufi Women*. Louisville: Fons Vitae.

Digby, Simon. 2001. *Sufis and Soldiers in Aurangzeb's Deccan: Malfuzati-i Naqshbandiyya*. New Delhi: Oxford University Press.

El-Rouayheb, Khalid. 2005. *Before Homosexuality in the Arab-Islamic World*. Chicago: University of Chicago Press.

Ernst, Carl and Bruce Lawrence. 2002. *Sufi Martyrs of Love: The Chishti Order in South Asia and Beyond*. New York: Palgrave Macmillan.

Faruqi, Ziya-ul-Hasan (tr.). 1996. *Fawa'id al-Fu'ad: Spiritual and Literary Discourses*. New Delhi: D.K. Printworld.

Feener, Michael and Terenjit Sevea, eds. 2009. *Islamic Connections: Muslim Societies in South and Southeast Asia*. Singapore: ISEAS.

Green, Nile. 2012. *Sufism: A Global History*. Chichester: Wiley-Blackwell.

Hanif, N. 2000. *Biographical Encyclopedia of Sufis in South Asia*. Delhi: Sarup and Sons.

Johns, A.H. (tr.). 1965. *The Gift Addressed to the Spirit of the Prophet*. Canberra: Australian National University Centre of Oriental Studies.

Khan, Sher Muhammad. 1997. *Tarikh-i Awliya-yi Kiram-i Burhanpur*. Pune: Sahar Art Press. Volume 1.

Kugle, Scott. 2007. *Sufis and Saints' Bodies*. Chapel Hill: University of North Carolina Press.

________. 2007b. 'Qawwali between Written Poem and Sung Lyric . . . or How a Ghazal Lives', *The Muslim World*, 97(4): 571-610.

________. 2009. 'Burhan al-Din Gharib: Enduring Sufi Example in the Eternal Garden of Khuldabad', *Deccan Studies Journal*, 7: 2.

Kugle, Scott and Siraj al-Haqq. 2010. *Homosexuality in Islam*. Oxford: Oneworld Publications.

Kugle, Scott and Stephen Hunt. 2012. 'Masculinity, Homosexuality and the Defense of Islam: A Case Study of Yusuf al-Qaradawi's Media Fatwa', *Religion and Gender*, 2(2): 254-79.

Lawrence, Bruce. 1994. 'Honoring Women through Sexual Abstinence: Lessons from the Spiritual Practice of a Pre-Modern South Asian Sufi Master, Shaykh Nizam ad-din Awliya', *Journal of Turkish Studies* 18: 149-61.

Lawrence, Bruce (tr.). 1992. *Morals for the Heart: Conversations of Nizam al-Din Awliya*. Mahwa: Paulist Press.

Manjhan, Shaykh. 2000. *Madhumalati: An Indian Sufi Romance*. Tr. Aditya Behl and Simon Weightman with Shyam Manohar Pandey. Oxford: Oxford University Press.

Papan-Matin, Firoozeh. 2010. *Beyond Death: The Mystical Teachings of 'Ayn al-Qudat al-Hamadhani*. Leiden: E.J. Brill.

________. 2009. 'Gisudaraz, an Early Chishti Leader of the Deccan and his Relation with Twelfth-Century Mystics of Iran', *Deccan Studies Journal*, VII (2): 112-32.

Pemberton, Kelly. 2010. *Women Mystics and Sufi Shrines in India*. Columbia: University of South Carolina Press.

Pourjawady, Nasrollah. 2005. 'The Witness Play of Ahmad Ghazali in Tabriz', in Todd Lawson, ed., *Reason and Inspiration in Islam: Essays in Honour of Hermann Landolt*. London: I.B. Tauris.

Safi, Omid. 2006. *The Politics of Knowledge in Premodern Iran: Negotiating Ideology and Religious Inquiry*. Chapel Hill: University of North Carolina Press.

Schimmel, Annemarie. 2003. *My Soul is a Woman: The Feminine in Islam*. New York: Continuum International.

Shaikh, Sa'diya. 2012. *Sufi Narratives of Intimacy: Ibn Arabi, Gender and Sexuality*. Chapel Hill: University of North Carolina Press.

Siddiqi, Muhammad Suleman. 2014. *The Junaydi Order in the Deccan*. Delhi: Midpoint Trade Books.

Tourage, Mahdi. 2007. *Rumi and the Hermeneutics of Eroticism*. Leiden: E.J. Brill.

Weischer, Bernd Manuel and Peter Lamborn Wilson tr. 1978. *Heart's Witness: The Sufi Quatrains of Awhaduddin Kirmani*. Tehran: Imperial Iranian Academy of Philosophy.

2

Religious Sects, Syncretism, and Claims of Antiquity

The Dashanami-Sannyasis and South Asian Sufis

MATTHEW CLARK[1]

Introduction

An intriguing feature of religions and religious sects (in general) is the apparent difference between, on the one hand, the almost universally and historically syncretic character of most sects; and, on the other hand, the claim (usually not directly stated, but implied and believed) of most sects to have been founded in antiquity with all the inherent components of belief and ritual intact. Syncretic elements—including the saints, sites, practices, legends, personalities, and philosophical and metaphysical elements—which in various combinations contribute to the identity and distinctiveness of the sect at a later time, have, in many instances, been borrowed and accumulated during a long period from other beliefs, philosophies, folklore and religions, but are assumed by orthodox adherents of the religion to have been *in situ* since the founding of their religion. While to the historian of religion (the etic view) one of the most ubiquitous features of religions is their historically syncretic character[2]—research attempts to reveal when components of the religion were included—the emic view of most religions is generally characterized by a view of the religion in which temporal change is not admitted, yet at the same time historical origins are often pushed back far further than any genuinely historical search would permit, in the pursuit of a crucially important antiquity, which generally provides an enhanced sense of validity for present beliefs and practices of adherents.

In my earlier study of the Dashanami-Sannyasis (Clark, 2006a), I tentatively explored some of the interesting parallels between the history, beliefs and practices of Sannyasis and those of South Asian Sufis. In this chapter, fully aware of the slim gains and potential pitfalls of any kind of comparativism, I return to this issue and reassess the extent to which the Sannyasis may have been influenced[3] by Sufi beliefs and practices; and also note, in passing, how both the Sannyasis and Sufis—in common with so many other sects—derive greater lineal legitimacy by extending their origins into antiquity. Another intriguing issue, briefly addressed towards the end of this inquiry, is the process behind the emergence in the sixteenth century of mercenary armies of *naga* Sannyasis, who, along with their Ramanandi (*vairagi*) *tyagi* counterparts, were virtually indistinguishable from marauding bands of Sufi *fakirs*.

The primary aim of this chapter is to explore the way a particular religious identity, that of the Dashanami-Sannyasis, may have emerged. Plainly, in the historical background of the Sannyasis are a number of South Asian sects, besides those of Sufis, whose ideas and practices are to a greater or lesser degree shared by many South Asian sects: Jains, Buddhists, Pashupatas, Kapalikas and Kalamukhas spring readily to mind. However, the political and social dominance of Sufi sects and institutions, particularly in north India during the fifteenth and sixteenth centuries, the time when I have suggested that the identity of the Sannyasis evolved, is the reason why this particular study has focused specifically on possible Sufi influence.[4]

While there have been several studies of how Sufism may have been influenced by other (particularly South Asian) religious traditions, there has been relatively little (or any?) exploration of how, the other way around, Hindu renunciate sects, such as the Dashanami-Sannyasis, may have been influenced by Sufism, which, from the time of its arrival in South Asia was widely influential on South Asian polity.

Regarding possible South Asian influences on Sufism, to give just a couple of brief examples, around a century ago Nicholson suggested (1963[1914]: 17) that Sufism may have been influenced through contact with Buddhism, which was widespread in Khurasan (Afghanistan and eastern Iran) at the time of the diffusion of Sufism in the later centuries of the first millennium. Nicholson believed that Sufis learned the use of rosaries from Buddhist monks and 'owe a good deal to Buddhism'. He noted the similarities between the Buddhist *nibbana* and the Sufi notion of *fana*, both terms having connotations of 'extinction' or 'passing away'.[5] There have been several studies of how the concepts of *yoga* found their way into Sufism, particularly in the Bengal region, where Sufis first arrived in the eleventh century.[6] The most famous text wherein Tantric *yoga* notions of *chakras*, *nadis* and yogic *pranayama* are to be found is the *Amritakunda* (The Pool of Nectar).[7] Within a decade of the Turkish conquest of Bengal, at the beginning of the fourteenth century, there were Persian and Arabic translations of this text, which was widely copied and circulated in Bengal and wider India, its ideas taught by some Sufi shaykhs to their disciples (Eaton 1993: 78-9).[8] For those Sufis who endorsed yogic practices and ideas, there is a familiar tradition that depicts 'Ali as receiving esoteric knowledge from Muhammad, the "Perfect Man", who is identified not only with creation but also with the Creator' (Tarafdar 1992: 103).

It needs to be emphasized that although in this chapter several striking parallels between Sufi and Sannyasi history, structure and practices are presented, in various aspects, this does not amount to demonstrating or proving any influence at all from Sufism on Sannyasis. A cogent criticism of the evidence hereafter presented of potential Sufi influence could be that nearly all of the aspects of influence presented in this chapter can readily be found in pre-Islamic South Asian beliefs and practices and that it is unnecessary to excavate Sufism for features of possible influence; that this study is effectively redundant, which is an entirely valid point of view. It is extremely difficult (if not impossible) to demonstrate causal influence in this kind of historical research. However, I leave it to the reader and other researchers to decide whether or not the cumulative parallels presented between the Sufis and Sannyasis provide sufficient evidence of possible influence or, alternatively, are merely coincidental. Perhaps less controversially, another way to analyse the emergence of sectarian religious identity in the sixteenth and seventeenth centuries—which I return to at the conclusion of this chapter—is to disregard notions of any direct influence and rather to understand the process in terms of the assembly of motifs of sectarian identity from a common pool of concepts and beliefs, to which Sufis may or may not have contributed.

Overview of the Historical Formation of the Dashanami-Sannyasis

Before turning to the possible influences Sufism may have had on the Sannyasis, it will first be necessary to outline what I have previously suggested are some of the processes that led to the formation of the identity of the Dashanami-Sannyasis as a sect.[9] The Dashanami-Sannyasis, one of the largest of the sects of South Asian *sadhus*, famously claim to have been founded by the legendary Advaita Vedanta philosopher Shankaracharya (*fl.c.*700), who is also believed to have founded, in the four corners of India, four monasteries (*mathas*/*pithas*), in which he installed four of his disciples, from which the incumbent Shankaracharyas claim lineal descent. I have suggested (Clark, 2006a; 2006b) that these claims are probably historically unfounded and that the identity of the Sannyasis as a sect developed in several stages, reaching its final and current form around the end of the sixteenth century.

In the first stage, Shankara, from relative personal and philosophical obscurity, was transformed by his hagiographers from a Vaishnava into a Shaiva.[10] Hagiographies of Shankara[11] were most probably first composed in the late fourteenth or fifteenth centuries in the region of the south-Indian Vijayanagara Empire, founded in 1336, providing the early rulers (the Sangama brothers)—based in the town that is now called Hampi—with a world-conquering patron saint, an incarnation of Shiva, for the re-branded monastic tradition at Shringeri:[12] a new Advaita Vedanta 'orthodox' Shaiva religion; 'orthodox' in the sense of being Brahmanical and acknowledging the Veda as the ultimate authority.

In the second stage several lineages of renunciates became integrated with other lineages pertaining to an Advaita Vedanta monastic tradition, into a scheme of the 'Ten Names'. The 'Ten

Names' (*dashanami/dashnami/dasnami*), one of which a *sannyasi* receives on initiation from his/her guru, is one of the distinctive marks of the Sannyasis. Of the eight hagiographies of Shankara examined by Bader (2000), the only one to mention the establishing of ten lineages—which is one of the earliest references I have found to the 'ten names'[13]—is Chidvilasa's *Shankaravijayavilasa* (24.36-37a).[14] (This is said to have occurred while Shankara was residing at Shringeri.) The dating of this text by Bader and Antarkar, who are the two foremost scholars of the hagiographies of Shankara, is imprecise. Antarkar (1973: 3) tentatively dates this text to before 1630, or possibly before the sixteenth century; while Bader (2000: 24) believes that although it is almost certainly post-fourteenth century it is from before 1740. The same phrase for the ten names used by Chidvilasa appears in the *Yatidharmaprakasha* of Vasudevashrama (66.14-15), dated by Olivelle (1976: 18) to between 1675 and 1800. In this passage, Vasudevashrama is referring to an earlier work, the *Yatidharmasangraha* of Vishveshvarasarasvati (pp. 102-3), who was the illustrious Advaita teacher of Maḍhusudanasarasvati (1540-1647); which allows us to date this reference to around the end of the sixteenth century.[15]

In the third layer of the process (which may have been almost simultaneous with the second stage), the legend of the founding of four *mathas* in the four quarters of India is added to the hagiographic picture. Only two of the eight hagiographies examined by Bader mention the founding of four *mathas*: Chidvilasa's *Shankaravijayavilasa* and the *Guruvanshakavya* of Lakshmanashastri, which may be dated to *c.*1740 (Bader, 2000: 52). Chidvilasa extolls Shringeri (24.31-33a),[16] where the *matha* (called Shri Matha) is said to have been established by Shankara, who installs his disciple Sureshvara therein. Shankara is then said to have founded other *mathas*: in the east, near the Jagannath Temple, presided over by Padmapada; in the west, where he installed Hastamalaka; and in the north, where he had a 'heavenly *matha*' built and where he installed Totaka. While there are specific references in Chidvilasa's *Shankaravijayavilasa* to Shringeri and Jagannath, and though the Gomati River (which flows near to the *matha* at Dvaraka) is mentioned as a *tirtha* (30.4), no mention is made of either Dvaraka or Badrinath, the sites now associated with the four *mathas* believed to have been founded by Shankara. However, it is apparent that the specific sites of the four *mathas* supposedly founded by Shankara have changed several times in the last few hundred years (Clark 2006a: 114-47).

In the fourth and final layer of the process, each of the ten names is assigned to one or another of the four *pithas*, integrating ten lineages into a scheme that establishes the four disciples of Shankara (who had become an incarnation of Shiva) in four specific *mathas* in the four quarters of India. This scheme is detailed in a series of short Sanskrit texts variously known as *(Shri) Mathamnaya, Mathamnayastotra,* and *Mathamnayasetu.* These texts specify, sequentially, the name of the *matha*, the pontiff assigned to it by Shankara, its regional jurisdiction (*mandala*), which of the 'ten names' belong to it, its sacred river, its deities, its Veda, its Brahmanical *gotra*, its *sampradaya*, and the name of *brahmacharis* attached to it.[17] When someone is initiated into the Dashanami-Sannyasi sect he or she is presented with a short Hindi text, the *Dashnam Vansh Vriksh*, which is similar in form to the Sanskrit *mathamnayas*, and provides a schema of the order. Described is an evolution from the 'cosmic void', through various gods and *rishi*s, to Shankara and his four disciples, who head the four *mathamnayas*. The new initiate, through his or her surname (one of the ten names), is assigned to one of the *amnayas*, with its associated specificities. The scheme of the *mathamnayas* is repeated (albeit with a few inconsistencies) in almost every publication on the Sannyasis that has been published in the last 150 years, and provides the primary emic and etic locus of identity for the sect.

The Integration of Lineages

It was mentioned earlier that, in what I have characterized as the second stage of a process of sectarian formation, it appears that several lineages of ascetics joined together to adopt a shared sectarian identity, with Shankara as their founder and patron saint. Numerous, prominent Vedantins, some of whom were directly connected to the Advaita-orientated monastic tradition, have borne one or another of the 'ten names' of the Sannyasis;[18] but I suggest that that those who were influenced by the philosophical heritage of Shankara did not consider themselves to be members of a sect of *sannyasis* founded by Shankara, a sect moreover that comprises lineages of radical, militant *nagas*.

The Sannyasi *nagas*, the *paramahansas* and the *dandis* (the three main divisions of the Sannyasis) are organizationally and administratively separate. The orthodox, Brahman *dandis* who carry a staff (*dand*) have no connection at all to the *akharas*[19] to which the *nagas* belong; and tend to regard the wild, ash-covered *nagas* disparagingly.[20] I have heard *dandis* remark that, 'we are not Dashanamis'. The only time that all branches of the Sannyasis properly convene is at Kumbh Melas, when initiations take place, under the auspices of a Shankaracharya.

I surmise that the adoption of Shankara as a tutelary saint by various lineages of *nagas*—who had attached themselves ideologically to lineages pertaining to the monastic tradition—provided groups of militants with a useful religious identity. During the heyday of the military campaigns of the large mercenary *naga* armies (up to 20,000 strong), in the seventeenth and eighteenth centuries,[21] a *raja* of Nepal complained in 1792 that, 'although the *fakir* is full of faults and deserving death', he could only expel them from his territory and could not confine or kill them, as that would be contrary to religious law (Ghosh, 1930: 9).[22] Bayly (1992: 184) comments that the *nagas*' religious status and fearsome reputation made them virtually immune from police prosecution or harassment. This is not to suggest that groups of mercenaries—many of whom between campaigns returned to small holdings and the like to tend agricultural plots—simply adopted Shankara as a saint to avoid prosecution when on military campaign; but that rather than engage in plain dacoity, there may have been an added attraction for the peasant farmer to become a religious mercenary with the benefit of relative immunity from potential criminal prosecution.

The Significance of the Framework of the *Mathamnayas*

The *mathamnayas* provide the prime locus of identity for the Dashanami-Sannyasis, providing a structure of a divine *avatara* (Shankara), four disciples and four regions (*kshetras*) over which each disciple has a jurisdiction. The jurisdiction of the *pithas* is not merely an issue of religious conception, as incumbent Shankaracharyas have legal rights to collect donations in their respective territories, which has led to many court cases in the last few hundred years.[23] However, many inconsistencies abound in the various lists of *acharyas* and the *guru-paramparas* pertaining to the *pithas* purported to have been founded by Shankara (see Clark, 2006a: 122-8), and there have been a number of claims by various *mathas* in several locations in India during the last three centuries to have been 'originally' founded by Shankara, providing further cause for skepticism about the authenticity of the scheme of the *mathamnayas*. I have been unable to determine the earliest date of the composition of the *mathamnayas* but speculate that the scheme may have crystallized towards the end of the sixteenth century.[24]

It has been suggested that one of the reasons for the enthusiastic adoption of the framework of the *mathamnayas* and the implicit hagiography of the world-conquering, orthodox, Brahman Shankara by various lineages of *nagas*, may have been that such an identity not only elevated the Sannyasis as spiritual descendants of an esteemed Brahman, but also provided useful protection to some degree from criminal prosecution, as *nagas*, upon initiation, become members of an orthodox religious sect. However, as I have previously speculated (Clark, 2006: 227-46), I believe that the impulse to form a Hindu sect of *sannyasis* with the specific frame-story embodied in the *mathamnayas* may have derived some inspiration from Sufi traditions and influence in South Asia.

Sufis in South Asia

Although scholars of Islam are not entirely unanimous about the origins of Sufism, there is broad agreement about the arrival of Sufis[25] in South Asia and the development of lineal teaching traditions, in a 'chain' (*silsila*)[26] of shaykhs.[27]

The first Muslim conquest in South Asia was of Sind by Ibn al-Qasim in 711/12 (Schimmel, 1980: 3-4), beginning a period of uninterrupted Muslim rule in Sind that lasted over 1,100 years. By the early tenth century there was a large and prosperous Muslim settlement near Bombay (Farooqi, 2004: 3). Also in the eighth century, the first Sufis[28] arrived in South Asia[29] (Siddiqi, 1989: 14), the first Sufi *khanqahs* (simple monasteries) in South Asia being established in the ninth century. Within a century or so, *khanqahs*, which also functioned as travellers' rest houses, were numerous throughout north India;[30] by the thirteenth century they had become widespread (Nizami, 2002: 62). In the thirteenth and fourteenth centuries there were up to 120 in Delhi (Digby, 1986).[31]

Sufi *silsilas* first developed in the twelfth century (Rizvi, 1978: 83; Nizami, 2002: 59), their institutional organization, which propagated particular Sufi paths (*tariqas*), superseding earlier instances of personal mysticism or what has been referred to as 'spontaneous individuality' (Ansari, 2003: 19),[32] and by the time of the founding of the Delhi Sultanate in 1206—by the *mamluk* (slave) Turk, Qutb-ud-Din Aibek—*silsilas* had taken root in South Asia, where they were more influential than in any other region under Muslim rule. Robinson (2003: 52) comments that the 'holy men' were pioneers and frontiersmen of the Islamic world in South Asia, who played a crucial role in drawing in people to Islam.

The first Sufi orders to have a significant influence in South Asia in the thirteenth century were the Chishti and Suhrawardi *silsilas*.[33] While the Chishti order emphasized the renunciation of wealth and subsistence on the receipt of unsolicited alms (*futuh*), many Suhrawardis became very wealthy and influential,[34] not only in Sind and Punjab, where they had their main centres at Multan and Ucch (Ansari, 2003: 19), but also at the court of the Delhi Sultanate.[35]

Besides pious Sufis, other waves of warrior (*ghazi*) Sufi shaykhs arrived in India from Khurasan around the beginning of the thirteenth century, their wrath leading to 'the discomfiture, misery and often death of those who presumed to oppose [them]' (Digby, 1986: 60). These warrior Sufis were very similar in many ways to Sannyasi *nagas*. Between 1296 and 1347, militant Sufis were extensively involved in Muslim military expansion in the Deccan.[36] Probably centred on *khanqahs*, they represented the only element of Islamic organization at the frontiers of expansion of the Bahmani state.

There is considerable evidence that in the thirteenth and

fourteenth centuries *ghazis* were still on the front line of Muslim expansion (Eaton, 1978: 34-46). Even though warrior Sufis had been active in India since the thirteenth century, the image of the *ghazi* only first appears in Indo-Muslim writing in the sixteenth and seventeenth centuries, an image that was then retroactively attributed to numerous individuals of previous centuries (Talbot, 2003: 107). By the middle of the fourteenth century, however, warrior Sufis, who at that time were not affiliated to any order, had almost disappeared from the Bahmani state, replaced by Sufis affiliated to various Sufi *silsilas*, notably the Chishti, Qadiri and Shattari orders (Eaton, 1978: 45ff.).

Sufi Regional Jurisdiction and Influence

The authoritative transmission of tradition (*silsila*)—a direct parallel to the Hindu notion of *guru-parampara*—is central to Sufi practices. After initiation, some Sufis were given a certificate (*ijaza* or *khilafat-nama*), authorizing them to act as deputies (*khalifas*) and to disseminate the principles and practices of their order (Rizvi, 1978: 102). In the process of political and religious expansion, leaders of *silsilas* dispatched *khalifas* to various provinces that fell within what they deemed to be their *wilayat* (territorial jurisdiction),[37] which was quite precise, but occasionally disputed, though less in South Asia than in other regions where *silsilas* flourished (Digby, 1986: 63-72). These *khalifas* in turn appointed subordinate *khalifa*s for cities and *qasbas*. Many *pirs* gained almost regal power and influence: they were invested with a turban and sat on a throne (*gaddi*), acquiring rights that were often legitimized in terms of wealth and social position. The *pir* would sometimes tour his region, on a palanquin (*palki*), in the style of a Shankaracharya's *digvijaya*, his progress resembling 'one of regal magnificence'. The *pir* would act as mediator in local conflicts, combining a regal and spiritual life (Ansari, 2003: 23-6), in a style also similar to that of incumbent Shankaracharyas. Indeed, in the same way that the Shankaracharyas are *sannyasis* (renouncers), yet head what are, in some cases, large organizations with high-level political connections, some Sufi shaykhs were, historically, in a similar socio-political situation, yet, at the same time *faqirs*: 'poor' (*faqr*) men.[38] 'Critics pointed out the contradictions between the Sufi ideal of poverty and the luxurious life possible for a *faqir* living in a sumptuously maintained lodge' (Ernst, 2011: 126).

Nizami (2002: 188) remarks that a hierarchy of saints came to be established in northern India. The chief saint at the centre—who was sometimes referred to as 'Sultan-ul-Hind'—stood at the apex of the whole system and controlled a network of *khanqahs*[39] throughout the country. Shaykh Mu'in-ud-Din Chishti and Shaykh Salim Chishti practically became patron saints of the Mughals,[40] their *wilayats* extending (theoretically) all over India (Digby, 1986: 72; Chandra, 1996: 145).[41] At the beginning of the fourteenth century, another shaykh of the Chishti *silsila*, Nizam-ud-Din Auliya (1238-1325), was so esteemed that he was identified with the fortunes of Delhi, over which his *wilayat* extended. Such was the status of some shaykhs that they were considered to be beyond the law in some aspects (Shackle, 1976: 162). By the sixteenth century, Mughal bureaucrats were dispensing royal funds and land to Sufi shrines that were generally regulated by appointed trustees (Ernst and Lawrence, 2002: 21). The influence of Sufis in South Asia was such that there was more Persian Sufi hagiographical literature produced in India than in all of Persia and Central Asia combined (Ernst and Lawrence, 2002: 48). The network of Sufi shrines in South Asia was extensive, and, as for Sannyasis, spiritual geography mirrored political geography.

Parallels between Sufi and Sannyasi Institutions

It was noticed (Clark 2006a: 234) that there was a coincidence in the formal institutionalization of aspects of both Sufi and Sannyasi orders in the fourteenth century. The first land grant by the Sangamas to the newly-founded monastic tradition at Shringeri was in 1346. The political significance of this event is commented upon by Nilakanta Sastri (1992: 125):

> The foundation of the [Vijayanagara] empire was the culmination of a strong wave of religious revival and political excitement caused by the Delhi Sultanate seeking to re-impose its sway on the Deccan and further south in the fourteenth century.

Subsequently, hagiographic accounts of Shankara presented him with a pan-Indian *wilayat*, expressed through his 'regal' *digvijaya*. I have suggested that the final layer of the hagiographic process was the specification in the *mathamnayas* of the jurisdictions (*kshetras*) of four of Shankara's disciples, in the four 'corners' of India, from which scheme the current Shankaracharyas derive the legitimacy of their jurisdiction.

In somewhat parallel circumstances, in 1347—just a year after the Shringeri grant—there was what was probably the first land grant to Sufis in the Deccan, at the founding of the Bahmani kingdom, adjacent to Vijayanagara, with which it shared a large number of structural similarities (Eaton, 2000: 160-75). In that year the coronation of Ala-ud-Din Hasan, the new Sultan—who had declared independence from the Delhi Sultanate—was assisted by Shaykh Siraj-ud-Din Junaidi (d. 1380), who was closely associated with the court. Junaidi was granted the village of Korchi, from which his descendants still benefit. Sultan Hasan subsequently distributed 400 pounds of gold and 1,000 pounds of silver, in the name of Nizam-ud-Din Auliya, facilitating the allegiance of all the Sufis in the territory to his successor, Muhammad Shah Bahmani (Eaton, 1978: 60-1). Just a couple of decades before the land grant to Sufis in the Deccan, in 1328 Shaykh Rukn-ud-Din Abul Fath, who was the grandson of Shaykh Baha'-ud-Din Zakariyya, accepted the largest land grant ever given by the Delhi Sultanate. He received a hundred villages and a large *jagir* for expenses for his *khanqah* for his support for Sultan Muhammad bin Tughluq during a rebellion (Huda, 2003: 124-6), illustrating the close ties between powerful Sufis and rulers in this period.

The rulers of Vijayanagara, in continuation of a practice that had been followed by kings for several hundred years, were all initiated by *raja-gurus* (*acharyas*), mostly from the Kalamukha order,[42] conferring power and protection on the king. Similarly, such was the symbolic power of Sufis that, as with the Bahmani rulers, Muslim sultans were often crowned by Sufis at the royal investiture ceremony. From at least the reign of Akbar, such was the influence of Sufi ideology, that Mughal emperors were referred to at court as *murshid* (teacher) and the courtiers as *murid* (disciple) (Green, 2008: 13, 16).

I mentioned previously that during initiation into the order that Sannyasis are presented with a Hindi document, the *Dashnam Vansh Vriksh* (Ten Name Lineage/Family Tree), in which the line of succession goes back through Shankara's disciples, Shankara, his teacher (Govindacharya), Bhattacharya, Gaudacharya, and then back through a line of *rishis*[43] and gods to a 'cosmic' void. These details and others in the document relating to the specific branch of the Sannyasis that the candidate is being initiated into are required to be memorized by the initiate. Similarly, during initiation, Sufis are required to recite the *silsila* of their order, a practice supplemented by the writing down of the names of chain of the masters of the order, resulting in a lineage/family tree, known as a *shajara* ('tree': Arabic). Knowing the names of the chain of masters in the *shajara* confers special merit (Ernst and Lawrence, 2002: 19-23). The *shajara* is a central feature of the Sufi's identity, often put on bold display at shrines (Green, 2008: 16), relating to both family ancestry (showing circles of minor disciples emanating from the major masters) and the initiate's ancestry. Some also contain brief biographical notes. Upon initiation, the disciple's name is added to the bottom of the list, which is sometimes many pages long. For both Sannyasis and Sufis the line of succession[44] stretches far into antiquity.[45]

Another parallel between the Sannyasi and Sufi orders—and indeed many other South Asian sects—is the way they trace their lineages back in antiquity to four 'rightly guided' preceptors; and prior to the four preceptors is a god-like figure: Shankara for the Sannyasis, and Muhammad for the Sufis. Subsequent to the formation of *silsilas* around the thirteenth century, most Sufi sects produced lines of succession back to the four 'rightly guided' Caliphs[46] and Muhammad. Most Sufi orders regard 'Ali as their shaykh and trace their descent from either 'Ali, or, via 'Ali, from Hasan al-Basri (642-728), who was born in Medina and settled in Basra.[47] The Chishti order, for example, has a tradition of masters that goes back through Hasan al-Basri and 'Ali.[48] However, a few Sufi sects, such as the Naqshbandi and Maulawi, retrospectively proclaimed a lineage going back to Abu Bakr.[49]

It was not only the Sannyasis who divided their order into a specific number of branches of their family (ten in the case of the

Sannyasis). In this connection, it is interesting to note the remarks of the author of the *Dabistan* (who wrote in 1645):

> [The Sufis], as they have heard that there are ten classes of sanyāsīs, and twelve of yogīs, they also pretend to be divided into fourteen classes; when they meet together, the questions which they ask are: who are the four sages, and which are the fourteen noble families? And they impose upon their disciples many years of service, before they reveal to them the four sages and fourteen families; they say: the sage of sages is the [1] illustrious Muhammed (may the peace of God be upon him!), and after him, devoted to godliness, [2] Ali (may the blessings of God be upon him!); from him the Khalifat devolved upon [3] Imam Hossain;[50] then [4] Khaja Hossen of Basora [Hasan al-Basri], also was his disciple and a khalif; these four personages are the four sages. (*Dabistan-i Mazahib*, pp. 220-1)

The text continues with a list of fourteen families[51] who are said to have descended from two Caliphs.[52]

Regarding the trope of four sage disciples, it is not only the Sufi and Sannyasi orders that trace their descent from four preceptors. Other instances in South Asian traditions include the four disciples of Lakulisha, four Vedic *rishis* who were disciples of Vaikhanasa, four disciples of Vyasa ('author' of the *Mahabharata*), four *kulas* of the Jaina Shvetambara mendicant community, the four Udasis who represent the four divisions of the Bara Udasi sect, and the four disciples of Ramanuja.[53] It has been suggested that the Sannyasis may have acquired elements of their sectarian identity from the Sufis. The idea of the four sages amongst Sufis was apparently known about in South Asia, assuming that the *Dabistan* is reliable in this respect, and other traditions of four sage preceptors may have added legitimacy to the Sannyasis' own project of identity.

Besides the similarities between the Sufi and Sannyasi overviews of their respective orders, features of initiatory procedures in both orders are also similar. *Sannyasa* initiation (when the candidate performs his or her funeral rites, which is the second and final stage of the initiation process; see Clark 2006a: 81ff.) is usually performed at Kumbh Melas. Subsequent to initial preparation through fasting, ablutions, *mantra*-recitation, and the payment of (usually) fifty-one rupees *dakshina*, and then after a ritual of being shaved (head, moustache, beard, armpits and pubic hair) the Sannyasi is renamed in the lineage of the initiating *guru* and presented with a *dand* (staff) (which is subsequently relinquished by all but *dandis*), a *kaupin* (loin-cloth) and a *kamandal* (water pot), the regalia conferring sectarian identity. Similarly, for Sufis the usual but not universal procedure for the initiation (*baiy'a*) is that after fasting, alms and prayer, the *pir* shakes the *murid's* hand (or touches his head),[54] the initiate's head is shaved, and the best disciples are invested with the patched woollen frock (*khirka*).[55] Their prayer carpet, wooden sandals, rosary and staff (*'asa*) constitute their identificatory regalia (Nizami, 2002: 188). Women are admitted to some branches of both Sannyasi and Sufi[56] orders.

Subsequent to initiation, both Sufis and Sannyasis are formally members of religious orders but may have a wide variety of roles in society. In my study of the Sannyasis I surveyed (Clark, 2006a: 3-22) the broad spectrum of activities that Sannyasis have engaged in—as mercenaries, bankers, traders, farmers, priests, administrators and householders—and challenged the oft-repeated motif of the Sannyasi as the lone, wandering renouncer. Lapidus (1967: 106) categorizes three kinds of Sufis: those who generally supported the *'ulama* (clerics), conservatives who vigorously opposed 'un-Islamic' practices (such as the consumption of wine and hashish), and those (such as the *harafish*: unruly beggars) following 'dangerous' and extreme beliefs and practices. But as Green (2008: 18) notes—in response to the complaint that 'real Sufis only exist in books'—that Sufis may have day jobs as bureaucrats, horse-dealers and soldiers: and these are, of course, 'real' Sufis.

Sufi and Sannyasi *Babas*

The visitor to South Asia may be struck with the similarities between the lifestyles and appearance of Sannyasi and Sufi *babas*. Seated by a *dhuni* (fire-place) presided over by a *pir* or *guru*, smoking *chilams* of *ganja* and *charas*, often sporting dreadlocks, roving extensively, and manifesting a proudly independent and generally antinomian style of behaviour, but for specific items of sectarian regalia, Sufi and Sannyasi *babas* are often practically indistinguishable; and indeed to many early British colonial recorders and administrators were indistinguishable.[57] Amongst Sannyasis, it is the branch of the Dashanami-Sannyasis from the *akharas*, in distinction from the more monastically-based *dandis*, who are more numerous and visible in north India, and who have a history of mercenary and militant activity.[58] That roving Sannyasi should even be customarily seated by a 'holy' *dhuni* is indeed somewhat curious given the Brahmanical injunctions that the traditional Sannyasi renouncer should—in that well-known Indological motif—'internalize' the sacred fire,[59] should beg for food and not use a fire at all. According to the rules of *dharmashastra*, even if resident in a *matha* cooked food for a Sannyasi must be brought in from outside.[60] But such is the association of renouncers with *dhunis* that the Hindi expression *dhuni lagana* also means 'to become a *yogi*' (which is a generic Hindi term for a *sadhu, sannyasi* or 'renouncer'). This is not at all to suggest that South Asian ascetics hadn't been sitting around 'holy' fires for millennia prior to the arrival of Sufis, but rather that the conspicuous presence and lifestyle of some sects of Sufis in South Asia for several hundred years may possibly have had an influence on the formation of the identity of the Sannyasis. What is being suggested is that elements of the lifestyle of Sannyasi, and indeed other sects of renouncers, such as the *vairagis* (Ramanandis) and Naths, may have been almost seamlessly adopted from wandering Sufi groups: all that might have changed within individual sects were sectarian marks and tutelary deities.

Amongst the different orders of Sufis who arrived in north India, during the thirteenth and fourteenth centuries, most prominent were numerous bands of roving antinomian Sufis (Digby, 2001: 25; Karamustafa, 2006: 60), who were generally referred to as *qalandars*. Several sects of these wild *dervishes* spread throughout the world of Islam between around AD 1200 and 1500, the most influential being the Qalandaris and Haydaris.[61] A great influence on the diffusion of *qalandars* throughout the Islamic world was the Mongol conquest of Khurasan in 1220/1 (Digby, 1984: 63). Within a decade of their appearance, members of these sects were portrayed as shameless charlatans. They spread rapidly to South Asia, being present in Delhi in the thirteenth century.[62] They emphasized celibacy, mendicancy, itinerancy and self-mortification, and openly rejected religious observances (they were *be shar:* 'outside the law').[63] Not only indigents but educated youths—children of the elite—joined the Qalandaris (Karamustafa, 2006: 93), whose members also included orphans, runaway children and adolescents, criminals escaping justice, and professionals who had 'dropped out' (Digby, 1984: 63ff.).

The Haydaris[64] wore iron necklaces and bracelets, garlands of teeth around their ankles, and had a lead ring through their penis.[65] They were often nearly naked and performed penances such as immersion in icy water in winter, and sitting by fire in the summer. Groups of *qalandars* usually carried banners, drums and tambourines and some used to sing and dance when performing *zikr*. Their begging for alms was often aggressive. Members of *qalandar* sects were often completely shaven of all body hair, including eyebrows, a shave known as the 'four blows' (*chahar zarb*).[66] They usually wore rough wool or sometimes animal hides and most went barefoot. Interestingly, some *qalandars* wore a reddish-ochre course garment (*palas*), characteristic of Indian ascetics (Digby, 1984: 64). The Madaris,[67] a South Asian sub-sect of the Qalandaris, smeared their naked bodies with ashes, wound chains around their heads and necks, and had matted hair and black turbans. By the end of the fifteenth century they had spread to all parts of northern India, Sind and Nepal, by which time social deviance had become a prominent religious option in South Asia (Karamustafa, 2006: 61). Several of the more conventional Sufi sects, including the Chishtis and Suhrawardis, developed *qalandar* sub-sects.

These *qalandar* sects usually travelled in groups for most of the year, returning to periodic residence of relative comfort in *khanqahs*. They sometimes dwelt in graveyards, were wild and unruly, and had a reputation for attraction to beardless boys (Karamustafa, 2006: 22).[68] Not infrequent are accounts of their attacks on shaykhs. They often attracted extreme opprobrium wherever they went—though there were voices of tolerance—and were famous for great consumption of hashish.[69] Both Sava and Haydar, who consumed hashish daily, were credited (of course, wrongly) with discovering it (Karamustafa, 2006: 19; Rosenthal, 1971: 49). Rosenthal (1971: 53) remarks that 'The use of hashish by Sufi fraternities and their presumably large role in the spread of hashish can be accepted as a fact in view of all the later evidence pointing in that direction'. Its use in the Muslim world accelerated in the thirteenth century, coinciding with the arrival in India of Sufi sects who used it. Sanderson (2003: 365-6, n. 43) notes the new appearance in some Tantric rites, particularly in the north-east of India, of an intoxicating cannabis drink known as *sanvit/sanvida* or *vijaya* (*bhang*), and comments that, 'It is probable that the use of cannabis for spiritual intoxication was adopted following the example of Muslim ascetics in India such as those of the Madariyya'.

To outsiders, hashish eaters were generally viewed as vagabond layabouts, while the intoxicated Sufis believed that hashish allowed access to the mystical inner secrets of the world that lay at the heart of their religion's revelation.[70] Some of these Sufis claimed that hashish was the master of Sufi teachings (Rosenthal, 1971: 149). The low cost of hashish (compared with alcohol) allowed the poor access to intoxication.[71]

Given the presence of bands of wild, roving, *bhang*-loving, antinomian Sufis in north India at the end of the fifteenth century, by which time they had lost something of their initial force and charisma (Digby, 1984: 91), it is tempting to speculate that the formation of the *naga* armies of Sannyasi and *vairagis* in the sixteenth century may have had a prior Sufi template, in the roving bands of *ghazis* and *qalandars*. Indeed, in subsequent centuries, the bands of armed, marauding raiders of Bengal that Warren Hastings so vigorously campaigned against in the late eighteenth century were both Sufi and Sannyasi.[72] Such, it would seem, was the attitude of relative liberality regarding traditional religious injunctions amongst some *nagas* that probably the most prominent, historically, of all Sannyasi *nagas*, Anupgiri and his brother Umravgiri (whose armies were active in the latter half of the eighteenth century) had several Muslim wives and courtesans (Pinch, 2006: 149-84).

Digby (1984: 99) remarks that by the end of the fifteenth century the Haydari name had practically disappeared from India, and that it is 'possible that similar devotees were absorbed into low-class Muslim groups bearing other names, the Madaris in northern India or the Rifa'is in the Deccan'. My speculation is that the *qalan-*

dar movement—if it can be so called—did not really decline, but was adopted by similar, roving, antinomian *babas* claiming allegiance to Shankaracharya, Ramananda or Gorakhnath.

Conclusion

Sufi terminology in most of the major languages of the Muslim world is identical (Green, 2008: 18);[73] and in this regard it is interesting to note how several Persian terms are used by Sannyasis for some of their most important institutions: *peshvai* (the 'reception' procession, as at a Kumbh Mela), *pir* (to refer to a *mahant* or guru), *shahi* (royal, as for a holy bath), *jamat* (wandering group), *julus* (procession), *baba* (*sadhu*), *akhara* (military division/wrestling ring: *akharebaz*, Persian). These terms were, of course, common currency in the late Mughal period,[74] but the use of non-Sanskrit terms for important procedures and honorary titles amongst newly emergent Hindi sects is perhaps noteworthy.

What has been suggested in this chapter is that out of a melting pot of traditions and religions that were current in the period, when the identity of the Dashanami-Sannyasis—and indeed several other sects—became fully crystallized, around the late sixteenth century onwards, motifs of identity were drawn from a pool of practices, terms and beliefs that were not 'new' but were common stock for many emergent Hindu sects; and substantial elements of this pool may have been contributed by several disparate sects of Sufis. Shankaracharyas represent the Sanskrit tradition in the modern world, yet it has been suggested that the history of their order is far more syncretic than it may appear at first glance.

Notes

1. Incorporating several comments that were made on first presentation, this is a slightly revised version of a paper that was delivered at the STIMW conference in Manchester (UK) on 25 May 2012.
2. In recent decades, the notion of syncretism in religions has been subject to some negative press (see, for example, Ernst, 2008: 246-51), the main objection being that those who find syncretic elements in a religion are assumed to believe that there is a 'pure' core that has

been (negatively) subject to syncretic influence. On the contrary, I would argue that explorations of syncretism have in many instances not gone far enough. One of the arguments against syncretism is that if nearly every component of a particular religion can be described as syncretic, then syncretism has almost no meaning. But to illustrate the almost universal pervasiveness of syncretism in the continuous process of development in religious traditions does not, in my view, void a description of syncretism—it merely illustrates the pervasiveness of syncretism: there was never a real essentialism (except in the minds of religious adherents) to argue either for or against it.

3. The issues of influence, borrowing and syncretism in the exploration of the history of particular religions are inherently complex, and although the analysis in this chapter occasionally uses the term 'influence', it is to be understood sometimes more as a term of convenience to describe what is often a rather opaque process, in which in some instances it is difficult to establish whether or not a particular component of a religion has been 'borrowed', is 'original', or was acquired almost simultaneously and independently by two or more religions, a conundrum that may afflict not only the study of religions but also sciences, arts and ideas in general.
4. South Asian religious sects are in a geographical situation to draw from a particularly rich and diverse pool of religious traditions, cultures and practices, and further insights would no doubt emerge from explorations (and many studies have already been done) of hybridity and syncretism in other religious traditions of South Asia, such as those of, for example, the Ismaili, Prannami, Sant, Sikh, Nath, and Kabirpanthi orders, to name but a few; but for the sake of brevity, this chapter is restricted to the broader impact and influence that Sufism may have had on the nascent sectarian identity of the Sannyasis. It should perhaps also be mentioned that this is but a preliminary inquiry into a complex process, for which the author is not fully linguistically competent and entirely reliant on secondary sources for the Islamic material in particular, from which infelicities doubtless issue.
5. Haq (1975: 157, 401) also believes that the 'stages' (*maqamat*) on the path of Sufis, leading to union with God, 'were fundamentally based on the Buddhist yoga'; and maintains that the Buddhist notion of *shunya* (void) also found its way into Sufism.
6. Haq notes (1975: 100-5) how Bengali Sufis may perform *zikr* ('remembrance'/'recollection') accompanied by concentration on *latifas* (centres of light), a technique probably introduced into South

Asia by Naqshbandi Sufis, though originating among Kubrawi Sufis (Ernst, 2008: 256). *Latifas*, unknown in Sufism before the twelfth century but widespread by the fifteenth century, are similar in function to the six *chakras* of Tantric yoga. This practice may also be performed with specific techniques of breath control (as in *pranayama*). Tarafdar (1992) considers four works written by Chishti Sufis from Bengal, dating from the fourteenth century onwards, which contain information on Tantric yoga practices and physiology: on *asanas*, *chakras*, *nadis*, *pranayama* and related concepts. All four works use specific yoga terminology, representing a syncretism in this type of Sufism of Islamic mysticism with elements of *hatha-yoga*.

7. Ernst (2011: 106-11), however, cautions the assumption that Sufi practices were necessarily acquired from Indian *yogis*, noting that breathing techniques, psychic points in the body, and visualizations were already current in Kubrawi Sufi circles in Central Asia in the thirteenth century. Ernst (2008: 273) also remarks that the term *yoga* rarely appears in the text.
8. Ernst (2008) provides a useful survey of the influence of yoga on Sufism in South Asia. It was particularly members of the Chishti and Shattari sects of Sufis who absorbed yogic ideas. However, amongst Sufis there were also reactions against yoga and yogic ideas (Ernst, 2008: 258, 272).
9. Although some of the material in the following sections of this chapter has been previously published (Clark, 2006a) it was thought to be necessary to present it again for those readers unfamiliar with the historical analysis previously undertaken, in order to provide the platform upon which the comparisons presented here depend. It should be emphasized that some of the conclusions arrived at remain tentative and on some points speculative.
10. This issue was first explored by Hacker in 1950 (Halbfass, 1995: 33-9); see also Hirst (1993: 131-9).
11. For studies of the hagiographies of Shankara, see Antarkar (1960, 1961, 1972, 1973, 1997, 2001) and Bader (2000).
12. The adoption of a saint as a figurehead for a political dynasty is not historically unusual. Considering Ireland in the seventh century, Stevenson (1995: 25) remarked that, 'By and large, each dynasty had its own saint, its own foundation, on a principle resembling the Continental *eigenkloster*. . . . Very clearly, the saints' lives, as propaganda for the power and influence of their subjects, had a crucial role to play in aggrandizing specific monastic centres at (inevitably) the expense of others.'

13. Tirtha, Ashrama, Vana, Aranya, Giri, Parvata, Sagara, Sarasvati, Bharati, Puri.
14. For the relevant verse, see the Antarkar edition (1973: 73).
15. For other early references to the 'ten names' in texts from this period, see Clark (2006a: 175).
16. This and the following references are to Antarkar's text (1973).
17. See Clark (2006a: 114-47) for further details of these texts and their publication. Some details in the various publications are not consistent, such as which one of Shankara's disciples was appointed to which *pitha*.
18. Amongst prominent Vedantins of the fourteenth to sixteenth centuries who bore one or another of the 'ten names' were: the first preceptors of Shringeri (Bharatitirtha, Vidyatirtha, and Vidyaranya); Madhva (the dualist) was initiated with the name Purnaprajna, but was called Anandatirtha when he was an *acharya*; Jayatirtha and Vyasatirtha (the early *acharyas* of Madhva Vedanta); Sadananda Yogendrasarasvati, Narasinhasarasvati, Brahmanandasarasvati, Jagannathashrama, Narasinhasarasvati: see Clark (2006a: 226) for further details.
19. The Dashanami-Sannyasis have seven *akhara*s (wrestling rings/military divisions): see Clark (2011).
20. *Paramahansas* are nominally affiliated to one or another of the seven Dashanami *akharas*, but are institutionally separate.
21. For accounts of the activities of these mercenary armies, see Sarkar (1958) and Pinch (2006).
22. Some ancient statutes in India provide special protection and legal dispensation for members of religious orders; see Olivelle (1987).
23. For details of some of these cases, see Antarkar (2001).
24. I have so far been unable to determine the primacy of either the Hindi or the Sanskrit texts.
25. Only rarely do Sufis refer to themselves, or are referred to by hagiographers, as 'Sufis'.
26. *Silsila* means 'chain of succession', equivalent to a *guru-parampara*. The term is not to be found in the Koran or classical Arabic literature (Habib, 2002: xxvi).
27. Arabic: *shaykh*; Persian: *pir*; meaning 'elder'.
28. One of the first Sufis to arrive in Sind was Shaykh Abu Turab (d. 788) (Farooqi, 2004: 7).
29. From the end of the twelfth century there was an influx of Sufis into Bengal (Haq, 1975: 2).

30. The earliest record of the construction of a *khanqah* in Bengal is in 1221 (Eaton, 1996: 71).
31. Nizami (2002: 187) cites the report from the early fourteenth century of a traveller, Shihab-ud-Din al'Umari, that there were 2,000 *khanqahs* and hospices in Delhi.
32. Many commentators still follow Trimingham's (1998) scheme of three (or four) phases of Sufism (though some offer critiques): 1. Individual mystics (*khanqah* stage); 2. Era of the *tariqas* (twelfth/thirteenth centuries); 3. (From the fifteenth century) rigid institutionalization and hierarchical organization; 4. Nineteenth century revival.
33. The Chishti *silsila* was founded by Khwaja Abu Ishaq Shami (d. 940) in Chisht (near Herat) and was brought to India, where it flourished, by Mu'in-ud-Din Sijzi (d. 1236) in the twelfth century. Ajmer became its main centre. Mu'in-ud-Din is a household name for almost all Muslims in India (Haq, 1975: 8). The Suhrawardi *silsila* flourished in South Asia simultaneously with the Chishti. It was founded by Shaykh Abu Najb al-Suhrawardi (1097-1168) in al-Jabal province (in Iran) and developed by his nephew, Shaykh Abu Hafs 'Umar al-Suhrawardi (d. 1234), who sent many disciples to India. It was Shaykh Baha'-ud-Din Zakariyya (b. 1182/3) who established the *silsila* in South Asia, primarily in Multan (Nizami, 2002: 60-2). Zakariyya certainly became wealthy, but the degree to which this was personal has been challenged (Huda, 2003: 141-6).
34. From the outset, the Suhrawardi order was politically engaged: Abu Hafs was deeply involved in the state affairs and policy of the Abbasid caliphate under al-Nasir (Huda, 2003: 17-18).
35. Many other *silsilas* subsequently developed. Abu'l Fazl, one of Akbar's court scribes, refers (1997: vol. 2, 393-420) to 14 orders of Sufis (see below). However, many of those sects listed were very minor in influence (Nizami, 2002: 187; Huda, 2003: 42ff.).
36. The first of several of these warriors to gain renown was Shaykh Sufi Sarmast, who with his army of 700 *ghazis* is said to have killed many Hindus and engaged in battle with a Hindu king, according to his hagiography. His death is stated to be in 1281, but he may have lived 50 years later (Eaton, 1978: 22-5). Disciples of Sufi Sarmast, Pir Khandayat, Shaykh 'Ali Pahalvan and Pir Jumna also fused militancy and mysticism, a phenomenon not unique to South Asia. Eaton (1978: 37-8) also refers to the *ghazis* of Anatolia.
37. '*Wilayat*' was also used by immigrants to refer to their 'country': usually Transoxiana, in Central Asia. During the time of British colonial

rule *wilayat* subsequently became used as 'Blighty', to refer to 'home' in Great Britain.

38. *Dervish* ('stretched out [sleeping] in door[ways]' = 'poor'/'indigent'), Persian = *faqir*, Arabic = *faqir*, Hindi.
39. Chishtis referred to their institutions as *jama'at-khanas*, while the Suhrawardis referred to theirs as *khanqahs*.
40. Babur, the founder of the Mughal dynasty (in 1526), was devoted to the Naqshbandi Sufi, Khwaja 'Ubayd Allah Ahrar, who was from the same region (Transoxiana) as himself. The Mughal imperial family continued to maintain cordial social relationships with the lineages of great Naqshbandi *khwajas* (Digby, 2001: vi).
41. Mu'in-ud-Din's tomb (*dargah*) at Ajmer became a great centre of pilgrimage, notably after Akbar's pilgrimage to the site on foot between 1562 and 1575. Nowadays the festival for the anniversary of the saint is the greatest Muslim festival in South Asia.
42. For further details, see Clark (2006a: 185-93).
43. Work is in progress to identify some of these obscure characters, whose legends are only preserved in oral tradition.
44. Social legitimacy conferred through established ancestry is not, of course, restricted to the religious domain: some Arabian clans and Maoris, for example, who have a strong sense of familial identity, are able to recite their ancestry.
45. As I have previously illustrated (Clark, 2006a: 122-47), the published lines of succession (the *guru-paramparas*) of the *pithas* that claim to have been founded by Shankara exhibit numerous inconsistencies. Moreover, the picture is further complicated by the contests between the various *pithas* that have claimed authenticity in the last few hundred years. So, omitting specific lines of Shankaracharyas between Shankara's disciples and the present day, a way to present an incontestable kind of chain of succession in particular Sannyasi branches, is to extend the chain into deeper antiquity to the spiritual ancestors of Shankara: to *rishis*, gods and voids. In this way the *Dashnam Vansh Vriksh* presents a similar chain of succession to that of the Sufis, without, in the case of the Sannyasis, one could speculate, running the risk of disagreement over the historical incumbency (or otherwise) of particular *acharyas*.
46. The four Caliphs reigned as follows: Abu Bakr (632-4); 'Umar (634-44); 'Usman (644-56); 'Ali [ibn Abi Talib] (656-61).
47. According to Sufi tradition, Hasan became 'Ali's disciple, though this is doubted by mediaeval and modern scholars (Rizvi, 1978: 27, 83).
48. Some Chishtis trace their lineage to the archangel Gabriel, and reckon

the twenty-first successor as Shaykh Nizam-ud-Din Auliya (d. 1325), and the twenty-second as Shaykh Nasir-ud-Din Mahmud Chiragh-i Dehli (d. 1356). However, the branch of the Chishti order that predominates in the Deccan starts with the Prophet Muhammad, and counts Shaykh Nizam-ud-Din's successor, Burhan-ud-Din Gharib (d. 1344) as the twenty-first successor, and Zayn-ud-Din Shirazi (d. 1369), as the twenty-second (Ernst and Lawrence, 2002: 23).

49. Hagiographers also retrospectively assigned lineages to famous Sufis, such as Jalal-ud-Din Rumi (1207-73), author of the *Masnavi*. In the *Al-Jawahir-ul Mudiyya* of Shaykh Muhi'-ud-Din Abdul Qadir (d. 1373), and other works, Rumi was attached to the lineage from Abu Bakr's family. However, this is contradicted by epigraphic and other evidence (Güven, 1991: 24-7).
50. Husain (624/5-669/70) was the son of 'Ali. His assasination—while opposing the Umayyads—was a decisive moment in the separation of the supporters of 'Ali (Shi'a) from the Sunni community.
51. In the eleventh century, Shaykh al-Hujwiri classified twelve Sufi orders, linking each to a famous Sufi master, despite the fact that there was seldom a correspondence between these early ascetics and the well-known Sufi orders of later times. Sultanate and Mughal *tazkira* (hagiography) writers added two more Sufi orders—to make fourteen—but the lists are not consistent in *tazkira* and other sources (Ernst and Lawrence, 2002: 24, 58).
52. The *A'in-i Akbari* of Abu'l Fazl (1972, vol. 2: 393-420) provides a list of the fourteen Sufi orders in India in the time of Akbar (r. 1556-1605): Habibi, Tayfuri, Karkhi, Saqati, Junaydi, Kazruni, Tusi, Firdausi, Suhrawardi, Zaydi, I'yazi, Adhami, Hubayri, and Chishti. The lives of the fourteen founding saints are also sketched. The scheme of fourteen families was the main taxonomy for Sufis in Mughal India. Abu'l Fazl's fourteen-family classification was based on that of Nizam-ud-Din Yamani, which he compiled between 1350 and 1378 (Ernst and Lawrence, 2002: 58).
53. For further details, see Clark (2006a: 245-6).
54. See Islam (2002: 385-96) on the *pir/murid* relationship.
55. This is the procedure for Chishtis. See Ernst and Lawrence (2002: 23-5) for further details.
56. Ernst and Lawrence (2002: 25) briefly describe the initiation rite for women entering the Chishti order. Women are admitted to a separate branch of the Juna *akhara* of the Dashanami-Sannyasis.
57. Ghosh (1930: 11) remarks: 'Now, who were these "Sannyasi Fakirs"? In the official records of the period the two words are used very

loosely, sometimes in juxtaposition and sometimes synonymously'. Ghosh then illustrates this point with several citations. Concerning religious identity in the eighteenth century, Pinch (2006: 97) remarks: 'The occasional success of joint *sannyasi-fakir* military action reflects, in my understanding at least, the location of historical armed asceticism beyond the boundaries of fixed, modern religious identities. . . . Macro-religious classification as Hindu or Muslim was, in the main, irrelevant to the world of Mughal ascetics, armed or otherwise. Sufis and *yogi*s interacted constantly on an individual basis—and interpenetrated at a communal basis—in the centuries preceding the upsurge of violence between company arms and joint *sannyasi-fakir* bands.'

58. See Pinch (2006); Clark (2011).
59. See, for example, *Manusmriti* 6.25, 38.
60. See Kane, vol. II, pt. II (1997: 933-4). As a *sannyasi* is not allowed to use fire, they are usually buried and not cremated (Kane, vol. IV, 1991: 229-31).
61. The Qalandaris were founded by Yunus Jamal-ud-Din Savi (d. *c.*1232/3), in Khurasan, and flourished also in Egypt and Syria, mostly under Iranian leaders (Karamustafa, 2006: 3ff.). The founder of the Haydaris was Qutb-ud-Din Haydar (d. 1221/2), Sava's disciple. Sava is described in several sources as a 'walking library'.
62. Digby (1984: 61) notes a *langar* (free food kitchen) there run by *qalandar*s in the thirteenth century.
63. Other similarly antinomian sects which emerged in the thirteenth century include the followers of Baba Barak (1257-1307), the Abdals of Rum, the Jamis, the Bektashis, and the Shams-i-Tabrizis; and, in the fourteenth century, in India, the Madaris and Jalalis (which were sub-sects of the Qalandaris). See (Karamustafa, 2006) for further details. One of the Indian sub-sects, the Juwaliqs, wore rings through their ears. Another sect of *qalandars* known in this period were the Muwallihs, who walked on fire.
64. Digby (1984: 61ff.) notes that the groups mentioned in the sources of the Delhi Sultanate are Qalandars, Haydaris, Juwaliqs and Muwallihs. Much less is known about the Muwallihs; the names of the other three groups are often used interchangeably.
65. Digby (1984: 86) notes that prior to the *qalandar* movement, Shaiva ascetics roamed in Khurasan, and that some *qalandar* practices may have been influenced by them.
66. This procedure has some resonance with the 'five area shave' of Sannyasis during initiation.

67. Badi'-ud-Din Qutb al-Madar, an immigrant who settled in Jaunpur, where he died in 1440, founded the Madaris, and became one of the most celebrated saints of Muslim India (Karamustafa, 2006: 60).
68. Digby (1984: 74) notes Sava's insistence on the practice of gazing at young good-looking boys.
69. The cannabis/hemp plant was referred to by many names throughout the Muslim world, including *kaff, ma'lum, zih, sahih* and *qinnab*. See Rosenthal (1971) for further details. Rosenthal's sources use the term 'hashish' to refer to the leaves of the cannabis plant. However, in general modern terminology, in both Islamic and non-Islamic worlds, 'hashish' refers to the pressed resin of the buds of female plants. The smoking of it only began, it is believed, after the Portuguese introduced tobacco to India at the beginning of the seventeenth century (*Indian Tobacco: A Monograph*, 1960: 1).
70. Brown (1968: 340) remarks on its use by Sufis: 'The first intention of *hashish* was evidently not as a stimulant. It was intended as a "spiritual" soporific producing that quiescence of soul so dear to Orientals.'
71. While there is little interest amongst commentators on its use by peasants, which may have been widespread, the use of hashish was noticed particularly amongst Sufis and scholars (Rosenthal, 1971: 142).
72. See Ghosh (1930); Moon (1947: 105ff.).
73. It is perhaps worth noting, in passing, how philosophically congruent in one respect were Sufis and Sannyasis. Around the time of the early Delhi Sultanate, Sufis introduced into India a mystic ideology that was already in a developed form (Nizami, 2002: 59). One of the most significant influences on mystical thought was the doctrine of Shaykh Muhi'-ud-Din 'Arabi (d. 1248). His notion of the unity of the phenomenal and noumenal worlds (*wahdat-ul-wujud*) was derived from his own experience of 'unity' (*tauhid*). All 'being' is said to be essentially 'one' and a manifestation of divine substance. His famous works (*Futuhat-i Makkiya* and *Fusus-ul Hikam*) reached South Asia early through Fakhr-ud-Din Iraqi (1213-89), attracted many commentaries, and provoked much interest (Nizami, 2002: 58). 'Arabi's influence extended to all levels of the Sufi orders and Islamic society (Chittick, 1992: 221). Some similarity between 'Arabi's philosophy and that of Shankara's Advaita is evident.
74. Akbar made Persian the official language of the empire in 1582 (Ernst and Lawrence, 2002: 61).

References

Abu-l-Fazl [-Allami]. 1997 [1927]. *The Āin-i-Akbarī* (being the third volume of the *Akbar-nāma*), tr. H. Blochmann and ed. D.C. Phillott. Delhi: Low Price Publications.

Ansari, Sarah F.D. 2003 [1992]. *Sufi Saints and State Power: The Pirs of Sind, 1843-1947* (South Asian Studies 50). Cambridge: Cambridge University Press.

Antarkar, W.R. 1960. 'Bṛhat-Śaṅkara-Vijaya of Citsukhācārya and Prācīna-Śaṅkara-Vijaya of Ānandagiri a/s Ānanda-Jñāna', *Journal of the University of Bombay*, XXXIX(2): 113-21.

________. 1961. 'Śaṅkara-Vijaya of Anantānandagiri', *Journal of the University of Bombay*, XXX(2): 73-80.

________. 1972. 'Saṅkṣepa Śaṅkara Jaya of Mādhvacārya or Śaṅkara Digvijaya of Śrī Vidyāraṇyamuni', *Journal of the University of Bombay* (n.s.), XLI(77): 1-23.

________ (ed.). 1973. 'Śrīcidvilāsamuniviracitaḥ Śaṅkaravijayavilāsaḥ, *Bhāratīya Vidyā*, 33: 1-92.

________. 1997. 'The Place of Śaṅkara's Final Disappearance', *Journal of the Asiatic Society of Bombay*, 71 of 1996: 1-22.

________. 2001. *Kāñcī Kāmakoṭi Mutt: A Myth or Reality?* (Post-Graduate and Research Department Series, no. 44). Pune: Bhandarkar Oriental Research Institute.

Bader, Jonathan. 2000. *Conquest of the Four Quarters: Traditional Accounts of the Life of Śaṅkara*. New Delhi: Aditya Prakashan.

Bayly, C.A. 1992 [1983]. *Rulers, Townsmen and Bazaars: North Indian Society in the Age of British Expansion, 1770–1870.* New Delhi: Cambridge University Press.

Brown, John P. 1968 [1898]. *The Darvishes (or Oriental Spiritualism).* London: Frank Cass & Co. Ltd.

Chandra, Satish. 1996. *Historiography, Religion & State in Medieval India.* New Delhi: Har-Anand.

________. 2003. 'Jizya and the State in India during the Seventeenth Century', in Richard M. Eaton, ed., *India's Islamic Traditions, 711–1750*, pp. 133-49. New Delhi: Oxford University Press.

Chittick, William. 1992. 'Notes on Ibn Al-'Arabī's Influence in the Subcontinent', *The Muslim World*, 82(3-4): 218-41.

Clark, Matthew. 2006a. *The Daśanāmī-Saṃnyāsīs: The Integration of Ascetic Lineages into an Order*. Leiden/Boston: E.J. Brill.

________. 2006b. 'The Curious History of the Daśanāmī-Saṃnyāsīs', in Anna S. King, ed., *Indian Religions: Renaissance and Renewal*, pp. 231-64. London/Oakville: Equinox.

———. 2011. 'Akhāṛās: Warrior Ascetics', in *Brill's Encyclopedia of Hinduism* (ed. Albert Hoffstädt), vol. 3. Leiden/Boston: E.J. Brill.

Dabistān-i Mazāhib (or School of Manners) [attributed to Mośul Fānī] (1843), vols. 1-3, composed in 1645, trs. from Persian by David Shea and Anthony Troyer. London: Allen & Co.

Digby, Simon. 1984. 'Qalandars and Related Groups: Elements of Social Deviance in the Religious Life of the Delhi Sultanate of the Thirteenth and Fourteenth Centuries', in Yohanan Friedmann, ed., *Islam in Asia* (vol. 1: *South Asia*), pp. 60-108. Jerusalem/Boulder, Colorado: The Magnes Press, The Hebrew University/Westview Press.

———. 1986. 'The Sufi Shaikh as a Source of Authority in Mediaeval India', in Marc Garborieau, ed., *Islam et Societé en Asie du Sud* (Editions de l'École des Hautes Études en Sciences Sociales, *Puruṣārtha* 9), pp. 57-78. Paris: Centre d'Études de l'Inde et de l'Asie du Sud.

———. 2001. *Sufis and Soldiers in Awrangzeb's Deccan: Malfūzāt-i Naqshbandiyya* (tr. from the Persian with an Introduction). New Delhi: Oxford University Press.

Eaton, Richard M. 1978. *The Sufis of Bijapur, 1300-1700: Social Roles of Sufis in Medieval India*. New Delhi: Munshiram Manoharlal.

———. 1996. *The Rise of Islam and the Bengal Frontier, 1204-1760*. Berkeley/Los Angeles/London: University of California Press.

———. 2000. *Essays on Islam and Indian History*. New Delhi: Oxford University Press.

Ernst, Carl W. 1999. 'Persecution and Circumspection in Shattārī Sufism', in Frederick De Jong and Bernd Radtke, eds., *Islamic Mysticism Contested: Thirteen Centuries of Controversies and Polemics*, pp. 416-35. Leiden/ Boston/Köln: E.J. Brill.

———. 2008. 'Situating Sufism and Yoga', in Lloyd Rigeon, ed., *Sufism: Critical Concepts in Islamic Studies* (vol. II: *Hermeneutics and Doctrine*), pp. 246-82. Abingdon, Oxon: Routledge.

———. 2011 [1997]. *Sufism: An Introduction to the Mystical Tradition of Islam*. London/Boston: Shambala.

Ernst, Carl W. and Bruce B. Lawrence. 2002. *Sufi Martyrs of Love: The Chishti Order in South Asia and Beyond*. New York/Basingstoke: Palgrave Macmillan.

Farooqi, N.R. 2004. 'Early Sufis of India: Legend and Reality', in Mansura Haidar, ed., *Sufis, Sultans and Feudal Orders (Professor Nural Hasan Commemorative Volume)*, pp. 3-22. New Delhi: Manohar.

Ghosh, J.M. 1930. *Sannyāsi and Fakir Raiders in Bengal.* Calcutta: Bengal Secretariat Book Depot.

Green, Nile. 2008. 'Emerging Approaches to the Sufi Traditions of South Asia: Between Texts, Territories and the Transcendent', in Lloyd Rigeon, ed., *Sufism: Critical Concepts in Islamic Studies* (vol. II: *Hermeneutics and Doctrine*), pp. 1-28. Abingdon, Oxon: Routledge.

Güven, Rasih. 1991. *The Absolutism of Sankaracarya as Compared with Mawlana Jalaluddin Rumi's School of Thought.* Ankara, Turkey: Rasih Güven.

Habib, Muhammad. 2002. 'Introduction' to Nizami 2002: see below.

Halbfass, William, ed. 1995, *Philology and Confrontation: Paul Hacker on Traditional and Modern Vedanta.* Albany: State University of New York Press. (The articles in this collection were first published—some in German—between 1948 and 1972.)

Haq, Muhammad Enamul. 1975. *A History of Sufism in Bengal* (Asiatic Series of Bangladesh Publications No. 30). Dacca: Asiatic Society of Bangladesh.

Hirst, Jaqueline Gaynor Suthren. 1993. 'The Place of *Bhakti* in Shankara's Vedānta', in Karel Werner, ed., *Love Divine: Studies in Bhakti and Devotional Mysticism*, pp. 117-46. Richmond: Curzon Press.

Huda, Qamar-ul. 2003. *Striving for Divine Union: Spiritual Exercises for Suhrawardī Sūfīs.* London/New York: RoutledgeCurzon.

Indian Tobacco: A Monograph. 1960. Madras: Indian Central Tobacco Committee (Ministry of Food and Agriculture, Government of India).

Islam, Riazul. 2002. *Sufism in South Asia: Impact on Fourteenth Century Muslim Society.* Karachi: Oxford University Press.

Kane, Pandurang Vaman. 1977-97 [1930-67]. *History of Dharmaśāstra*, vols. 1-5. Poona: Bhandarkar Oriental Research Institude, 3rd edn.

Karamustafa, Ahmet T. 2006 [1994]. *God's Unruly Friends: Dervish Groups in the Islamic Middle Period 1200–1550.* Oxford: Oneworld Publications.

Lapidus, Ira Marvin. 1967. *Muslim Cities in the Later Middle Ages.* Cambridge, Massachusetts: Harvard University Press.

________. 1988. *A History of Islamic Societies.* Cambridge: Cambridge University Press.

Manusmṛti (The Laws of Manu). 1991. Trans. and ed. Wendy Doniger and Brian K. Smith. London: Penguin Books.

Moon, Penderel. 1947. *Warren Hastings and British India.* London: Hodder and Stoughton Limited.

Nicholson, Reynold A. 1963 [1914]. *The Mystics of Islam*. London/ Boston: Routledge & Kegan Paul.

Nizami, Khaliq Ahmad. 2002 [1961]. *Religion and Politics in India during the Thirteenth Century*. New Delhi: Oxford University Press.

Olivelle, Patrick. 1976-7. Trs. and ed. *Vāsudevāśrama Yatidhatmaprakāśa: A Treatise on World Renunciation* (Parts 1 and 2). Vienna: De Nobili Research Library.

________. 1987. 'King and Ascetic: State Control of Asceticism in the *Arthaśāstra*', *Adyar Library Bulletin*, vol. 51 (Festschrift for Professor Ludo Rocher), pp. 39-59.

Pinch, William R. 2006. *Warrior Ascetics and Indian Empires*. Cambridge: Cambridge University Press.

Rizvi, Saiyid Athar Abbas. 1978. *A History of Sufism in India* (vol. 1: *Early Sufism and its History in India to AD 1600*). New Delhi: Munshiram Manoharlal.

Robinson, Francis. 2003 [2000]. *Islam and Muslim History in South Asia*. New Delhi: Oxford University Press.

Rosenthal, Franz. 1971. *The Herb: Hashish Versus Medieval Muslim Society*. Leiden: E.J. Brill.

Sanderson, Alexis. 2003. 'The Śaiva Religion among the Khmers, Part 1', *Bulletin de l'Ecole française d'Extrême-Orient*, 90-1 (2003–4), pp. 349-463.

Sarkar, Jadunath. 1958. *A History of the Dasnami Naga Sanyasis*. Allahabad: Sri Panchayat Akhara Mahanirvani.

Sastri, K.A. Nilakanta. 1992 [1963]. *Development of Religion in South India*. New Delhi: Munshiram Manoharlal.

Shackle, Christopher. 1976. 'The Pilgrimage and the Extension of Sacred Geography in the Poetry of Khwāja Ghulām Farīd', in Attar Singh, ed., *Socio-Cultural Impact of Islam on India*, pp. 159-70. Chandigarh: Publication Bureau, Panjab University.

Schimmel, Annemarie. 1980. *Islam in the Indian Subcontinent*. Leiden/ Köln: E.J. Brill.

Siddiqi, Muhammad Suleman. 1989. *The Bahmani Sufis*. Delhi: Idarah-i Adabiyat-i Delli.

Stevensen, Jane. 1995. 'Early Irish Saints: Some Uses of Hagiography', in Clyde Binfield, ed., *Sainthood Revisioned: Studies in Hagiography and Biography*, pp. 17-26. Sheffield: Sheffield Academic Press.

Talbot, Cynthia. 2003. 'Inscribing the Other, Inscribing the Self: Muslim-Hindu Identities in Pre-Colonial India', in Richard M. Eaton, ed., *India's Islamic Traditions, 711-1750*, pp. 83-117. New Delhi: Oxford University Press.

Tarafdar, Momtazur Rahman. 1992. 'Influence of the Natha Cult on the Growth of Sufism in Bengal', in Frederick De Jong, ed., *Shī'a Islam, Sects and Sufism: Historical Dimensions, Religious Practice and Methodological Considerations*, pp. 97-104. Utrecht: M.Th. Houtsma Stichting.

Trimingham, J. Spencer. 1998 [1971]. *The Sufi Orders in Islam*. Oxford/New York: Oxford University Press.

3

Mingling of the Oceans

A Journey through the Works of Dara Shikuh

MRIDULA JHA

Introduction

Born in 1615 CE, Dara Shikuh is remembered not so much as an emperor's son but as a mystic philosopher. The great dream of his life—a dream shattered by his untimely death—was the brotherhood of all faiths and the unity of mankind. Despite being the son of the mighty Mughal ruler Shah Jahan (r. 1628-58 CE), his lifelong passion was directed towards broadening of his understanding of different religions. He wrote extensively and all his writings are a reflection of his journey as a Sufi, from a novice who wrote hagiographies to a full fledged mystic thinker who tried to tackle some very complex and vital issues related to religion in his later works. Traversing through his various works an attempt has been made to comprehend how he evolved as a 'Sufi thinker'.

Moving away from the Chishtis, Dara Shikuh's interest in the Qadiriyya order had first been kindled by his tutor, the revered Mirak Shaikh bin Shaikh Fasih-ud-Din. A scholar and an ascetic, the Shaikh had received instructions from Miyan Mir (Dara's Murshid) and was the first to enthuse him about Sufism, later to become the overwhelming interest of his life. Later this interest was deepened through his association with Miyan Mir and Mulla Shah Badakhshi, a disciple of Miyan Mir. The first of his visits to Miyan Mir was in April 1634 in Lahore. Shah Jahan took Dara Shikuh along with him as he had been suffering from syphilis. After touching Dara's hands, Miyan Mir filled the *kuza* (earthenware cup) with water and recited the first verse of the Koran. Dara was then given some of the water which he claimed cured him of his illness.[1]

After returning from Kashmir at the end of December 1634, Shah Jahan and Dara Shikuh revisited Miyan Mir at Lahore. Shah Jahan offered him a turban and a rosary. Miyan Mir accepted the rosary but returned the turban. While Shah Jahan and Miyan Mir talked, the latter chewed some cloves and spat out the remains of this on the floor. Dara Shikuh respectfully picked up those and ate them. When the emperor left, Dara placed his head at the feet of Miyan Mir. Raising him up, Miyan Mir hugged the young prince and showered him with his blessings.

In 1635, Miyan Mir passed away without having had time to make Dara a disciple. In 1640 Dara remained with the emperor in Kashmir for about seven months (22 March 1640–14 September 1640) and during this time he became a disciple of Mulla Shah Badakhshi.[2] Though Dara Shikuh received instruction and inspiration from several saints (discussed later on) and addressed them in his letters as his *pir* and *murshid*, it was Mulla Shah who retained the allegiance of the prince to the last. After his initiation into the Qadiriyya order, Dara Shikuh designated himself as 'Qadiri' and 'Hanafi'. All his works bore these two titles along with his name.

According to Dara Shikuh, Mulla Shah advocated that every individual had an innate capacity for gnosticism which he believed they should use. That was the reason that he never asked his disciples to perform any ascetic exercises or undergo any forms of mortification or renunciation. Dara Shikuh believed his own spiritual progress was due to Mulla Shah's contemplation and meditation.[3]

Other than Miyan Mir and Mulla Shah, Dara had great reverence for Shaikh Muhibullah Allahabadi (d. 1648).[4] Dara wrote in a letter that the greatest pleasure as governor of Allahabad had been that Shaikh Muhibullah resided in the same province. In the same letter Dara requested the Shaikh to answer in detail sixteen questions on Sufism. The Shaikh wrote back in reply a very long letter answering all the questions on Sufism. These questions in themselves reflect Dara's mind which was bubbling with so many ideas and queries as he tried to unfold the mystery of *wahdat-ul-wujud* (unity of being).

Dara Shikuh was so deeply impressed by the answers he received from Shaikh Muhibullah that in another letter he expressed his gratitude and wrote that there were very few persons like the shaikh who had mastered the concept of *wahdat-ul-wujud* and were fully practicing it in their lives. In a candid confession he wrote that he understood some of the shaikh's replies in the light of his own spiritual attainments, some in the light of Koran and Sunna. He even requested the shaikh to sharpen his spiritual perception through the shaikh's own mystical experience.

Another close Sufi guide of Dara's was Shaikh Bari whom he called Hazrat Bari in his writings. Bari's concept of *wahdat-ul-wujud* was such that he refused to divulge to his disciples even his name (he was known by the name of his native village) for the reason that ascetics had no need of an individual name as all names were related to one reality (unity of being), so much so that his *pir* and *silsila* also remained a secret. He asserted that he owed spiritual allegiance only to his order, but he candidly confessed that he could not improve upon the spiritual advancement of Miyan Mir.

Another significant influence on Dara Shikuh's mystical development was Shah Dilruba. Six letters written by Dara Shikuh to Shah Dilruba are extant in a collection of letters, entitled *Fayyaz-ul-Qawanin.*[5] These letters were written by Dara in reply to letters received by him from the saint, which are unfortunately lost. Since these letters are without dates, it is uncertain when Dara came into contact with Shah Dilruba. In *Hasanat-ul-'Arifin*, which was written around 1654, Dara Shikuh referred to Shah Dilruba, so it seems likely that they might have known each other long before that date. These letters are a reinforcement of Dara's firm belief in *wahdat-ul-wujud*, by then his all consuming passion.

Dara Shikuh not only tried to comprehend the perspective of a *majzub* like Sarmad, but he also tried to interact with almost all contemporaries who believed in *wahdat-ul-wujud*. It was not as if he just interacted with the creamy layer of mystic saints who were more renowned than others, but like a genuine seeker he also interacted with *yogis* and *sannyasis* of Benaras who did not have the privilege of being famous. It seems that initially his understanding of *wahdat-ul-wujud* was based on ideas expressed by Ibn-ul-Arabi, but later, after his contact with Hindu saints like Baba Lal Das and other *yogis* and *sannyasis*, this concept became wider and he tried to assimilate the Hindu thoughts in it.

Love for Learning and Search for Truth

Dara Shikuh had imbibed two things from Mulla Shah; the first was his passion for the idea of unity of being and the second was his passion for writing. In this section various works of Dara Shikuh will be discussed. At the age of twenty-five, in 1640, Dara Shikuh wrote his first hagiography, *Safinat-ul-Auliya*. He writes in the preface itself that he always cherished reverence and obedience for this great body of saints, and the work includes biographical descriptions of some 400 saints, both Indian and non-Indian. Preceding his account are other biographies of Muslim notables, beginning with the Prophet Muhammad, the first four caliphs, the eleven *imams* (successors to the fourth caliph, Ali) and the four founders of Sunni legal schools.

Dara's genuine respect and love for the saints is evident everywhere in *Safinat-ul-Auliya*. He places the Auliyas next to the prophets of God. To him no one could be more compassionate, magnanimous, independent, learned, perfect and erudite and yet at the same time practical, humble, polite and heroic. That is why he cautions laypersons that these Auliyas walk the earth in many guises, and so long as one has not insight and truthfulness of intellect, he should not criticize anyone, because criticism is in reality doing injustice to one's own self.

The most remarkable part is that the last chapter has been devoted to 'women saints'. It is very obvious that there were hardly any 'women saints' who became 'saints' totally on their own. That is why prophets' wives, daughters and other saintly women have been taken up. Those women must have played a vital role in the making of saints. The final outcome which the world was witnessing had the loving, careful nurturing by those women in the form of mothers, wives and daughters.

Sakinat-ul-Auliya is the second hagiographical work by Dara Shikuh; it deals with the lives of Miyan Mir and his disciples. The disciples have been discussed under two sections—the first about those who were already deceased, and the second about the ones who were alive at the time of completion of the work. Mulla Shah, who was a disciple of Miyan Mir and Dara Shikuh's *murshid*, has also been discussed in great detail in the section dealing with the saints who were still alive. This hagiography was completed in the year 1642[6] when he was about twenty-seven years old. In this work, Dara appears totally awed by the lives of his *murshids*. For the modern mind, it is difficult to accept this kind of narrative but this is what the world of medieval Sufi saints had been like! It's an outpouring of sentiment which Dara had for both of his *murshids*. In a very captivating way he portrays them as two of the most distinguished saints of their times. A prince being their *murid* (disciple) not only must have given a fillip to their popularity amongst the masses, but also must have established them as 'prominent ones' in their own fraternity of saints.

This hagiography helps one comprehend the lifestyle of Sufi saints of medieval times. Dara Shikuh gives graphic details of their lives. One may not agree with the kind of miracles associated with these saints, but such asceticism where they deny themselves even the basic requirements of human life can't be overlooked. The works of this kind serve us as a window through which one visits the world of medieval Sufi saints. Along with it is unfolded the mystery of their immense mass appeal.

According to Dara Shikuh, Miyan Mir always insisted on adherence to *shari'at*. To him this was the first stage of a Sufi. The second stage was *tariqat* where an effort could be made to purify the soul (*nafs*) fully, which in turn might prompt Allah (God) to withdraw the veil from being human, and thus introduce an understanding of the *haqiqat*. In the *haqiqat* there would be annihilation of the self in the divine. Miyan Mir postulated that human heart and spirit is initially unrefined like an animal soul. It can be reformed through following the *shari'at* and then by fulfilling the obligations of the *tariqat*; then one would think of treading on the path of *haqiqat*.[7]

Dara believed that he received instructions from the spirit of the deceased Miyan Mir. He felt intense restlessness while sleeping and just before dawn he saw a *rauza* (tomb). He took this as the tomb of Miyan Mir. When he entered into it he noticed that it was very well decorated and in the middle there was a grave. Hazrat Miyan Mir stepped out of that grave and seated himself on a chair. The moment he saw Dara, he called him and made him sit beside himself. Dara continuously kissed his feet and then rubbed his hands on his eyes. Afterwards he was given some sweets by Hazrat Miyan Mir, symbolizing his initiation into the Qadiriyya order, after which he proceeded to press Dara's ears with his finger tips and hug him so tightly that he felt his whole body transformed into *sultan-ul-azkar*[8] and he felt himself drowning in a wave of mysterious sounds. Dara always ascribed Hazrat Miyan Mir's spiritual grace as being a gift from God.[9]

In *Sakinat*, Dara Shikuh also wrote quite at length about Mulla Shah's early life, and then how ultimately he found a perfect *pir* in Miyan Mir and then remained with him in Lahore. In 1628-9, Miyan Mir, in view of the difficulties faced by Mulla Shah, allowed him to stay in Srinagar during the summer and to spend the winters with him in Lahore.

Mulla Shah was so much engrossed in *wahdat-ul-wujud* that it was said that his utterances began to match Bayazid and Hallaj. Miyan Mir cautioned him to restrain himself but in 1634 the court *ulama* persuaded Emperor Shah Jahan to sentence Mulla Shah to death for blasphemy. Dara Shikuh, who later became his disciple advised the emperor to postpone the order until he had consulted Miyan Mir. Miyan Mir's intervention caused the decision to be cancelled, but through it Dara Shikuh first got interested in the man who was to become his *pir*.

In 1639-40, Shah Jahan visited Srinagar and stayed in the palace built in Zafrabad garden. The emperor invited Mulla Shah to visit him and impart spiritual guidance. Initially Mulla Shah was reluctant but later on relented. In the same year, Dara Shikuh and his sister Jahan Ara became Mulla Shah's disciples. Mulla Shah never called Dara Shikuh by his name but would call him *jawan* or *admizada*.[10]

Dara firmly believed that his *pir* was endowed with such powers that he could make gnostics of the young, the old, the Muslim and the infidel without asking them to perform any ascetic exercises or undergo any forms of mortification or renunciation. Mulla Shah believed that every individual had a hidden capacity for gnosticism which he believed they should use. Dara Shikuh confessed that he owed his own spiritual progress to his *pir*.[11]

Like his *pir*, Miyan Mir, Mulla Shah advocated an obedience to the Holy law. He summed up his teachings in the remark that Sufis who concentrated their attention truly in Allah and wanted total annihilation of the self in divine unity never indulge themselves in frivolous debates about Muslim and *kafir*, heaven and hell, reward and punishment.

In another of his works, *Risala-i-Haq-Numa*, Dara writes about the events which inspired him to write *Safinat-ul-Auliya* and then *Sakinat-ul-Auliya*. He wrote that after writing those two books he felt that God had opened for him the doors of unity (*tauhid*) and wisdom and he was the lucky one to have been endowed with his special grace and victory. *Risala-i-Haq Numa* is a pamphlet where he describes the four planes of existence, namely, the physical (*nasut*), the super physical (*malakut*), the blissful (*jabarut*) and the divine (*lahut*), corresponding respectively with the four states of human consciousness, known as waking, dreaming, deep sleep, and trans-consciousness. He asserted that the practices taught herein have their origin in the holy prophet himself and revealed only to a few well-known disciples.

Dara wrote that there are two paths that lead to God. The first path is that of grace and second that of exertion. If god wills the seeker is taken to *insan-i-kamil* (perfect individual), that is, *faqir*. And this *faqir* by one glance at the disciple removes the veil from his eyes, rouses him up from the sleep of worldliness and indifference, and without any effort, pain, austerity or penance on the part of the disciple, shows him the face of the True Beloved, and this frees him and takes the seeker to that stage which neither the eyes have seen nor ears heard. This would be the grace of God. He bestows it on those whom he likes! And the second path is that of exertion, austerity, pain and penance till a seeker finds a perfect *faqir* and walks on the path through which the former seekers of wisdom have trod. Then ultimately descends the grace of God and finally the union.[12]

Another of Dara Shikuh's works, *Hasanat-ul-'Arifin*, is also known as *Shath-hiyat*, which means ravings of Sufi saints during spiritual ecstasy. He completed this work in the month of Rabi-ul-Awwal in 1062 AH (1654 CE). It would not be out of place if one quotes Dara from the very beginning of *Hasanat-ul-'Arifin* in which he amply explains why he wrote this tract.

As I had become dissatisfied with the current books of the men of the path, and at times used to utter words containing the highest truth, in my ecstatic states and some ill natured and insincere people, out of shallow knowledge, began to taunt and accuse me of heresies, it struck me that I should collect sayings called *Shath-hiyat* of high souled and eminent men of sanctity as authorities for my profession, to convince those who are imbued with the spirit of Dajjal instead of that of Christ or with that of Pharaoh instead of that of Moses or with that of Abu Jahl instead of that of Muhammad. Some sayings had been no doubt collected by Baqli but as they were in allegorical style, I have added more and simplified the language so that it may be properly understood.[13]

Shath-hiyat were not approved by the conservative sections but with this narrow mindedness he could never come to terms. He could never comprehend why the statement uttered by Mansur Hallaj should be berated when he said *An-al-haqq* (I am the Truth). He could never accept these statements as 'blasphemy'. Rather he suggested that one should make an effort to understand the implicit meaning in it instead of just clinging on to the mere statement.

It is indeed remarkable and very daring that Dara concluded his biographical account of the celebrated Muslim saints, *Hasanat-ul-'Arifin*, with the lives of Hindu ascetics, like Kabir, Baba Lal Das and Baba Piyare, whom he venerated as eminent followers of the only God. It is a testimony to the fact that he wanted to empathize with the Hindu ascetics' idiom as well. For the *ulama* class who were not ready to relate to statements made by saints like Mansur Hallaj and many others of his kind, this was a sacrilege and nothing less. But here was a 'Prince' who not only wanted to comprehend *Shath* of Muslim ascetics but was very much willing to explore this stream in Hindu ascetics also. For the *ulama*, Dara Shikuh committed a 'double sin' by proceeding in this direction.

Writing about Kabir, Dara Shikuh wrote that he was one of the prominent *'arifs* (gnostic) of India. It appears that he was quite impressed by the fact that Kabir had written extensively about *'irfan* (divinity) and *tauhid* (unity of being). Muslims claimed that he was a Muslim and Hindus claimed he was a Hindu. But he was above all these claims. Muslims wanted that he should be buried whereas Hindus wanted him to be cremated at the time of his death. Dara Shikuh wrote that he told people that these rituals would take place only if you would ever find me out! After saying so, he locked himself in and died. When the door was opened, nothing could be found except some soil. The fuss over the last rites was now over.[14]

Dara wrote at length about the unique methodology followed by Baba Piyare and his followers. He could find nothing at all about him in the books of references, but he remembered meeting two of his disciples. He recollected from their reminiscences that Baba Piyare belonged to a very different category of saints. Once Shaikh Husain asked him, 'Who are you'? To this, he said, 'Neither a *muqim* (the one who has a permanent residence) nor a *musafir* (passenger); neither a Muslim nor a *kafir*'![15]

Dara Shikuh also had great regard for Baba Lal and had fairly long sessions of dialogue with him which were scattered over almost seven meetings. His queries were those of a 'truth seeker' in whose mind the feeling that they belonged to different religion was the remotest. Baba Lal Das, like a gnostic, pours out his wise and clear thinking about the matters related to mysticism, evil, suffering, detachment from the world, cosmology, metaphysics, and Hindu mythology. While writing about aphorisms of Baba Lal, one finds the very interesting remark that 'Truth is not the monopoly of any one religion'. Dara himself frequently observed that the method of Hindus and Muslims may be entirely different, but the destination point, where both of them want union with the supreme authority, is the same. In fact, he found the difference between these two religions superfluous.

He writes in the introduction to *Sirr-i-Akbar*[16] that his spiritual quest which took him in the direction of the comparative study of Hindu scriptures began in 1641, when he was absorbed in understanding some *marmuz* (mysterious) topics of Koran in the light of other scriptures like the Old and New Testaments. At this juncture it seems that the urge to explore the Hindu religious thought began. Till then he was ignorant of the Hindu religious thought although it is possible he may have already met some Hindu mystics and ascetics. His concept of *wahdat-ul-wujud* (unity of being) was strictly based on the ideas expressed by Ibn-ul-Arabi. But his later contact with *yogis* and *sannyasis* refined his understanding of *wahdat-ul-wujud* and he began interpreting them in a terminology understood by Hindus and Muslims alike.

Dara Shikuh wrote *Majma-ul-Bahrain* in 1657 at the age of forty-two. It is an effort to prepare a lexicon through which he brought forth an idea that the truth of divine unity is everywhere the same. Different religions may define and explain their terms in a different manner but the ideas and the focal points are similar. It was the first attempt of its kind to reconcile the two apparently divergent religions.

Dara Shikuh remarks in his *Majma-ul-Bahrain* that

> this unafflicted, unsorrowing *faqir*, Muhammad Dara Shikuh, after knowing the truth of truths and ascertaining the secrets and subtleties of the true religion of the Sufis and having been endowed with this great gift (i.e. Sufistic interpretation), thirsted to know the tenets of the religion of the Indian monotheists; and having had discussions with the perfect divines of this (i.e. Indian) religion who had attained the highest pitch of perfection in religious exercises, comprehension (of God), intelligence, and (religious) insight, he did not find any difference, except verbal, in the way in which they sought and comprehended truth.[17]

Bikramajit Hasrat[18] has suggested that *Majma-ul-Bahrain* is 'poor in spirit, largely verbal and devoid of any deep insight or great spirituality'. Here one would not agree with Bikramjit Hasrat. Actually it is not a philosophical discourse but an effort to underline the similarity of basic ideas in two seemingly different religions. After having collected the views of two religious groups (Hindus and Muslims) he resolved that the nuclei are similar in both of them. That is why he claimed that it is a collection of truth and wisdom of two truth-knowing (*haq shinas*) groups.

The hypothesis which he had set forth was very challenging in the sense that there was no literature available at that time which could have helped him to prove it. The treatment of the subject matter has been dealt with by comparing the technical terms of these two religions. The ultimate authorities like the Vedas from the Hindu side and Koran from the Muslim side are often mentioned. Keeping in view the ethos of seventeenth century the very idea in itself was novel, though Hindu and Muslim mystics were also involved in exploring the common grounds.

In *Hasanat-ul-'Arifin,* which he penned just before *Majma-ul-Bahrain,* one can find him quoting one of the aphorism of Hindu ascetic Baba Lal where he declared that 'Truth is not the monopoly of any one religion'. It seems this was the premise on which *Majma-ul-Bahrain* was based upon. It is a clear reflection of the openness of Dara's mind that he not only believes but tries to prove that the focal points are same, there is no such major difference. Words may differ, terms may differ, but the ideas around which human imagination revolves are one and the same. There is no denying the fact that sometimes Dara has gone too far and his ideas seem quite far-fetched like when he equates Mikhail (or Michael) with Vishnu, Israfil with Mahesh and Jibrail with Brahma. Similarly, he equates the complete soul of the chief (i.e. Muhammad) with that of Hiranyagarbha, whereas Hiranyagarbha in Indian religious thought is not a Prophet (real or living) to guide and inspire but rather a figurative name given to an aggregate of souls. Thus he has no similar importance as that of Prophet Muhammad.

But its amazing that Dara was very well aware of the implications this work would have for the orthodox sections of both the religions. At the time when this work was written he was a declared 'heir apparent,' even then he was not under any illusion that this pamphlet would be welcomed by people at large. That is why, perhaps, he wrote at the end of it that it was the outcome of much painstaking and considerable research and 'is in accordance with my own inspiration, which, although you may not have read in any book or heard from anyone, is also in conformity with the Qur'an'.[19] Moreover, there were many secrets concealed in the Holy Koran and the sacred books whose interpretation was difficult to find. So he desired to read all the revealed Books, for the utterances of God elucidate and explain one another.

In the preface to his *Sirr-i-Akbar*, Dara quotes a verse from Koran in which a reference is given of *Kitab-i-Maknun* (the hidden book):

That (this) is indeed a noble Qur'an.
In a book kept hidden
which none toucheth save the purified.[20]

A revelation from the lord of the worlds—Dara was sure that the reference to the 'book kept hidden' (*Kitab-i-Maknun*) refers to the Upanishads.

Dara believed that the translation of Upanishads would be very helpful to both Hindus and Muslims alike who were interested in *wahdat-ul-wujud* (unity of being). He observed that conservative Hindu scholars had even deprived a majority of Hindus by not portraying the fact that this was an ocean of pantheistic philosophy.[21] Dara Shikuh completed this translation of Upanishads (*Sirr-i-Akbar*) in 1657, a year before the succession struggle started. But it appears that he was very well aware of the opposition it might evoke despite the fact that he was the favourite son of Emperor Shah Jahan. That is why he wrote that he had translated the text for his own spiritual benefit and for the religious advancement of his children, his friends and the seekers of truth and not for the general public.[22]

Dara Shikuh's urge to explore the 'Truth' was such that he took pains to learn Sanskrit himself so that he could translate the essential parts of the Upanishads which were deeply related to the philosophy of pantheism (*wahdat-ul-wujud*).[23] Dara also got *Gita* and *Yoga Vasistha* translated again because he was not satisfied with the existing translations. These translations do not mention any date, but it appears that they were not done before 1657, the year in which Dara translated the Upanishads (*Sirr-i-Akbar*). He was sure that the translations would be of great help to all those who believed in the ideology of *wahdat-ul-wujud* (unity of being).

In conclusion, one is left wondering why Dara Shikuh dabbled into the domain of court politics and bid for the throne when he was much preoccupied with the matters like the fundamental unity of different religions. Why could he not decide to carve out a separate niché for himself by withdrawing from the struggle for the throne? Maybe, by sitting on the throne he wanted to achieve the kind of world which would be a replica of his 'vision of perfect world' where all human beings would be seekers of 'truth' only, irrespective of their religion. Destiny had something else in store for him, however. Contemporary European travellers like Manucci and Bernier opine that it was *Majma-ul-Bahrain* which procured a decree from the legal advisers of Aurangzeb that Dara Shikuh had 'apostatized from law and having vilified the religion of God, had allied himself with heresy and infidelity'. He was executed in the year 1659 CE.

Notes

1. *Sakinat-ul-Auliya*, p. 55.
2. Ibid., pp. 152-3.
3. Ibid., pp. 169-70.
4. Qanungo, 1935: 359.
5. Ibid.: 360.
6. *Sakinat-ul-Auliya*, p. 7.
7. Ibid., p. 83.
8. *Sultan-ul-Azkar* or *Sultan-i-Zikr* is a process of mystic transformation in the Sufi tradition which leads towards annihilation.
9. *Sakinat-ul-Auliya*, pp. 54-5.
10. Ibid., p. 186.
11. Ibid., pp.169-70.
12. *Risala-i-Haq Numa*, p. 2.
13. *Hasanat-ul-'Arifin*, p. 2.
14. Ibid., p. 49.
15. Ibid., p. 53.
16. *Sirr-i-Akbar* (the Great Secret) is a Persian translation of fifty Upanishads done by Dara Shikuh, completed in the year 1657 at Delhi.
17. *Majma-ul-Bahrain*, p. 114.
18. Hasrat, 1982: 216.
19. *Majma-ul-Bahrain*.
20. Rizvi, 1992: 423.
21. Hasrat, 1982: 265.
22. Ibid.: 269.
23. Ibid.: 266.

References

Bernier, Francois. 1983. *Travels in the Mogul Empire 1658-1668*, vol. I. New Delhi: Munshiram Manoharlal.

Dara Shikuh.1640. *Safinat-ul-Auliya*. Kanpur: Naval Kishore Press, 1884.

________. 1642. *Sakinat-ul-Auliya*. Ed. Tara Chand and Sayyid Muham-mad Raza Jalali Na'ini. Reprint 1965. Tehran: Muwassa-e-matbuat-i-ilmi.

________. 1646. *Risala-i-Haq Numa*. Tr. S.C. Vasu. 1912. Allahabad: Panini Office.

________. 1654. *Hasanat-ul-'Arifin*. Lithographed copy at National Museum. New Delhi.

________. 1657. *Majma-ul-Bahrain*. Tr. Mahfuz-ul-Haq. Reprint 1982. Calcutta: Asiatic Society.

________. 1657. *Sirr-i-Akbar*. Ed. Tara Chand and S.M. Raza Jalali Na'ini. 1961. Tehran.

________. Date not known. *Mukalima Baba Lalwa Dara Shikuh*. Delhi: Mewar Press, 1891.

________. Date not known. *Diwan*. Ed. Ahmad Nabi Khan. 1969. Lahore: Idarah-i-Adbiyat.

________. *Bhagwad Gita*, ed. 1980. Mohammad Reza Jalalina'ini, Tehran: Kitab Khan-i-tahuri.

________. *Yoga Vasistha*, ed. Tara Chand and Dr. S.A.H. Abidi, 1948. Aligarh: Aligarh Muslim University.

Elliot and Dowson. 1877. *The History of India as Told by its Own Historians*, vol. VII. London: W.H. Allen and Co.

Hasrat, Bikramajit. 1982 (2nd edn). *Dara Shikuh: Life and Works*. New Delhi: Munshiram Manoharlal.

Khafi Khan. 1975. *Muntakhab-ul-Lubab*. Tr. S. Moinul Haq. Karachi: Pakistan Historical Society.

Manucci, Niccolao. 1981. *Storia do Mogor or Mughal India*. Tr. William Irvine. vol. I, New Delhi: Oriental Books Reprint.

Qanungo, K.R. 1935. *Dara Shikuh: Biography*. Calcutta.

Rizvi, S.A.A. 1992 (rpt.). *A History of Sufism in India*, vol. 2, New Delhi: Munshiram Manoharlal.

Ruqaat-i-Alamgiri. Letters of Aurangzeb. 1972. Tr. J. Billimoria. Delhi: Idarah-i-Abadiyat-i Delli.

Storey, C.A. 1972. *Persian Literature: A Biographical Survey*. London: Routledge, pp. 992-6.

Sarmad. 1991. *The Rubaiyat of Sarmad*. Tr. Syeda Saiyidain Hameed. New Delhi: Indian Council for Cultural Relations.

Saqi Mustaid Khan. 1947. *Maasir-i-Alamgiri*. Tr. Jadunath Sarkar. Calcutta: The Asiatic Society.

4

Contested Religious Identities in Prannathi Textual Discourses during the Reign of Emperor Aurangzeb

SANDHYA SHARMA

The Prannathi Nijanand Sampraday represents a literary-religious tradition in Mughal India. Dev Chandra (1581-1655) was the founder Guru of Nijanand Sampraday but it was established in institutional form and propagated with missionary zeal across Gujarat, Rajasthan, Delhi, Maharashtra and Bundelkhand by Prannath (1618-94). The Sampraday, popularly known as Shri Krishna Pranami Sampraday in the contemporary world, had its beginning in Bhuj Nagar, Kutch and established the seat in Jam Nagar (Nautan Puri in scriptures) in Gujarat. The tradition manifested many diverse religious currents prevailing in Mughal India but conferred singular identity to its adherents through consecration.

Literary discourses based on holy scriptures of various traditions and *kirtans* were dominant modes of propagation of the beliefs and practices of the Sampraday. The preceptor Prannath himself authored many texts, some renditions of older scriptures from established traditions and some representing his own beliefs. All the fourteen texts written by Prannath are compiled in the sacred scripture named *Kuljam Sarup* or *Kuljam Sharif.* I will discuss in this paper that both titles represent the same text but different perspectives. In the vibrant and conducive environment for formulation of identities during the period, a number of cults, sects and *silsilas* were attracting people to their fold.[1] There were not always major ideological differences and it was the charismatic character of the guru, *pir* or diviner which determined the place of his institution among competing rivals. Issues of identity crept into the domain of religion and spirituality. Contest was not simply binary, between Hinduism and Islam, as it emerges in the recent research on past religious movements.[2] Propagation of one's faith was almost a struggle for survival, which called forth a specific agenda. The modes of communication had to be chosen deliberately. Prannath adopted a literary and argumentative approach for propagation. He wrote in Sindhi, Gujarati and Hindvi or Hindustani languages. Each of his texts represented old philosophies anew to make his tradition inclusive. His ideology was beyond the union of Hinduism and Islam or syncretism. More significantly, his use of the terms Hindu and Muslim carries radical connotations and makes it evident that his ideology was transformational. Whenever the situation demanded convincing people to embrace his faith, he offered a text consisting of innovative meaning of the sacred scripture of those who were being addressed, or at least he provided concrete reference for his argument. Most of his texts were written in Hindustani because he believed that it was the language of the common man in Hindustan. Apart from these scriptures, a number of hagiographies were penned by the immediate, intimate disciples.

In spite of the rich literary heritage, Prannathi tradition has long remained marginalized for different reasons. The custodians of the scriptures in Padmavati Puri Dham in Panna, Madhya Pradesh (popularly known as Panna Dham, and the most sacred place for Prannathis) were rigid and feared pollution through the hands of non-believers, informs Vimla Mehta, the founder of Shri Prannath Mission. For the same reason and also because this literature defied all literary boundaries, Hindi scholars have ignored this significant literature. Moreover, it was perhaps the radical ideology involving deep philosophical interpretations of tenets of diverse religions which could not be communicated convincingly by the successors of Prannath, made the tradition lose its mass appeal. In academic circles, where oral and folk traditions have been given adequate space, this religious tradition enveloping socio-political and identity issues deserves more attention. This chapter explores the ways in which Prannathi spiritual and reform movement became political when Prannath appealed to regional rulers to accept his faith and even challenged the Islam of Emperor Aurangzeb (1658-1707). I depend largely on *Bitak* of Swami Laldas, an intimate disciple of Prannath. He composed this hagiographic text just after his mentor's departure for Ultimate Abode. *Sanandh* and *Kirantan* constitute my reading of works by Prannath, and lend me a few citations in support of my argument. My focus here is to situate the movement in the Mughal context, and deep philosophical themes are not explained.

The history of Nijanand Sampraday dates back to the birth of Dev Chandra on 11 October 1581 in Umarkot. The place, now in Pakistan, is described as a town in Marwar province in *Bitak*.[3] This place is also known as a town in Sindh, the birthplace of Mughal Emperor Akbar. Dev Chand was born to affluent Kayastha parents, Matu Mehta and Kunwar Bai. Myths have been attached to the birth of Dev Chandra. All stories identify child as the moon and the son thus born was named Dev Chandra. The moon signified Chandravanshi lineage which perhaps legitimized his embodiment as Lord Krishna. To Laldas also, the arrival of this divine soul was predicted in both Ved and Kateb.[4] The hagiographer introduces Dev Chandra as an incarnation of Ruh Allah or Jesus who came to this mundane world for revealing the mystery of the Trinity:

E nidh jo lyaiaya, Ruh-Allah chauthe asmaan.[5]
Tin seti prapat bhai trigun sist pehchan.

Fortune brought Ruh-Allah from the fourth sky: the knowledge of Trinity was revealed through Him.

The birth of Dev Chandra signified the arrival of Ruh-Allah, i.e. Jesus. The theme is significant for understanding the philosophy of the tradition. Lal Das introduces Dev Chandra as the personification of Lord Krishna, the Prophet and Ruh-Allah who mediated the connection between the Creator and Creation. Laldas situates Trinity in the Bhagwat tradition when he writes that Shukdev Muni had revealed the arrival of Dev Chandra to King Parikshit.[6] The concept of *avatar* and prophets is clearly visible in these verses. Laldas employs the term to present Dev Chandra as a messenger of God and not God Himself. He is an apostle sent by God, in the same way that Jesus and Muhammad were sent. Laldas expounded cyclic notions of time and described the famous kings, saints and messengers of God in the four ages as accepted in Hindu mythology, namely, Satyug, Treta, Dwapar and Kaliyug. He again stresses on the cycle when he writes that a Messenger of God will come again after completion of nine hundred and ninety years after the Prophet. And this Messenger was born as Dev Chandra. The tradition is introduced with presumptions of similarities between diverse religious currents—Brahmanical, Islamic and Christian.

The author then narrates the life history of this Messenger. When Dev Chandra was just eleven years old, he began to contemplate the deep philosophical questions pertaining to the existence of human beings and the Ultimate Reality.[7] The anxiety motivated him to renounce his family and leave along with a marriage-party going to Bhuj Nagar. Late in joining the caravan, he decided to follow the footsteps of the camels and horses. It became dark and the wind also removed animal footprints from the sand. Desperate, Dev Chandra felt himself in the grips of a serious stomach-ache. Here he had a vision of some divine soul who cured his stomach-ache and showed him his way. He soon disappeared after giving Dev Chandra his sword.[8] Dev Chandra realized that the person was his Lord. The identity of this mysterious figure has been interpreted differently by scholars. Dominique Sila-Khan perceives the miraculous figure as the Prophet Muhammad.[9] Laldas however used the word *khawind* for this supernatural figure. The literal meaning of *khawind* is lord. The lord could be the Prophet or Guru or even Lord Krishna who came to reside later in the person of Dev Chandra. *Bitak* contains detailed references to saints, ascetics, *sadhus*, *bairagis* and *mullas* in temples, mosques and other hospices in Kutch, Bhuj Nagar with whom Dev Chandra interacted for getting answer to his queries.[10] The mystery of the Supreme Lord was still not revealed.

Lastly, he found a true preceptor in Vallabhi Guru Haridas who worshipped Lord Krishna in the form of Bal Mukund or child Krishna. Pleased with the servitude and inquisitiveness of the disciple, the guru decided to entrust him with the idol of Bal Mukund. The *Gazetteer of India*, Gujarat State, Surat District, also states that there was a tradition of distributing the image of Lord

Krishna among the disciples in Vallabhacharya's Sampraday in Gujarat. Laldas then narrates that the idol disappeared the same night leaving the guru in disgust. He began to fast till Bal Mukund was restored to his seat. Bal Mukund appeared in the dream of Hari Das and instructed him not to transfer the idol to Dev Chandra because the latter himself was the Supreme Lord and his divinity would be undermined if He served Lord Bal Mukund.[11] The Lord was childhood Krishna of Gokul. The roots of Nijanand Sampraday may thus be traced in Krishnaite Bhakti and Vallabhi tradition in particular.

It is known that Vallabhi Sampraday was well established in Gujarat and Hari Das propagated the faith aggressively. The Pushti Marg as preached by Vaishnavas of Vallabhacharya's sect, the rituals and the guruship are explicit in the verses of Laldas. The rituals of prayer, cleanliness and devotion of Swami Haridas and formal initiation of Dev Chandra through a *mantra* present both of them as ardent Vallabhis. Dev Chandra's training as a Vaishnav of Vallabhi sect was still incomplete in terms of learning and experience. His migration to Jam Nagar was instrumental in the formation of the Nijanand Sampraday. The visions of Lord Krishna in dreams and his conversations with the divinity legitimized his spiritual authority. The Lord became immersed in his person and granted him *tartam mantra*, which had to become the key to initiation into the tradition. The dream or vision had been an integral part of Islamic Sufi *silsilas* where the spiritual authority of the *pirs* was attested through such visions of the Prophet or God. The dream of Dev Chandra has to be interpreted contextually and it would be appropriate to borrow Marshall Hodgsons's explanation of dreams as expression of one's own desires and social expectations.[12] Dev Chandra's vision was symbolic of his environment too. The Lord in Vallabhi tradition was visible to the Vaishnavs. Lord Krishna could be seen through Dev Chandra whose spiritual authority was derived through a dream. The tradition began from divine ordinances transforming Dev Chandra, the disciple and learner into Divinity.

The existence of the Lord on earth could not be a secret for long. People discussed that the Lord appears thrice a day for accepting his meals, distributes goods to people and performs miracles.

The community of the believers known as *saath* or *sundar saath* in *Bitak* was initially the family of Dev Chandra. Laldas recounts the names of those who were consecrated. Gangji was the first disciple who joined with his family. The family included his sons, daughters-in-law, daughters and sons-in-law, and their relatives and friends. Dev Chandra held discourses or *charcha*. Looking for divine vision, whosoever came got consecrated by persuasion and through commendable discourses. Beginning with acceptance by the family, relations and kinfolks, the number of adherents continued to swell. The discursive sessions were attended by the gathering of both male and female devotees. It was alarming for the conservatives and the *kotwal* of the city was informed:

Chugli khai kotwal se, ek kayath ke ghar.[13]
Joru marad baithat hain, tum kyun na let khabar.

The *kotwal* was asked, in the house of a *kayastha*, men and women sit together, why don't you investigate?

Once the devotees adopted membership and the bond between the guru and disciple became strong, Islamic themes were introduced in the discourses. Reference was made to Koran and *tafsir* (probably *Tafsir-i-Husaini*, a commentary of the Koran, which was cited in the context of Prannath's Delhi visit) for justification. The quotes from these texts suggested immersion of Nur of Khuda into the person of Dev Chandra, who already embodied Lord Krishna and Ruh-Allah. The three divinities were not different but were the Messengers of the Supreme God; the Lord performed Ras in Braj first, and then went to Arabia, and finally came to dwell in Ruh-Allah, Dev Chandra. A new chapter in the history of Prannathi tradition began with the joining of Meheraj Thakur, who became Prannath at a later stage.

Prannath's original name was Meheraj Thakur. He was born in Jam Nagar, Gujarat, in 1618. His mother was Dhan Bai. His father Keshav Thakur, a Kshatriya by caste, held the post of prime minister of Jam Nagar. He was introduced to Dev Chandra at an early age through his brother Govardhan in 1630. Both Dev Chandra and Meheraj sensed mutual attraction and the guru-disciple relationship thus marked a significant development.[14] Prannath developed a strong emotional bond as a servant and soon became a favoured disciple. Dev Chandra perhaps believed in striking a balance between the worldly life and renunciation, and observing his disciple renouncing worldly life, sent him to Gujarat (probably Ahmedabad) on some pretext. Later, he was commissioned to visit Arabia where Gangji's brother Kheta Bhai was operating business. Meheraj was told to bring him back. Meheraj went to Arabia in 1643 where he stayed for four years. Meheraj's return, and imprisonment due to a conspiracy hatched by Dev Chandra's son Bihariji, his joining of Dharol court for two years, and his last meeting with his guru who entrusted him the task of spiritual awakening have been dealt at length by Laldas.

After Dev Chandra, the spiritual life of Nijanand Sampraday became feeble. The guruship was essential for the Sampraday and Bihariji was given *gaddi*, though Meheraj was more popular and learned. Meheraj began to consecrate devotees and guide them to meet the guru. Bihariji, however, disapproved of Meheraj's independent ventures on many grounds. He instructed Meheraj to be selective in recruiting disciples. The low caste, widows and others of that ilk were not to be given *tartam mantra*:

Ek to neech jat ko, sunao nahi tartam.[15]
Dujo raand istri ko, teeje kahen ham tum.

First to the low born, do not impart *tartam*. Second to widowed women, and third not to everyone.

Such an approach was incongruent with Dev Chandra's ideals and therefore Meheraj decided to proceed independently. His opponent communicated disapproval through a conspiracy which put Meheraj into prison. When in prison, the aggrieved Meheraj expressed his grief in verses and the journey of the preacher took the shape of books. Till now, the tradition was connected to the past through literary texts like the *Bhagvat* and Koran but *Shri Ras/Injil* and *Prakash/Zabur* were new elements. Another text *Shat Ritu* was also produced in this prison:

E doy kitaben utarin, Anjir and Jambur.[16]
Shat ritu bhi in samia, isq viraha ka utra nur.

These two books were revealed, *Injil* and *Zabur*. In *Shat Ritu* also at this point was immersed the light of love and separation.

The prison was termed as Prabodh Puri. *Injil* was the Holy Book given to Jesus by God, whereas *Zabur* was revealed by God to David before *Injil*. We also have references to *Torah*, the Holy Book revealed to Musa, in the same section. All these scriptures preceded Koran but altogether are referred to as Ketab. The interpretation of the original canons of Semitic tradition and reproduction in book form was new to the religious world in medieval India though the Holy scriptures had already been introduced in Thatta.[17] Jadunath Sarkar writes that Sarmad the *faqir* venerated Prophet Muhammad, but was critical of those Christians who misinterpreted the Old Testament. Sarkar further notes sectarian conflicts involving Emperor Aurangzeb. The execution of Muhammad Tahir, a Shia, in 1672 by the imperial *diwan* and killing of Sayyid Qutbuddin of Bohra sect and his 700 followers might have caused unrest. These circumstances perhaps motivated Meheraj to reproduce *Injil, Zabur* and *Torah* in local languages and to acquaint the masses with the commonality of these faiths.

Meheraj dedicated these texts to Bihariji after his release to be utilized for propagation, but the latter never revealed them in public fearing ascent of Prannath. In 1659, Meheraj went to Junagarh where he met Kanhji Bhai, a Vallabhi, who played a vital role in the accomplishment of the mission of Meheraj. The providence of Meheraj was demonstrated in providing sustenance to his group, both worldly and spiritual. He revived contacts with the old disciples of Dev Chandra in Diu and began preaching with zeal. Div Bandar was his next destination for preaching for about two years till 1667. The community continued to swell there amidst hostile and scandalous preachers from other cults and sects. They mobilized an informer to disparage the popular figure and frame accusations of blasphemy against Meheraj. Interestingly, the *firangis*, apparently Portuguese, were to be reported to and their intervention was to be sought for expulsion of the community from Diu. The presence of Portuguese in this region during the period and their violent ways were known facts.[18] The informer was, however, shown the right path by some miraculous figure who disappeared soon after. During his travels and halts, he revived old contacts reminding them of their affiliations and commitments to Guru Dev Chandra, and Meheraj initiated new believers also.

Thatta, 1667, became decisive in the history of Prannathi tradition. Seth Laxman Das, himself delivering discourses on *Bhagvat*, was introduced to Meheraj through Chaturdas. Laxman, once proselytized, adopted the pseudonym Laldas. An affluent merchant owning ninety-nine ships, he renounced the material life to become the favoured disciple and accompanied Meheraj for all of his life. He also composed the first *Bitak* of the tradition.

Meheraj's travel to Muscat was scheduled both for rescue of Prannath's wife and many other people from the Arab pirates and also for propagation. He soon reached Abbasi Bandar where one Bhairav Seth provided for ransom to get the hostages back from Muscat, arranged their stay and facilitated the discourses. Bhairav Seth and other aspirants were instructed to observe some restrictions forbidding consumption of meat, wine and refraining from theft and lies:

Parhej karaya char baat ka, e Kabool kar let.[19]
Ek to haram khya maans ko, dusra haraam sarab.
Tisre aurat birani tajai, so paavai haiyati aab.
Chori jhooth bolna inka chhodna udrak.

Abstinence from four things is to be promised. Meat was the first forbidden thing, the second was wine. The third was to detach from paramour to get the water of Heaven and the fourth was not to steal or telling lies is wise.

In spite of these restrictions, men and women flocked to the venue of discourse. Such sessions were unknown in the region, writes Laldas. *Bitak* contains a long list of adherents in Abbasi Bandar. The themes were still from *Bhagvat* and largely about Braj Ras. The change of kingship here became inevitable and people anticipated an intolerant rule.[20] Thus, Meheraj needed to move on and his ongoing journey of initiation and consecration through discourses and *kirtans* passed through many places of prominence. During the absence of the preceptor, the task was then performed by Laldas independently. Bihariji was also informed about the progress.

Meheraj's visit to Nalia was significant. Here, the inclusion of Dhara Bhai, an 'outcaste', provoked Bihariji and he sent word for Meheraj's immediate expulsion. It resulted in a split between

Bihariji and Meheraj. Meheraj was to be enthroned on the *gaddi* in Syed Pura, a locality in Surat, the temple to become Mahamangal Puri Dham in the tradition. The temple became the shelter for Bihariji's expelled devotees. Meheraj further added that *Sundar Sath* intended to accommodate and extend support to all disabled and helpless people. Caste and creed were no bar, as Dev Chandra had himself conferred *tartam* upon a widow Khoji Bai. Financial support to the separated wing was extended by Govardhan, an ardent believer, who had arrived from Abbasi Bandar. Meheraj thus justified his claim of guruship on social grounds. In 1671 Meheraj was ritually proclaimed the new guru and he became Prannath for his disciples. Laldas offers interesting comparisons of Surat with Medina and of Prannath with Hazrat Muhammad. The immigration of Prannath to Surat from Jam Nagar is symbolic.[21] *Sundar Sath*, the 'beautiful community', was styled as *Muhajir*, Prophet Muhammad's companions who migrated with him from Mecca to Medina. Prannath, frequently addressed as Shri Ji by Laldas, stayed in Surat for seventeen months and then left for Merta. He consecrated a large number of devotees from different social backgrounds in Merta who flocked to listen to the sermons and have a vision of the guru:

Ab in samai Merte me, bada jo padya sor.[22]
Charcha or didar ko, khalak chali aavai in thor.

Now at this time in Merta, there was much publicity. For discourses and vision, the entire population turns up at his place.

With a large following, the audacious preceptor aspired to higher goals. He intended to seek political sanctions. Laldas records his mentor's sensitivity to political developments and his attempts to utilize them for construction of the identity, both personal and institutional. During his stay in Merta, he heard about Jaswant Singh (1629-78) and decided to have a communication. The latter was in Kabul at this juncture. Prannath wrote two letters for Jaswant and commissioned his disciple Govardhan Bhatt to go across Attak and transmit the message:

Suni baat jab Jaswant ki, tab pati likhi doy.[23]
Bhatt Govardhan le chale, paigam pahunchavane soy.

Hearing the details of Jaswant, (He) wrote two letters. Govardhan Bhatt carried them, to deliver the message.

Govardhan had sent the response from there only. *Bitak* and other texts leave some queries unanswered. One may presume that Jaswant was invited to join the faith to add political support. How a Rathor who fought against Aurangzeb in the battle of Dharmat, and then was posted at Kabul as a Mughal *mansabdar* could help Prannath is ambiguous in *Bitak*. Laldas furnishes philosophical explanations for a negative response when he writes that Jaswant's soul was not the chosen one (divine seed or *ankur*) and thus he declined to accept their faith. A historical explanation may suggest that the guru attempted to play the rivals against each other, but Jaswant held a rank of 7000/7000 in the Mughal empire and did not want to disturb his relation with Aurangzeb. Prannath now targeted the imperial power directly. It was a challenge to see if the divine soul of the emperor immersed in worldly infatuations could be awakened. The guru had to make hectic deliberations both ideologically and materially.

Ab ladai karne ko, jaaiye paas sultan.[24]
Inko pratham dawat Karen, e lyave iman.

Now to fight, we go to the sultan. He should be invited first, to adhere to the faith.

There are other references in *Bitak* which indicate a premonition of conflict with the emperor. In Merta, Prannath heard a Mulla's call for prayers from the top of the mosque, in which was the pronouncement, *la ilah illulullah* (there is no God but God). Laldas uses *kalma* (word, words of the Koran, words used in prayer, words of the profession of faith) for it. It sounded to Prannath strikingly similar to the idea of Ultimate Reality or Aksharatit Brahma. He realized that the Prophet had brought down this message for him. So the Prophet is none but their Messenger Dev Chandra. It is difficult to say if guru began to see striking similarities between his philosophy and the one manifest in *kalma* because the idea of proselytizing Emperor Aurangzeb had clicked. Moreover, if we traverse through the verses in *Bitak*, Dev Chandra had already instructed Prannath to communicate the message of Koran to people:

Ham to in ke quran ko, bahut kiya padhan.[25]
Par jahiri lok jo, hamko na deve levan. E baat tumse hoygi. . . .

I have read their Koran meticulously. But it can be revealed externally, you will do it. . . .

The response in Merta was overwhelming. The first task was to reformulate the notions of existing guru, who then addressed a larger community. In the initial phase, Guru Dev Chandra represented Ruh-Allah, Lord Krishna and the Prophet. Prannath manifesting his guru and implicitly Muhammad also, then claimed Imamat too:

Rasool, moman, Ruh Allah aur Mahdi Imam[26]
Ye charon ek tan hain, tako naam islam

The Prophet, the Devotee (Prannath), Ruh-Allah and Mahdi Imam are one and they all are called Islam.

Inducting the erstwhile portrayal of Dev Chandra as Lord Krishna also in his own person, he manifested Dev Chandra, Lord Krishna, the Prophet, Ruh-Allah and Imam. Thus empowered, he was well equipped to wage a religious war with Emperor Aurangzeb. They travelled via Agra, Gokul and Mathura, and reached Delhi in 1678.

A number of adherents accompanied Prannath to Delhi. Interestingly, many followers were already there to welcome, host or assist their guru. The number was floating as some stayed temporarily and quit after some time. All these devotees engaged in discussion with people around them and mobilized them at least to think about their understanding of Islam. The believers wandered in the Urdu Bazar also. Laldas and Prannath drafted the letter to be delivered to Aurangzeb carrying twenty queries. Asajit, the new recruit from Delhi suggested that Aurangzeb might not even receive the letter because he was hostile to Hindus. Even if received, the emperor would not read the Hindvi content.[27] I however see it as a contest between the region and empire; the regions resisting the Mughal authority deployed Braj as a literary device to challenge the empire. Prannath therefore deliberately chose to write in the vernacular.

It is evident from these references that Prannath encouraged his disciples to create a public sphere for his faith. Grocers, shopkeepers, wage-earners, Vedanti, Sufi, Syed, and many others offered their services. The ideas were transmitted through these people. In previous references, Laldas furnishes a long list of names with a confession of omissions of so many others who deserved notice. He does not, however, indicate initiation of a large number in Delhi. The entourage was apprehensive of hardships and threats and therefore did not hold discourses and *kirtans* in Delhi. The details of enthusiasm and publicity are missing for this period. The discussion was interpersonal, one to one. The discussions took place on the roof top, in an isolated place:

Maas doy yahan rahe, hoye charcha Ved Vedant.[28]
Upar Atari ke, baithe the ekant.

Stayed here for two months, engaged in discussions on Ved Vedant. Sat on roof top, in isolation.

Something was indeed conspicuous in their message. It remains a matter of speculation why the discourses on Ved-Vedant were opposed by the families of the Hindus. But the concepts were complex; the intertwined themes were probably beyond the reach of common man. Assessing the situation during these eight months, the guru was still not confident to send his message to the emperor. Some eminent and strong connection was desired. A certain Shaikh Badl had joined them for a few days only. An appropriate time was still awaited.

Leaving a few disciples in Delhi, Prannath went to Shahjahanpur where one disciple Laxmidas had arranged the guru's stay. In the house of Laxmidas, the Lord began to appear and he came to take his meals regularly; he cracked jokes and assured Prannath that Aurangzeb would be contacted the eighth day from then. His disciples surveyed the vicinity and even visited some local ruler. The mentor was informed that the environment was not conducive for the growth of the Sampraday. A letter was also written in Persian, and Bhim Bhai and Laldas were to leave for Delhi for delivering the letter to Aurangzeb. The angel Gabriel warned Prannath that the task might not be accomplished at this stage:

Peechhe tain Jabrailen, diya jab ilham.[29]
Yah paigam jo bhejiya, par hovega nahin kaam.

Promptly Gabriel gave the indication.
The message you have sent but task will not be accomplished.

A word was sent forbidding the move. Important is to note that once Koran and the Prophet were invoked and propitiated, Gabriel here and Israfil later replaced Lord Krishna. Prannath's visit to Shahjahanpur assumes significance for a paradigm shift, redesigning the strategy to convert the emperor. The guru himself set out for Hardwar to attend Kumbh fair, to indulge in religious debates and discussions to demonstrate supremacy of his Nijanand Sampraday in 1678. He had to reach Delhi to join his group to complete his mission.

Prannath's text *Sanandh* would be the tool for teaching striking similarities between Nabi and Narayan. They came back to Shah Ganj in Delhi, with their *Sath*, and reached Lal Darwaza to meet Asajit. An adept of Delhi's culture, Asajit doubted if the radical interpretation would be tolerated in the imperial circle. He expressed his contempt for their struggle against orthodoxy who professed *shari'at*. Prannath saw no reason to convince Asajit and began to hunt for a new connection, some close associate of the emperor. One Shaikh Sulaiman was approached by the trusted devotees who asked him to fix their meeting with the emperor.[30] The Shaikh asked if their leader had some political agenda, the disciples explained their mission was simply religious. They further told the Shaikh to accept Prannath as Hazrat Imam Mahdi.

Prannath was also continuing with the process of understanding the doctrines of Koran. He depended on Laldas and Govardhan Bhatt for bringing information from some *mulla* of a mosque. Laldas found the doctrines quite similar to their beliefs but Govardhan was scared:

Govardhan ke dil me, dar rahe Musalman.[31]
Pohra Aurangzeb ka, jin koi sune kan.

In the heart of Govardhan, rests fear of Muslims.
During the reign of Aurangzeb, none would hear them.

Prannath therefore entrusted Laldas to read and interpret the Koran and a feeble Govardhan was sent to Surat and the guru himself went to Anup Shahr. Despite his ill health, he composed many sections of *Sanandh*. Shaikh Badl was sent to Delhi to intimate Aurangzeb about the faith. He went to Idgah on Friday where a crowd had gathered for the congregational prayer. People heard him patiently and realized the Truth but the content in Hindvi created suspicion:

Koi kahe Hindvi mine, likhe eh kalam.[32]
Baaten to barhak hain, par name raba nahi is tham.

Someone said, the verses are composed in Hindvi.
The content sounds truthful, but we can not accept it right now.

He came back to *haveli* of Gani Beg in Lal Darwaza and recited verses from *Sanandh* aloud. Prannath also reached Delhi and asked Govardhan and Laldas to meet Shaikh Sulaiman. The Shaikh continued to evade them for many days. He then told them that their dress code was not fit for meeting the emperor. They had to change their attire. After listening patiently to all the objections and suggestions, they shifted to Sarai Rohilla Khan. Daya Ram brought one Mulla Qayam who was employed on monthly salary for writing their text in Persian and Arabic. The five documents were prepared to be handed over to the close friends of the Emperor:

Thaur Thaur pahunchayen, jo they sultan ke yaar.[33]

Door to door might be sent, to those friends of the Sultan.

Their ideas still demanded modifications in the light of Islamic texts. The possibility of getting *Dajjal Nama*, a text on anti-Christ themes containing reference to *qayamat* (Day of Judgement), was uncertain, but the availability of *Tafsir Husaini*, a Persian commentary on Arabic Koran, gave them hope.[34] A copy was purchased for forty rupees and handed over to Prannath. Mulla Qayam, a salaried scholar of Prannathis in Delhi, read and interpreted the *Tafsir* for the guru, who utilized it for his claims of *Imamat*. Prannath believed that their beliefs might be comprehended by the people in like-minded groups. Who constituted 'like-minded' groups is not explained, and is problematic because both Hindus and Muslims rejected their ideas in Delhi. The conflict at this juncture was multi-dimensional involving orthodox Sunnis, Shias and Hindus. It was not a matter of communal or linguistic divisions but a matter of distinct identity for the community of Nijanandis who infused a Shiite element also. Political patronage was desired for situating the Sampraday at a higher platform in hierarchy; among the competing Sampradays by placing rival political groups against each other, Jaswant Singh earlier and Rana Raj Singh now against Aurangzeb.

Prannath met his intimate followers at Sarai Rohilla Khan to decide the further course of action. The emperor was not to be approached directly. Dominant nobles of the court were given a copy of the message from Prannath and were asked to support Prannath's claim of Imamat. The nobles however declined to consider their appeal on one or the other pretext.[35]

The exasperated disciples met Prannath in a garden and the mentor guided them to be resolute. They began to sing the *Sanandh's* verses in a nearby mosque regularly, and Nandlal, the clock setter of the palace, was induced to paste the letter of appeal at the door of *gusalkhana,* the inner audience chamber of the imperial bath where the emperor met the most trusted nobles regularly to discuss official and personal matters. The appeal was an invitation to all true Muslims to be faithful to Prannathi religion. The matter came to Aurangzeb and Shaikh Sulaiman was called for explanation. He was charged with not reporting the appeal in a proper way. He was proved guilty and his *mansab* (rank) of 2000 was withdrawn. Shaikh Nizam's son Abdullah replaced him. On Friday, when Aurangzeb came to Jama Masjid for congregational prayer, all appellants waited for their turn, Abdullah interrupted their move. Emboldened by the confidence of his delegates, he designated Laldas, Shaikh Badl, Bhim Bhai, Mulla Kayam, Somji Bhai, Nagji, Khimai, Daya Ram, Chintaman, Chanchal, Ganga Ram and Banarasi to meet the emperor. Two of them were Muslims and ten were Hindus, writes Laldas. On a Friday, they succeeded in approaching Aurangzeb. They asked him to surrender his faith and accept their version of Islam:

Kaha maange din Mahammadi, aur na chahen ham.[36]

Told they demand the faith of Muhammad, nothing else.

Aurangzeb, however, deputed Siddi Faulad and the *qazi* in turn to talk to them. He also instructed them to treat the delegation properly, feed them nicely and ensure that they were not troubled. Siddi Faulad got suspicious when he came to know of their food habits. The people talking of Muhammad and Imam were vegetarians.

Prannath was perturbed over the detention of his devotees. He says that in the first section, on page 62 of the Koran, and on the fourteenth page of *Tafsir Husaini*, the curse for rejecting the divine message is written. The Hindus, like the Jews, had opposed Muslims earlier but the same Hindus had now become the custodians of the Koran.[37] Laldas reprimands the nobles for treating all Hindus like Jews and calling them *kafirs*. He further tells the dissenting nobles that God had sent *Ahl-i-Kitab* for Jews and he has now sent Prannath to disseminate the divine message and therefore all those who accept the faith should not be persecuted. Detaining the devotees is again repetition of those sins. He reprimanded Aurangzeb and his nobles for renouncing the true spirit of Islam which his disciples were disseminating on his behalf. The mentor then wrote a letter called *Bari Patri* to the confined disciples encouraging them to continue their struggle and also to suggest ways and tactics they should follow. Laldas says the letter was brought to them when they were under arrest:

E patri Dilli minay, the qaid me ham.[38]

This letter came in Delhi, when we were imprisoned.

The *Patri* is lengthy and it is not possible to furnish the details. Still, the idea was to guide the disciples to convince Aurangzeb somehow. Laldas argues in one verse for the need for imperial acceptance; if the emperor comes to their fold, all will follow:

. . . *Ab patsah ko sunay ke, jo aave ine iman. . . .*[39]
Sab daurenge aap se paithne Islam me.

Tell the emperor (the beliefs), he might come to this faith.
All will hurry themselves to join Islam.

The *Chhoti Patri* was a supplement to the *Bari Patri*. The disciples had sent a reply through Shaikh Badl. They had written that it was difficult to have personal talk with the emperor for there was strict security around him. They were still there to seek an opportunity. They suggested that Prannath should continue to remain in hiding and send letters to *Sundar Sath* in Siddhpur, Merta, Bharuch, Jam Nagar, Surat, Thatta, Porbandar, Nautan Puri and Ahmedabad. All the believers might acknowledge his struggle with Aurangzeb. Meanwhile, Prannath left Kama rock in Delhi to reach Amber, and then went to Sanganer. Ladhu Masani, a Jargi Panthi in Udaipur joined Nijanand Sampraday with his flock. Prannath attracted crowds through his eloquent discourses there. At this point, the twelve devotees were told to leave Delhi with the permission of the emperor, receiving one hundred rupees from him. They reached Udaipur to join the guru.

Rana Raj Singh (1654-81) was informed about the presence of Nijanandis and their discourses. People told different stories about them. They were identified by some as great ascetics with a broad vision. Some believed they were *thugs* in the guise of *sadhus*. They were even accused of being agents of Aurangzeb sent for converting people. In spite of all odds, they attracted the Pathans there. A Pathan merchant Inayat Khan, and Abdul Nabi and Murad Khan joined the community. Aulad Khan, Yar Khan, Iliyas Khan, Abu Bakr and Mihin Khan joined *Sundar Sath*.[40] Laldas then writes that imperial forces landed in Ajmer for an expedition against Udaipur. A message was sent asking Rana Raj Singh to accept Islam and receive a reward of five *paraganas*. Prannath wanted to mediate and exploit the occasion for proselytizing Aurangzeb. He assured the Rana that he would be able to negotiate with the emperor:

Tum kachhu na bolio, rad badal Karen ham.[41]
In rah se din ki, e aaven tale hukam.

You do not speak at all, I will negotiate.
Through this track of religion, he will submit.

A significant point was presented by the guru. Political victory was to come through religion. The Rana, however, did not find the proposal practical and projected himself as a believer stuck to his own faith. He would never seek conversion either way. He rather requested Prannath to leave Udaipur. The guru also surrendered to the divine will and decided to move wherever the Almighty wished. He conferred a robe of honour (*siro paav*) upon Maha Singh who came to see the guru. All in attendance were also given the robes. They all wore the dress of Nirgun *bairagis*, coloured salmon pink and left their belongings in order to travel like wandering ascetics.

Their first halt was at Mandsor. Prannath engaged himself in discussions on Koran. Ibrahim and Laldas transcribed Koran here at nights. They were also carrying *Tafsir Husaini* and Ibrahim wanted to take it home. When his request was denied, he threatened to provoke the Pathans, but the matter was resolved. Once again we find the guru sharpening his literary tools for asserting the commonality of all the faiths, the focus being largely on Koran and *Tafsir* in Mandsor. Mukund Das was sent to Aurangabad, to the court of Bhav Singh Hada (1651-81), who held a *mansab* of 1000/500 in the Mughal court.

Laldas describes the torturous journey to Aurangabad. After violent encounters with *pandits* there, debating sessions were held between Prannathis and the *pandits* in the presence of Bhav Singh. Royal transport was arranged for bringing Prannath to Aurangabad. Bhav Singh arranged the guru's stay in his own *haveli*. After getting a passage, the guru revealed the themes of Qayamat and Koran. Bhav Singh thoughtfully asked him to convince the Muslim courtiers of his court. The king assured him of support in their struggle with Aurangzeb after approval from his Muslim nobles:

Tab mai Aurangzeb saun, bandh kai kamar.[42]
Laraun waste din ke, sir saunpa in baat par.

Then I will confront Aurangzeb, with all preparations.
Will fight for religion, I swear upon my head.

However, Bhav Singh died in 1681, forcing Prannathis to migrate and protect their lives from violent attacks in Aurangabad.

The death of Bhav Singh did not dishearten Prannath and his followers. They continued their struggle against Aurangzeb from

Burhanpur and Akot through Kapastani, Eilach, Devgarh and then to Ramnagar asking people to join the Sampraday. The meeting with Dev Karan, the *diwan* in Garha was pivotal in the history of the Tradition. Garha was destroyed by Ramnagar forces and Dev Karan had to migrate to Mau. Dev Karan became instrumental in the meeting of Chhatrasal Bundela (1649-1731) and Prannath. Chhatrasal had been engaged in the contest for power since 1671 and Prannath was facing deterrents for his religious identity. Laldas uses the metaphors Musa, Harun and Pharaoh for Prannath, Chhatrasal and Aurangzeb respectively. Koran's sixteenth section was cited by Laldas for producing evidence:

Tab khudai ne diya, Muse ka bhai Harun.[43]
Ab Ferun ka na chale, kar na sake khoon.

Then Khuda sent Musa a brother, Harun.
Now Pharaoh cannot govern, cannot kill anyone.

Chhatrasal, having acknowledged Prannath as guru, won all battles against local and imperial forces with the blessings of Prannath. In 1683 Chhatrasal gave a warm welcome to Prannath in Panna and the servility of Chhatrasal is hyperbolic in *Bitak*.[44] He identified the guru and his wife Tej Kunwari as Infinite Divinity (*Aksharatit*). Hence the Apostle assumed the form of the Lord.

It may be accepted in this context that Chhatrasal, who was fighting against the emperor, connected himself with a religious tradition identifying itself as Krishnaite to legitimize his position as a great king protecting the Hindu faith. Heidi Pauwels has observed a similar motive when Madhukar Shah patronized Braj bhakti in order to ensure upward social mobility.[45] Shahabuddin Iraqi has also observed that the relation of Prannath and Chhatrasal was similar to that of Ramdas and Shivaji.[46] Both the gurus exploited religious prejudices against Aurangzeb. I, however, find that Ramdas never rose above guruship but Prannath came to be worshipped as a god in Panna court. Sections 62-73 in *Bitak* deal with Asht Prahar (eight intervals of a day) or the routine rituals attributed to the Lord eight times in a day, in similar fashion as are ascribed to Lord Krishna by Vallabhis in Vrindavan.[47]

The long narrative abounds in interesting details of locality, region and the empire, each being accorded significant space. Mobilization of masses, approaching the people in the remotest villages, attempts to consecrate the regional rulers, big or small, and persistent attempts to convert the Emperor Aurangzeb present different contexts in which texts were situated. The empire is revealed to be more powerful than the regions when all local magnates refuse to extend support on one or the other pretext. It must be noted that Prannath's choice of kings was strategic. All the potential allies of Prannath who were against Aurangzeb could be mobilized to accept the discipleship and could become instrumental in challenging Aurangzeb. Maharaja Jaswant Singh, Rana Raj Singh and Bhav Singh had a history of enmity with Aurangzeb. It may not, however, be denied that all the targeted regional powers were by then subdued and integrated into the Mughal administration and were not capable of defiance. Laldas also admits this in the context of Ramnagar when the ruler tells Prannath to leave his territory:

E patsahi dabdaba, sah na saken ham.[48]

This imperial pressure, we cannot endure.

Still, the visionary Prannath continued his struggle by mobilizing the support of the masses. The religion he preached needed political backing, at least regional, if not imperial. The identity for the Sampraday in Bundela court was the culmination of textual encounters between the guru and his disciples and the political and religious authorities at different social levels. The ideological issues in this contest resulted in aggressive literary encounters between Prannath and the *ulama* on one hand, and with *pandits* in various courts on the other. The masses could be mobilized through *kirtans* and sermons, but textual knowledge would be decisive in defeating the theologians. Each move was in writing, whether communication between Bihariji and Prannath, or between the guru and disciples, or between the Sampraday and the masses. Written documents were incessantly sent to individuals, to the locals in the places guru visited, and to the emperor and his eminent nobles. These documents always contained reference to one or the other scripture in support of their faith. The Islam thus preached by Prannathis was the religion of all, though claims of Hindu identity were still retained. One may understand it as Hinduization of Kateb tradition because original Islam was subordinated once the patronage by Chhatrasal was assured in Panna.

A brief note on Aurangzeb's attitude towards this movement is essential here.[49] There is enough evidence in *Bitak* and also in *Kirantan* to suggest antagonism between the Hindus and Muslims and Aurangzeb's suppression of non-Muslims. However, careful reading of 'textures' of the texts reveals that Aurangzeb was not a fanatic. The way he permitted discussion with the Prannathi delegation and ordered decent treatment for them indicates his tolerance. Interestingly, Shaikh Islam and Rizvi Khan believed that Shah Jahan, the father of Aurangzeb, would have got these people beheaded for preaching unorthodox Islam:

Jo Sahjahan ke bakhat me, koi aisa lyave tufan.[50]
To tab hi mare gardan, aur baat na sune kaan.

If during the times of Shah Jahan, someone induced such storm,
Then he would have got him beheaded without giving a hearing.

It was not a matter of Hindu or Muslim faith. As noticed here, 'Tafseer', 'Dawat' and 'Imam Mahdi' indicate different contexts within Islam. In spite of open debates and discussions in Delhi, Aurangzeb set them free. Aurangzeb ordered their arrest in Ramnagar only when he was informed of their popularity and sway in the region and their attempts to provoke regional and local powers against him:

Naurang akas rakhat hai, hai ladai Islam.[51]
Dawat sab thauraun karo, bulao apne tham.

Aurangzeb is hostile, the fight is for Islam.
Send invitation to all destinations, call them to your place.

Also, a highly active network of communication is discernible in *Bitak*. With such developed modes of communication, the emperor might have been well informed about the developments. Still, he did not interfere so long as his own authority was not threatened and reflects his indifference to the religious issues.

To conclude, Prannathi movement was a struggle for deciding

identities, both religious and political. Prannath succeeded in his mission of formulating a radical identity for his Sampraday and for himself as a human divine in Hindu tradition. His definition of 'Hindu' was perhaps inclusive which included people of diverse faiths who adhered to a universal Islam.[52] The duality of titles of the texts (*Shri Ras/Injil*, *Prakash/Zabur* and *Kuljam Sarup/Sharif*) conveyed that the texts were addressed to all social groups. The movement was far from being Hindu, Islamic or a shared faith; it was a matter of unique identity that hegemonized the power and authority of Prannath.

Notes

1. Bahuguna, Dutta & Nasreen, eds., 2012. The volume addresses the issues of identity in various religious traditions represented through literary and hagiographic texts. See also, Lorenzen, 2004.
2. For different interpretations of Prannathi Movement, see, Wilson, 1976: 351; Ali, 1989: 136-48; see also, Mukharya, 1989: 113-26; Imhasly, 2007: 3-4; Sikand, 2003: 136-8; Gupt, 1997: 92. In many books on Mahatma Gandhi where his mother's connection with Pranamis is highlighted, the Pranamis have been portrayed either as Hindus, Muslims or adherents of a religion of shared beliefs; see for example Toffin, 2011: 1-29.
3. Ram, 1996: 37; Dhami, tr., 1991: Section 1, v. 16.
4. *Bitak*, Section 1, v. 21 reads:

   Soi Ved Kateb me, inon ki likhi saakh.

   (This is written in Ved and Kateb, He is eulogized in these texts). The verse further clarifies the forecast of his incarnation.
5. Ibid., v. 27.
6. Ibid., v. 19. Laldas identifies Ruh Allah/Jesus, the Prophet and the founder guru Devchandra (and later Prannath) as one and the same. This symbolism also attempts to explain the Creator, the creation and the Agency between the two. Laldas writes Aksharatit Bramha as the Ultimate Reality and Prannath as the Messenger. The notions of Trinity in the religious traditions Laldas addresses need extensive research.
7. The commonly asked question 'Who am I' has been a query in Indian philosophical traditions. See Openshaw, 2010; Granoff and Shinohara, eds., 1994.
8. *Bitak*, Section 2, vv. 52-7.

9. Sila-Khan, 2002: 209-31. See also, idem, 2008. It must also be noted that Khan is conclusive about the Nizari Ismaili character of the Sampraday. Asghar Ali Engineer also proffers similar views; see Engineer, 2008.
10. Bhattacharya, 1989: 97-105. She calls the medieval period in Gujarat an age of renaissance because many religious cults and sects had flourished there. See also, Burger, 1992: 56-64.
11. *Bitak,* vv. 44-59; the portrayal of Lord Krishna as a living human being who talks to his devotees, and often gets annoyed due to the negligence of believers is the key theme in *Chaurasi Vaishanavan ki Varta*. The text, composed by Vitthaleshwar Gosain, the son of Vallabhacharya, exhibits the Vallabhi tradition of treating Krishna as living divinity. See for this discussion, Gosain, 1986.
12. Hodgson, 1974: 466. See also Felek and Knysh, eds., 2012. The section 'Dreams in Sufi Literature' and Meenakshi Khanna in particular explains the meaning and significance of dreams in Indian context in her chapter. Bakshi Hansraj, a Prannathi and Braj bhasha poet of the same period versified the dreams of Radha and Krishna in *Saneh Sagar.*
13. *Bitak,* Section 2, v. 23
14. Barz, 1969: 3-16; Gold, 1987: 3-6; Mangalwadi, 1977: 16-17; Brent, 1972: 30. The studies of other scholars like Lorenzen and Vaudeville also suggest that the gurus, not necessarily the Brahmans, also wielded power in various ways. See, Lorenzen, ed., 1976; Vaudeville, 1996. For the authority of Sufi *pirs*, see Rizvi, 1997: 97-101.
15. *Bitak,* Section 28, v. 50. These regulations were inconsistent with Vallabhi ideology. *Do Sau Bawan Vaishnavan ki Varta* informs that Vallabhi Sampraday in Vrindavan was open to widows, prostitutes and all low-born people. See Gosain, 2008.
16. *Bitak*, Section 17, v. 58.
17. Jadunath Sarkar informs that the mystic Sarmand had immigrated from Persia as a trader in 1640s. He was a Jew and had studied the Hebrew Scriptures. In Thatta he induced Abhay Chand to become his disciple and taught him Pentateuch and the Psalms. Abhay Chand translated a few chapters of Psalms into Persian. Sarmand went to Hyderabad and Delhi for propagation but was ultimately put to death by Aurangzeb. See, Sarkar, 1972: 62-5. For literary compositions of the gurus during medieval period, see Novetzke, 2008: 135-9.
18. Mannucci, 1966: 123.
19. *Bitak*, Section 24, vv. 16-17.
20. Sarkar informs about the reshuffling of administrative positions in

Basra, with the arrival of refugee Husain Pasha in Delhi. His son Yahya Pasha also resigned from his post in Basra and came to Delhi in 1671. Laldas mentions Prannath's stay in and around Basra at the same time and apprehensions of persecution of immigrants from Hindustan. Sarkar, 1972: 77-8.

21. *Bitak*, Section 31, vv. 1-2 reads:

 Hazrat ne hijrat kari, lene ko Macca. . . . Sahar Medina Surat, yahan seti chale jab. Mahajaron maddat kari, jo saath seva me chale tab.

 (Hazrat migrated to take Mecca. The city Surat is Medina, he departed from here. All *muhajirs* supported him and also went along.)

 The claims of being a prophet were already expressed in Section 12, verse 3 succinctly:

 Ham aaye hain aras se bheje parvardigar

 (I have been sent from sky by God.)

22. Ibid., Section 33, v. 63.
23. Ibid., Section 33, v. 66.
24. Ibid., Section 34, v. 5.
25. Ibid., Section 13, vv. 55-6.
26. Ibid., Section 45, v. 16.
27. Aurangzeb's preference for Persian as a matter of politics has been discussed by Muzaffar Alam. He, however, does not suggest the emperor's aversion to Hindvi, because Braj was accommodated in the Mughal court in the wake of assertive regional forces. For Mughal responses and attitudes to language and ascent of Persian in the Mughal court, see Alam 1998. See also, Cohn, 1997.
28. *Bitak,* Section 34, v. 39.
29. Ibid., Section 36, v. 25.
30. Shaikh Sulaiman Fazil Khan was Indian by birth and held a *mansab* of 1500/1500 in the court of Aurangzeb. See, Ali, 1970: 255. He was one among five selected nobles of Aurangzeb who were to be given a copy of the written message for the emperor.
31. *Bitak*, Section 39, v. 6.
32. Ibid., v. 39. Verse 46 in this section again also elaborates the apprehension for the message in Hindvi.
33. Ibid., v. 56.
34. Many *Tafseers* were available in Mughal India by this time but the verses give us the impression that these were not widely circulated. Laldas did not record the author of the *Tafseer.*
35. The following nobles are mentioned. Saiyad Ali Rizvi Khan, whose ancestors had migrated from Bukhara, held a *mansab* of 3000/500

zat-sawar rank. He is categorized as Indian of Turani origin. In his capacity as Sadr-us-sudur of the empire, he acted as an advisor of Aurangzeb; see Ali, 1970: 237 and Bhatia 2006: 129. Shaikh Nizam held a high *mansab* of 7000/7000; see Ali, 1970: 217. Bhatia also writes that Shaikh Nizam headed the team appointed for the compilation of *Fatwa-i-Alamgiri*, a *shariat*-based penal code for imparting justice; see Bhatia, 2006: 184. Mir Askari Aqil Khan held a *mansab* of 1500/500; see Ali, 1970: 128. Siddi Faulad or Faulad Khan was a *mansabdar* of 1500/1200, and was *kotwal* of Delhi.

36. *Bitak*, Section 43, v. 38. In *Bari Patri*, Prannath sends a message for Aurangzeb challenging his knowledge of Islam. Section 47, v. 73 suggests that Islam as professed by Prannath is also the same as Islam of the emperor:

    E bhi wohi Islam hai jis par khade ham tum.
    Tum chahat Din Mahmmadi, Bari karat talab.

37. Ibid., Section 44, vv. 10, 12.
38. Ibid., Section 47, v. 3.
39. Ibid., vv. 66-7.
40. Ibid., Section 49, vv. 79-80. Sarkar writes that the Afghans were disgruntled as Aurangzeb had not assigned them high ranks even though they had supported him in the war of succession. The Afghans were spread all over India and were turbulent; see Ali, 1970: 20-1. An anti-Aurangzeb attitude perhaps drove them to the side of Prannath, who was already trying to gather support against Aurangzeb.
41. *Bitak*, Section 50, v. 11. Rana Raj Singh and Aurangzeb initially had good relations. Rana was awarded a *mansab* of 6000/6000 by Aurangzeb. The cause of the war given here is exclusively religious, a matter of conversion. In another contemporary source, *Raj Vilas*, the reasons besides religion were economic disputes, the Rathor rebellion, and Aurangzeb's forcing marriage upon a local Hindu princess. For this discussion, see Sharma, 2010: 168-74.
42. *Bitak*, Section 53, v. 48.
43. Ibid. Section 59, v. 45.
44. Ibid. Section 60, vv. 48-60.
45. Pauwels, 2009.
46. Iraqi, 2009: 227.
47. *Chaurasi Vaishnavan ki Varta* contains the details of eighty-four Vaishnavas of Vrindavan during the reign of Mughal Emperor Akbar (1556-1606), men who served the living Lord Krishna. These devotees lived with him and performed assigned duties with complete devotion.

48. *Bitak*, Section 58, v. 55.
49. Jadunath Sarkar and Sri Ram Sharma are two well-known historians who were obsessed with depicting Aurangzeb as a religious bigot and discussing at length the 'Hindu Reaction' by citing examples of forced conversions, temple demolition and persecution of Shiites. These views need review in the light of recent research which negate orthodoxy of Aurangzeb. See Chandra, 1986-7: 88-101; idem, 2003; Habib, 1999: 390-405; Bhatia, 2006: 109-15. More recently, Katherine Butler Brown has revealed misconceptions about the ban on music imposed by Aurangzeb. For the discussion about how Aurangzeb directly or indirectly facilitated growth of music, see Brown, 2007: 77-120.
50. *Bitak*, Section 43, v. 54.
51. Ibid. Section 60, v. 5.
52. The terms 'Hindu', 'Muslim', and 'Hinduism' have received much attention from historians and have been interpreted differently in the context of the colonial period in India. See Oddie, 2006: 42-3; Lorenzen, 2010: 25-40; Oddie, 2010: 41-55. Both Lorenzen and Oddie believe that 'Hindu' and 'Hinduism' represented a way of life and inclusiveness wherein all other religions were accommodated even before the colonial period. The terms 'Hindu' and 'Musalman' were frequently used by Prannath and Laldas. The Hindus and Muslims denoted socially stratified communities. One might decipher multiple identities of Hindus and Muslims in Prannathi literature and they were still either Hindus or Muslims. The Prannathis during the last phase in Panna identified themselves as Hindus. Laldas clearly identified all adherents in Akot in Section, 57, v. 8 of his *Bitak*:

    Ham lakhon kabile Hinduan ke, hot dakhil din Islam.

    (We, the lakhs from Hindu families, have taken initiation into the religion of Islam.)

References

Books

Ali, M. Athar. 1970. *The Mughal Nobility under Aurangzeb*. New Delhi: Asia Publishing House.

Aslam, Adnan. 1998. *Religious Pluralism in Christianity and Islam*. Richmond: Curzon.

Bahuguna, Rameshwar Prasad, Ranjeeta Dutta and Farhat Nasreen, eds. 2012. *Negotiating Religion: Perspectives from Indian History*. New Delhi: Manohar.

Barz, Richard. 1969. *The Bhakti Sect of Vallabhacharya*. New Delhi: Munshiram Manoharlal.

Bhatia, M.L. 2006. *The Ulama, Islamic Ethics and Courts Under the Mughals: Aurangzeb Revisited*. New Delhi: Manak.

Bloch, Ester, Marrianne Keppens and Rajaram Hegde, eds. 2010. *Rethinking Religion in India: The Colonial Construction of Hinduism*. Oxfordshire: Routledge.

Brent, Peter. 1972. *Godmen of India*. London: Penguin Books.

Chandra, Satish. 2003. *Mughal Religious Policies, the Rajputs and the* Deccan. New Delhi: Vikas Publishing House.

Dhami, Manik Lal, tr. 1991, *Mahamati Prannath Prerit Swami Laldas Virachit Bitak*. Delhi: Shri Prannath Mission.

Felek, Ozgen and Alexander D. Knysh, eds. 2012, *Dreams and Visions in Islamic Societies*. Albany: State University of New York.

Gold, Daniel. 1987. *The Lord as Guru*. New York: Oxford University Press.

Gosain, Vitthaleshwar. 1986. *Chaurasi Vaishnavan ki Varta*. Bombay: Shri Krishnadas.

Gosain, Vitthaleshwar. 2008. *Do Sau Bawan Vaishnavan ki Varta*. Bombay: Shri Krishandas.

Granoff, Phyllis and Koichi Shinohara, eds. 1994. *Other Selves: Autobiography and Biography in Cross Cultural Perspective*. Buffalo: Mosaic Press.

Gupt, Bhagwan Das. 1997. *Mughlon ke Antargat Bundelkhand ka Samajik, Arthik aur Sanskritik Itihas*. New Delhi: Hindi Book Centre.

Habib, Irfan. 1999. *The Agrarian System of Mughal India*. New Delhi: Oxford University Press.

Hansraj, Bakshi. *Saneh Sagar*, ed. Bhagwandeen. 1972. Nagri Pracharini Sabha: Varanasi.

Hodgson, Marshall. 1974. *The Venture of Islam: Conscience and History in a World Civilization*. Chicago: The University of Chicago Press.

Imhasly, Bernard. 2007. *Good Bye to Gandhi? Travels in New India*. New Delhi: Penguin Viking.

Iraqi, Shahabuddin. 2009. *Bhakti Movement in Medievall India: Social and Political Perspectives*. New Delhi: Manohar.

Loenzen, David N., ed. 2004. *Religious Movements in South Asia 600-1800 (Debates in Indian History and Society)*. New Delhi: Oxford University Press.

________, ed. 1976. *Bhakti Religion in North India. New* Delhi: Manohar.

Mangalwadi, Vishal. 1977. *The World of Gurus*. New Delhi: Vikas Publishing House.

Manucci, Niccolao. 1966. *Storia do Mongor (1653-1708)*, tr. William Irvine. Calcutta: Editions India.

Morris, Brian. 1994. *Anthropology of the Self: The Individual in Cultural Perspective*. London & Boulder: Pluto Press.

Novetzke, Christian Lee. 2008. *History, Bhakti and Public Memory*. New Delhi: Permanent Black.

Oddie, Geoffrey, A. 2006. *Imagined Hinduism: British Protestant Missionary Constructions of Hinduism, 1793-1900*. New Delhi: Sage.

Openshaw, Jeane. 2010. *Writing the Self: The Life and Philosophy of a Dissenting Baul Guru*. New Delhi: Oxford University Press.

Prannath, Mahamati. 2013. *Sanandh*, tr. Raj Kumar Arora. New Delhi: Prannath Mission.

Ram, Shiv Mangal. 1996. *Swami Laldas Krit Mahamati Prannath Bitak ka Madhya Kalin Bhartiya Itihas ka Yogdan*. Delhi: Hindi Book Centre.

Rizvi, S.A.A. 1997. *A History of Sufism*, vol. I. New Delhi: Rupa & Company.

Sarkar, Jadunath. 1972. *History of Aurangzeb*, vol. III. New Delhi: Orient Longman.

________. 1974. *History of Aurangzeb*, vol. V. New Delhi: Orient Longman.

Sharma, Sandhya, 2010. *Literature, Culture and History in Mughal North India: 1550-1800*. New Delhi: Primus.

Sikand, Yoginder. 2003. *Sacred Spaces: Exploring Traditions of Shared Faith in India*. New Delhi: Penguin.

Vaudeville, C. 1996. *Myths, Saints and Legends in Medieval India*. New Delhi: Oxford University Press.

Wilson, H.H. 1976. Selected Works Collected and Edited by Reinhold Rost, *Religions of Hindus*, vol. 1. New Delhi: Asian Publication Services.

Articles in Edited Volumes

Bhattacharya, Manjula. 1989. 'Medieval Bhakti Movements in Gujarat', in N.N. Bhattacharya, ed., *Medieval Bhakti Movements in India*. New Delhi: Munshiram Manoharlal.

Burger, Maya, 1992. 'The Hindu Model of Social Organization and the Bhakti Movement: The Example of Vallabha's Sampraday', in R.S. McGregor, ed., *Devotional Literature in South Asia Current Research, 1985-1988*. Cambridge: Cambridge University Press.

Cohn, Bernard. 1997. 'The Command of Language and the Language of Command', in Ranajit Guha, ed., *Subaltern Studies IV: Writings on South Asian History and Society*. New Delhi: Oxford University Press, pp. 276-329.

Khanna, Meenakshi. 2012. 'The Visionaries of a Tariqa: The Uwaysi Sufis of Shahjahanabad', in Ozgen Felek and Alexander D. Knysh, eds., *Dreams and Visions in Islamic Societies.* Albany: State University of New York.

Lorenzen, David N. 2010. 'Hindus and Others', in Esther Bloch, Marrianne Keppens and Rajaram Hegde, eds., *Rethinking Religion in India: The Colonial Construction of Hinduism.* Oxfordshire: Routledge.

Muhammad Tahir. 1989. 'Influence of Islam and Sufism on Prannath's Religious Movement', in N.N. Bhattacharya, ed., *Medieval Bhakti Movements in India.* New Delhi: Munshiram Manoharlal.

Mukharya, P.S. 1989. 'Sant Prannath and Pranami Sect', in N.N. Bhattacharya, ed., *Medieval Bhakti Movements in India.* New Delhi: Munshiram Manoharlal.

Oddie, Geoffrey, A. 2010. 'Hindu Religious Identity with Special Reference to the Origin and Significance', in Esther Bloch, Marrianne Keppens and Rajaram Hegde, eds., *Rethinking Religion in India: The Colonial Construction of Hinduism.* Oxfordshire: Routledge.

Sila-Khan, Dominique. 2002. 'The Prannathis of Rajasthan: Bhakti and Irfan', in Lawrence Babb, Varsha Joshi and Michael W. Meister, eds., *Multiple Histories: Culture and Society in the Study of Rajasthan.* Jaipur: Rawat Publications.

Articles in Journals

Alam, Muzaffar. 1998. 'Pursuit of Persian: Language in Mughal Politics', in *Modern Asian Studies,* 32(2): 317-49.

Brown, Katherine Butler. 2007. 'Did Aurangzeb Ban Music? Questions for Historiography of His Reign', in *Modern Asian Studies,* 41(1): 77-120.

Chandra, Satish. 1986-7. 'Religious Policy of Aurangzeb during the Later Part of His Reign: Some Considerations', in *Indian Historical Review,* 13(1-2): 88-101.

Engineer, Asghar Ali. May 2008. 'On Sufi Approach to Islam', in *Progressive Dawoodi Bohras: Islamic Perspective.* Mumbai: Centre for Study of Society and Secularism.

Pauwels, Heidi. 2009. 'The Saint, the Warlord, and the Emperor: Discourses of Braj Bhakti and Bundela Loyalty', in *Journal of Economic and Social History of the Orient,* 52: 187-228.

Sila-Khan, Dominque. 2002. 'The Tale of the Hidden Pir', in Newsletter, *ISMI,* 11, 2.

Toffin, Gerrard. April 2011. 'Propagation of a Hindu Sect in India and Nepal: The Krishna-Pranami Sampraday', in *Journal of South Asian Studies,* 35(1): 1-29.

5

Ballads, Public Memory, and History in the Littoral Zone of Eastern Bengal

DAVID L. CURLEY[1]

Introduction

This paper is an attempt to use local ballads as sources of history in the littoral zone of eastern Bengal. My primary sources for ballads from this micro-region are the volumes edited, translated and published by Dineshchandra Sen, and then recollected and edited by Kshitish Candra Moulik.[2] This chapter will examine plural social bonds, boundary transgressions, identity changes, and social conflict in 'romantic' and 'historical' ballads that Sen and Moulik collected.

Sen's work was part of his project to recover a Bengali 'national identity' based on a Bengali 'literary archive'.[3] One limitation of his archive lies in the selection of its texts. He used ballads to support ideas about shared moral sentiments that he thought had formed the long-enduring social bond of the Bengali nation. Biases shaped his unitary idea of the nation, and are reflected in two explicit standards for selection of the ballads. The first eliminated versions of ballads that were too much influenced by contemporary Muslim Bengali print culture, and the second eliminated ballads that were too crudely humorous, or too explicitly erotic for the taste of contemporary educated elites.[4] This essay will use ballads to explore not a unitary national identity, but many representations of local social bonds in their plurality.

Another problem with Sen's archive is inaccuracy in transcription. Sen's informants had transcribed recitations of people who still remembered ballads, rather than taking them from existing printed versions. To great advantage on the other hand Moulik when possible used manuscripts of the ballads kept by the performers themselves. His invaluable Bengali volumes correct many confusing errors of transcription and spelling in Sen's Bengali texts, and inaccuracies and elisions in his translations, and I will rely on his version of the ballad that will be most important to this discussion.[5] Moulik, however, did not live to re-edit Sen's final volume.

The third problem is that by nature the ballads are not documents. They can be seen as memories that become public through performance, and like all public memories they rely on a shifting penumbra of public amnesia.[6] They also have been shaped by expectations of their genre shared by authors and audiences; their narratives often represent 'formulaic content' rather than 'immediate experience'. Reading the ballads as historical sources requires understanding shared expectations about the genre and their complex relation to public memory.[7]

A final problem has to do with the time represented by the ballads. Although Sen was convinced of the ballads' historical value, and cited them as evidence for enduring features of Bengali society, many of the ballads he collected simply do not belong to pasts that they purport to narrate. I will pay careful attention to circumstantial evidence of dates of composition, and evidence that ballads were altered during the course of being performed. I will argue that literary and rhetorical purposes shaped such alterations. By recognizing 'historical' ballads with late dates of composition, and patterns of their alteration, we can recognize changes in the ways some historical ballads were plotted in the early twentieth century.

Having tried to understand some features of the genre and its relation to public memory, I will examine a ballad representing characters who can be placed in the littoral zone of Noakhali in the 1760s, when the English East India Company and its servants took control of revenue collections and trade in the most profitable commodities of the south-eastern littoral zone, and faced a campaign of resistance led by officials in Nawab Mir Qasim's government. I will suggest that the earliest core of this ballad probably dates back to the first three decades of the nineteenth century.

The hypothesis of this essay is that in the 1760s conflict between Company servants, and Nawabi officials and local zamindars drew on existing social identities, and exacerbated local social conflicts.

Marriages as Rituals of Social Integration

In ballads from eastern Bengal transgressive and contested marriages introduce familial and political conflict. Couples may be united by a seeming 'abduction' (*apaharan*), a theatrical action in which brides secretly choose their husbands, and even arrange the time and place of escape from their parents. With respect to the Christian-Muslim frontier in Spanish ballads, Adriano Duque has argued that a man's journey across the frontier results in his meeting a girl from the opposite religious community, her abduction, their transgressive marriage, and the bride's conversion to a new religious identity.[8] But the littoral zones of eastern Bengal were 'permeable', and religious frontiers were vague or non-existent; rather, the whole subregion was a 'space of interaction' characterized by ethnic, religious and cultural diversity. People from different localities, ethnicities, and religions routinely met for exchange in small ports, where they also could form partnerships, work together, and sometimes participate in religious practices that sought divine protection from the special dangers of life at sea and along its margins.[9] In ballads from eastern Bengal, meetings of lovers who have different social identities take place in the public space of the river landing. But according to one ballad, without shared ideas about gender roles and about modesty codes for women, enduring marriages with Burmese women are not possible: 'these women have no *parda* [seclusion, modesty]—no self-respect, no affection, or sympathy in their soul', and the men do the cooking.[10]

In 'The Tale of Bhelua, the Beautiful One' from Maimensingh, a 'love' marriage transgresses marriage rules for preserving the superior *kulin* identity of the bride's family. Madan was the son of a merchant from a village on the Ujani River, who had crossed the sea on a trading voyage to reach the 'golden city' of Kanchanpur in eastern Bengal.[11] From his boat he saw Bhelua bathing in the river with her friends. She was the daughter of a merchant equally rich, but as *kulin* her family claimed a status that Madan's family lacked. Bhelua's father refused a marriage proposal from Madan's family, and then, after Madan had abducted Bhelua from the river landing with her permission, and had taken her to his home, his own father disowned him for this 'theft', and commanded him to return Bhelua to her father, and never to return.

Journeys by boat on treacherous rivers emphasize the danger of this couple's estrangement from both sets of natal kin, and their vulnerability as they fail to find protection beyond the family. After plot complications involving a pirate Abu Raja, Madan's faithless friend Hiren, and Hiren's faithful sister Menaka, the couple boarded Madan's ship and came in a storm to a vast intersection of four rivers (*chau-ganga*), pursued by male antagonists in three separate boats. To save the truth of her vow to be faithful to Madan, Bhelua threw herself into the confluence, and her girlfriend Menaka followed. Her pursuers—her father, Abu Raja, and Hiren—all drowned in the storm. From a melodramatic sacrifice of antagonists the ballad contrives a comic ending. The retreating tide left both girls alive on a sandbank. They and the possibility of nuptial love itself were saved by a dispassionate and 'grave looking old merchant of saintly character'. In the ballad's conclusion, Madan, with the approval of his chastened father, married both girlfriends in a double wedding. A nineteenth-century composition seems probable, because while criticizing *kulin* restrictions on marriage within the same caste, the ballad both allows a double wedding, and avoids the 'intimate scandal' of polygamous *kulin* grooms who had dozens of wives, a topic that elite, educated Hindu Bengalis did not want to broach publicly in the nineteenth century.[12]

We may contrast this ballad to a ballad that Sen collected from Chittagong, where a Muslim marriage is contested but not transgressive, and subsequent abductions are real, not feigned. Its heroine also is named Bhelua.[13] Sen thought that the ballad was based on an event that took place during the reign of Nusrat Shah (r. 1519-32), and he believed that the historical origin of the ballad was proved by its many geographical references to the district of Chittagong, and by a local, Persian history.[14]

The ballad opens with a description of the eastern port of Saflapur belonging to a merchant-prince named Manik, who enjoyed 'landed properties, annually fetching him many lakhs of rupees,' and who employed 'a large retinue of soldiers and troops besides revenue collectors and officers', and who had 'mastered the Koran'. The little port was ruled by its merchant prince, it apparently was independent of any superior state, and the ballad's opening passage describes a busy traffic of ships, cargoes, sailors, and buyers.[15]

The bride Bhelua and the groom Amir of this ballad were cousins. There is no religious or status bar to their marriage, and a plot of river journeys and social conflict first requires excessive conjugal passion, Amir's departure on a trading voyage, and intervention by Amir's unmarried and jealous sister to destroy Bhelua's honour in her affinal family. Reduced to an unprotected servant who must draw water for her husband's kin, Bhelua then can be abducted against her will from the river landing. The result is similar to the first ballad: a woman without family protection and a clear identity is imprisoned by two men in positions of power and authority who want to possess her, a river pirate and a lecherous *kazi*.

Both the river pirate and the *qazi* violate norms for proper exercise of authority, and neither comes under the discipline of a superior state. It therefore is crucial to the plot that the groom's father was a merchant prince with a military force. He summoned his army and navy, and defeated the combined armies of the pirate and the *qazi*. Despite the promise of this military success, however, the plot ends in tragedy. Bhelua had undertaken a vow of starvation to prevent a coerced 'widow marriage' (*nikah*) to the *qazi*, and she died from illness during the voyage home.

Both ballads uphold sentiments supporting conjugal love against opposing kin and against indisciplined men in positions of power and authority. The first ballad criticizes excessive concern for honour associated with *kulin* rank, while the second criticizes a husband's excessive passion, intrafamilial jealousies, and hasty and mistaken condemnation of the bride's conduct by the groom's family. Transgressive and contested 'love' marriages threaten familial bonds between parents and children, and between brothers and sisters. Without protection from their affinal families brides are exposed to capture, confinement, and shame, and grooms also may suffer predatory attacks from treacherous friends or powerful strangers. Marriage bonds survive opposition and separation because couples make and keep promises to remember each other, and because 'saint-like' men intervene on love's behalf. The death of antagonists affirms sentiments that approve romantic conjugal love. A tragic end for the bride or groom, on the other hand, affirms sentiments that support the authority of parents, social order against individual happiness, and caste boundaries against love's unruly passions.

Interreligious Marriages in 'Historical' Ballads

This section will consider historical ballads that treat marriages between Hindus and Muslims, and that probably were composed in the late nineteenth or early twentieth century.[16] We can date some of these ballads by their novel themes, and by their intertextual relations with local print culture. We also can identify some passages that probably were added after their initial composition. I will argue that after the turn of the twentieth century, some 'historical' ballads were reshaped in a new context of conflict between Hindu and Muslim religious nationalism. Forced abductions, especially of low caste Hindu women by powerful Muslim men, replace voluntary, staged abductions, and forced abduction stories are countered by stories about Hindu women who have married Muslims and converted to Islam voluntarily.

Set in the distant past, the ballad 'Malua' describes a 'Muslim abduction' of a Hindu woman against her will.[17] Sen responded to criticism of this and other ballads by 'some Mohammedan gentlemen of culture and position' by denying that composers of the ballads had 'any sinister or racial motives', and by pointing out similar criticisms in the ballads of both Muslim and Hindu rulers.[18] Pradip Kumar Datta, however, has analysed features of public discourse about a threat to the 'Hindu community' posed by 'Muslim abductions'. Hundreds of stories of abductions were published in the early twentieth century, both in Hindu Bengali works of fiction, and in Hindu nationalist newspapers. Datta lists stereotypical features of stories in this discourse. They include a new focus on the vulnerability of low caste Hindu peasant women whose husbands have departed to find work. Other features include, in addition to the wife's abduction by a powerful Muslim man, her rescue by her heroic brothers who take up clubs against the Muslim man and his henchmen, her husband's return after the wife's release and his rejection of her for having lived with a Muslim man, the wife's appeal to a caste council and her rejection also by her caste, and her final *sati*-like suicide to resolve all doubts about her 'purity'. Collected in 1921 at the peak of Hindu agitation about Muslim abductions, and published in 1923, Sen's version of the ballad 'Malua' contains each one of these stereotypical features. It demonstrates that Hindu nationalist discourse about the need for an 'organized' Hindu response to the 'problem of Muslim abductions' influenced a late version of a ballad about interreligious marriages.[19]

In two 'historical' ballads that feature interreligious marriages, intense political competition between Hindu and Muslim politicians, and new discourses of religious nationalism have shaped stories about violent conflict between organized communities of Hindus and Muslims.[20] The refusal of Hindu men to recognize marriages of their women to Muslims is answered by 'purificatory sacrifices' of war and execution, through which sacrifices a society divided by religious identities and sentiments can be 'bloodily deconstructed'.[21]

Several ballads about Isha Khan and his descendants, a family known as the Dewans of Jangalbari, were revised for local publication in the late nineteenth and early twentieth century. Like 'Malua' these ballads are marked both by religious nationalism, and by the influence of local print culture. Sen published two of them: a version of 'The Ballad of Isha Khan Mashnad Ali' and 'Firoz Khan Dewan'.[22] One impetus for composition and publication of this set of ballads was a new genealogical claim by the Jangalbari Dewan family that their ancestor who first converted to Islam was the Afghan Sultan Sulaiman Karrani (r. 1564-72), a claim that also had been corroborated by the family in several recent, local histories.[23] Although Sen believed that he had found an earlier version of the ballad than those that had been printed, Moulik found a single printed source that contains most of Sen's version.[24] Whatever may be the date of the ballad's original composition, the versions printed by both Sen and Moulik date from the end of the nineteenth century at the earliest.[25]

The ballad of Isha Khan describes how an ancestor of the Jangalbari Dewans had converted to Islam, and how the family had resettled in eastern Bengal. According to Sen's version, before converting to Islam Isha Khan's father Kalidas had served as the chief minister of Sultan Jalaluddin at Gaur in Bengal. Because of their different religions, Kalidas declined the Sultan's daughter's invitation to marry her, and she therefore decided to 'destroy his caste' by arranging to feed him beef without his knowledge. Kalidas threatened suicide in response to her exposure of his 'sin', but Sultan Jalaluddin proposed that he choose instead to complete a conversion already involuntarily begun, and promised not just his daughter in marriage, but inheritance of the kingdom of Gaur as well. Thus Kalidas eventually became 'Sultan Sulaman'.

In the second generation Sultan Sulaman's son Isha Khan lost the kingdom of Gaur to the Mughals, and was forced to acknowledge fealty to Emperor Akbar. He escaped to 'Jangalbari' in eastern Bengal, and later was installed by a Mughal decree in this 'home in the wilderness'. Isha Khan then chose a Hindu bride.[26] She was the sister of Kaidar Ray, the Hindu ruler of the wealthy river port of Shripur. By her suggestion, Isha Khan secretly abducted her from the river landing where they had first met. With her full consent the girl was given a Muslim name, Niamat Jan, they were married in a Muslim ceremony, and in due course two sons were born.

In the crucial third generation, Kaidar Ray came to visit his widowed sister Niamat Jan in Jangalbari with a proposal that her two sons should marry his two daughters, a marriage of cousins lawful for Muslims but not for Bengali Hindus like him. Suspicious, Niamat Jan temporized. Kaidar Ray then arranged to abduct his nephews back to Shripur, where he put them in prison and tortured them. A battle followed between the armies of Kaidar Ray and his sister's army commander. Kaidar Ray's daughters accepted their cousins as husbands to be, and saved them from an execution ordered by him. The girls then told their aunt's army commander where their father was hiding. He killed their father, returned in triumph, and paraded Kaidar Ray's severed head through the city of Jangalbari. The two pairs of cousins were then married in a Muslim ceremony.

By showing that Hindu women took the initiative in arranging abductions and marriages with the Dewan family's men, and that the women readily accepted conversion to Islam, this late ballad tries to counter stereotypical Hindu narratives about violent abductions of Hindu women by Muslim men.[27] The conflict between Kaidar Ray and Niamat Jan therefore is resolved by the execution of Kaidar Ray through the agency of his own daughters.

Moulik briefly summarized a different, 'Hindu version' of events in the crucial third generation. In this version Kaidar Ray's daughters were abducted against their will by the Dewan family, and to preserve their honour and that of their natal family they immolated themselves, in the process burning down the quarter of the palace in which their aunt Niamat Jan dwelt.[28] In this version Hindu women responded to real abductions by immolations, both voluntary and forced, that purify all women in the family who have been made impure by contact with Muslims. Ultimately in this ballad the new, nationalist identity boundary between Hindus and Muslims could not be negotiated in a single narrative satisfactory to both religious communities.

'The Ballad of Surat Jamal and Adhua' by Faizu Fakir also treats the theme of marriage across religious boundaries.[29] Its historical subjects are a similar family of converts to Islam, the Dewans of Baniachang in Sylhet. The ballad's narrative frame has been extended to explain causes and consequences of the core story, and the final scene again is marked by religious nationalism.

Fictional elements of the ballad's opening taken from folklore[30] explain how the Muslim prince Surat Jamal came to be adopted by the Hindu ruler, Raja Dubraj, and how Surat Jamal and Adhua, the daughter of Dubraj, formed a deep bond. When Surat Jamal regained his father's kingdom, Adhua proposed marriage. Refusing to 'steal' her, Surat Jamal sent his minister to make a formal proposal to Raja Dubraj, with the argument that 'Hindus and Muhammadans are the children of the same God'. Instead of consenting, Dubraj imprisoned, dishonoured, and tortured the minister, and then drove him out of the city. To avenge this insult

Surat Jamal prepared to invade and destroy the realm of Raja Dubraj.

The plot then develops through escalating threats of violence between Surat Jamal and Raja Dubraj, and between Surat Jamal and his father Alal, who suddenly returned home, and briefly formed an alliance with Raja Dubraj to dethrone and punish his son for the sinful marriage proposal. The ballad seems to be resolved by parallel sacrificial deaths of the bride and groom, but Sen's version extends the narrative frame to answer questions about the fate of the two fathers. Alal recognized his son's diamond ring on the finger of Adhua's dead body, and through it the 'truth' of their love. He called her father Dubraj and the two 'friends' were 'united in common grief'. Alal became a fakir, and Dubraj converted to Islam, and the two departed for Mecca. Marked by Muslim religious nationalism, the conclusion enacts a triple erasure of the Hindu identity of the family of Dubraj, by marriage, by conquest, and by conversion.

These two 'historical' ballads performed functions of public memory in relation to local places, events, and characters. The versions we have do not negotiate a boundary within a 'space of interaction' characterized by ethnic, religious and cultural diversity. Instead they serve as proof texts to demonstrate the superior moral character of one religious 'community', and they erase opponents from the other side by death or conversion. As print culture began to reshape written and oral composition, ballads incorporated novel material from recently published genealogies and histories, and commented on contemporary religious nationalism. Performing public memories in new and changing contexts, recently composed versions of 'historical' ballads were shaped by public amnesia, allowing new, fictional material in extensions of narrative frames, in evocation of intense sentiments of religious identity and hostility, and in violent plot resolutions that represent a purified and truncated society.

Memories and Rhetoric in 'Rangamala Sundari'

We now can consider 'Rangamala Sundari or Chaudhuri's Larai', a romantic ballad (with several alternative versions and titles) that is about historical conflict within the *zamindari* family of Babupur. Babupur was located a few miles from the Noakhali coast, between the Meghna and Feni rivers. The ballad's Babupur conflict entered into British records in the 1760s, when the British first established the East India Company's economic and political dominance in eastern Bengal. The ballad narrates a struggle between an uncle, Rajendra Chaudhuri, younger brother of the previous zamindar of Babupur, and Rajendra's nephew, Rajchandra, the deceased zamindar's son. 'Rangamala Sundari' is interesting because its powerful and dangerous male characters include the lover in the romance, the nephew Rajchandra. The ballad invites its audience to consider threats to love from the disparity of power between Rajchandra and his beloved, and it provides us with an especially rich picture of marginal but mobile subjects and their strategies for dealing with *zamindari* power.

Between Sen and Moulik we have two quite different versions. While Sen's version follows Moulik's in many verses, it also rearranges some events, adds many new details, and is clearly a later version. Moulik discovered that Sen's version was similar to printed versions by five Muslim authors who wrote around the turn of the twentieth century.[31] Moulik obtained his version in 1953 from the copybook of the son of a man whom he had heard perform the ballad in 1920, and who, according to the family's genealogy, was in the eighth generation of descent from the ballad's original author. Judging by the copybook's paper, Moulik thought that the manuscript itself dated to the mid-nineteenth century.[32] Internal evidence suggests that Moulik's version can be no earlier than the first third of the nineteenth century.[33]

The uncle Rajendra had taken control of the entire Babupur property when his elder brother died and Rajchandra was still a boy.[34] Subsequent conflict between uncle and nephew was caused by an informal, but increasingly public union between Rajchandra and Rangamala. Rangamala belonged to the 'Nar' caste (a caste of musicians whose boys, but not girls, also performed dances). Although both families were Shudras, the Nars belonged to the 'depressed' category of Shudras from whom water cannot be accepted. Intimate contact with the Nars would make the Shudra Babupur family 'lose caste'.[35]

Moulik's version directly criticizes the Babupur zamindars' oppression, and it also suggests that the family could have acknowledged their nephew's informal marriage to the beautiful Nar woman. In this version the Babupur family's arbitrary power consistently was enforced by violence. Poor and low born men and women were beaten as a matter of course by the nephew and his strongman (*bir*). Twice the nephew Rajchandra's strongman violently extorted valuable gifts that Rajchandra had bestowed on others. In fact, beatings are represented as being common throughout the local society of Babupur, and given a response of submission, they might form a kind of social bond. In a repeated formula the preferred response is to utter no cry, and while circling around the beater to clasp his or her feet. Men and women might be struck with fists and kicked, or they might be butted to the ground or beaten with clubs (*lathi*), or hit with shoes as a sign of special debasement. One poor, low caste woman was beaten by Rangamala's maidservants. Brahmin men were not immune, and once Rajchandra presumed on his family's prestige to beat his uncle's strongman, and the strongman silently bore it.[36]

Given the Chaudhuri family's power, high- and low-caste women were vulnerable to young Rajchandra's lust. In two stereotypical stories of a spoiled prince, Rajchandra first laid his hands on a Brahmin bride, and then attempted to rape an untouchable weaver's wife in her own house. In both cases the Chaudhuri family simply refused to hear appeals for justice. To seek justice by force, an 'army' of Brahmin men assembled to fight against the Chaudhuris, but they disbanded at once when one member wisely described them (and himself) as 'a hundred or two of mice'. Local Brahmins could not even enforce a threatened ritual boycott of the Babupur zamindars.[37] The weakness of Brahmins in 'the tidelands' east of the Meghna River allowed the Shudra Babupur family to ignore Hindu sentiments and caste identities, and to violate moral norms.

A beautiful and very low caste woman's vulnerability to men is the theme of formulaic stories that introduce us to the heroine Rangamala. Both of her natural parents had died. Her adoptive 'father' and her younger brother had agreed to marry her off to a high caste hunchback in return for his promise of large monetary rewards. After seeing her deformed husband in the course of the wedding, Rangamala refused to accept the marriage, and we are told in an aside that 'because of that day' she 'knew who were her own people and who were not' (*chinlo apan poro*). Later, after meeting and falling in love with Rajchandra, Rangamala told her 'father' and brother that with their permission, she would marry again by an exchange of garlands, without summoning any Brahmin, and 'without caste laws' (*samajar bebastha nai*). First to himself and then at their private and informal marriage Rajchandra in turn vowed before Dharma that he would not count anything equal to her, neither *zamindari* rule, nor family, nor honour, nor lines of learned Brahmins, and he promised never to desert her in life.[38]

Another set of stories centre on two sets of killings by Chand Bharali, the uncle Rajendra's strongman and 'hero', his chief advisor, and the acting agent of his military power. Inga Chaudhuri, a Muslim zamindar, had been appointed as the provincial governor's (the Nawab's) supervisor of local 'rajas of the tidelands', of which local people Inga was not at all afraid.[39] It is important to note that despite Inga's Muslim identity, in Bengali slang his outlandish name suggests someone 'English' or 'English-like'.[40] The nephew Rajchandra had formed an alliance with Inga in order to force his uncle to divide the *zamindari* property. In return for Inga's assistance Rajchandra had to promise to give this 'English-like' superior a quarter of the Babupur *zamindari*. The uncle Rajendra's strongman Chand Bharali discovered the alliance and its terms, and on his own initiative staged a surprise attack, and killed Inga and his young brother in their fort. (We will see that the surprise attack by Chand on the fortress of Inga is a fictionalized version of victories over Company sepoys in which Rajendra participated.)

The second set of killings immediately follows. Rajendra feared revenge by Inga's extended family, and therefore gave his nephew Rajchandra nine-sixteenths of the *zamindari* estate. Rajchandra immediately hired Maghs (Arakanese) to dig a very large tank that he had promised to Rangamala's 'father'. He then invited his uncle Rajendra to take part in a ritual feast at the Nars' house for the opening rite performed upon filling their new tank. This feast would have raised the Nar family to the rank of Shudras from whom water is accepted.[41] To save his master from 'loss of caste', Chand

Bharali drugged Rajchandra, and fought and killed the headman Ramya Magh and other Maghs who were guarding Rangamala. He sacrificed Rangamala and her brother by beheading them, and set fire to the Nars' house. Chand then brought Rangamala's head back to his master Rajendra, who, upon seeing her beauty wished that he had allowed and paid for the marriage, foresaw his nephew's ensuing 'madness', and hid with his strongman.

When Rajchandra awoke from his drugged sleep, he saw flames at the Nars' house. Rushing there he discovered Rangamala's decapitated body and the bloody site of her beheading. He removed her body. In his uncle's courtyard he discovered Rangamala's severed head, brought it outside and vowed to kill both Rajendra and Chand, and then set fire to his uncle's house. However, Chand attacked him in the darkness, and Rajchandra mistaking Chand for a ghost (*bhut*) fled. Unable to fulfil his vow, Rajchandra ordered his strongman Ram Bharali to secure a Brahmin priest to build a funeral pyre at the Nars' house, and to tie Rangamala's head and body together and set her upon the pyre. He compelled the Brahmin to recite *mantras* for her cremation. Weeping, Rajchandra himself touched the flame to her mouth, fulfilling a promise he had made to Rangamala to cremate her if she should die before he did.[42]

Here Moulik's version abruptly ends. Four unusual, imperfect, or violently inverted rites frame its narrative: the imperfectly integrative, informal, and private 'wedding' between Rajchandra and Rangamala, the public feast planned for the opening of her family's new tank (radically transformative and reintegrative for the Nars, but aborted by their massacre), Chand's sacrificial staking and beheading of Rangamala and her brother, and finally, Rajchandra's cremation of Rangamala's mutilated corpse, an act he apparently performed as her husband in the absence of her son, father, or brother. Moulik's version leaves unresolved both Rajchandra's relation to his uncle and to Chand Bharali, and the Babupur family's relation to the family of the slain and powerful zamindar Inga Chaudhuri.

Like Moulik's version, Sen's version coordinates its quite different representations of marriage and *zamindari* rule. In it Rangamala is only a concubine. Her dealings with Rajchandra are manipulative and motivated by greed,[43] and her 'marriage' with Rajchandra is condemned. Sen's version normalizes only formal marriage, excluding concubines from the approval of marriage bonds and sentiments, and so it is in accord with changes in family law that had been introduced by the British.[44] It does not make discovery of Rangamala's body the ballad's climax, and in it Rajchandra does not perform Rangamala's cremation. Instead, Sen's version extends the narrative frame in order to resolve the larger political conflict between Rajendra and Inga Chaudhuri's family.[45] In this extension, Inga's uncle—a still more powerful official and zamindar—installed the nephew Rajchandra as zamindar of the entire estate, and then decided not to pursue further vengeance against Rajendra and Chand. The emotional climax of Sen's version is a scene in which Rajendra (who had abdicated) forgave Rajchandra, and Rajchandra in turn forgave Chand.

Sen's conclusion rehabilitates both of the Babupur Chaudhuris, and softens the earlier version's criticism of their violent oppression of subjects. Having excused Chand's murder of Rangamala, however, Sen's version adds lurid details to Chand's attack on Inga's household, including his killing of one of Inga's wives despite the command of his chosen deity, Goddess Kali. We may speculate that a new story about violence against a different woman had to be inserted to maintain the remembered opprobrium attaching to Chand's character. A still later addition that Sen only summarizes provides Chand with Kali's divine punishment.[46] In general Sen's version reflects a later, and more elite colonial mentality in affirming the Babupur men's solidarity as a family, and in representing their upholding of 'caste law' in marriage.

The Babupur Conflict and Amnesia

I now turn to Company letters and documents that described the events at Babupur in the early 1760s, and to related events in Dacca, Chittagong, Tripura, and on the three alluvial islands of Sandwip *pargana*. My purpose is to place events in Babupur in the context of conflict between Company servants and officers of the Nawab's government that occurred when the English East India Company and its servants took control of revenue collection, and of trade in the most profitable commodities of south-eastern Bengal, and when Mughal officials and some zamindars mounted a campaign against the English, aimed at ruining their trade.[47] We can then identify what remained in local memory about these events, and what had been forgotten when the ballad of a double murder—Inga's and Rangamala's—was composed several decades later.

In eastern Bengal the Company's control of territorial revenues, and their use of political power to alter terms of trade began with a palace revolution in 1760. Governor Vansittart secretly negotiated with Mir Qasim on terms by which the latter would be appointed Deputy Nawab under Nawab Mir Jafar, but have full executive responsibilities of the Nawab. Mir Qasim in turn promised to cede permanently to the Company the revenue administrations of three 'provinces', Burdwan and Midnapur in the west, and Chittagong in the east. When Mir Qasim's appointment was announced, Nawab Mir Jafar abruptly abdicated, and Mir Qasim became Nawab in name as well as in fact. The Company's 'gentlemen' in Chittagong and Dacca then aggressively expanded both the Company's trade and their own private trade into the eastern littoral.[48]

The actions of the Company's Dacca gentlemen in Babupur generated charges about the coercive nature of private trade by Company servants, and about their 'interference' in the Nawab's government. In addition to Rajendra and his nephew Rajchandra, two other characters had central roles: W. Billers, the Company's Chief at Luckypore (Lakshmipur), and Muhammad Ali Beg, the Nawab's *faujdar* at Dacca, who had been given responsibility for police and criminal justice throughout the eastern half of the province of Bengal. Billers and the Company supported the nephew Rajchandra. Muhammad Ali Beg, however, supported Rajendra, and in 1762 the Company could do nothing against the Beg's superior force.

According to Billers, Rajendra Chaudhuri, the uncle of the 'rightful heir', twice had 'dispossessed' his nephew Rajchandra, and was a 'noted dacoit', a 'plunderer', and a 'nuisance and a terror to every zamindar in the country'. The Company had advanced large sums to weavers in and around Babupur, and Billers warned that Rajendra might 'greatly molest our business, he being a very notorious plunderer'. Billers applied to Chittagong for reinforcements, and captured the Babupur fort, and stationed sepoys to defend it, but Rajendra in the meantime received the support of

Muhammad Ali Beg. With that support Rajendra retook his fort at Babupur.[49] This battle seems to be the basis for local memories of a battle between the uncle and the nephew. Despite Billers' request for 'some effectual method' to seize Rajendra, Governor Vansittart only directed him to report the complaint fully to Muhammad Ali Beg.[50]

During the following months there was intense conflict between Muhammad Ali Beg and his subordinate officers, and Company servants on the Noakhali coast and on the islands of Sandwip, Bamini, and Hatia. The Beg ordered his subordinates to revoke the privilege of tax-free trade claimed by Company servants. He also tried to thwart Company servants' use of advances to control textile production, and he tried to stop altogether their private monopoly in salt made on the Noakhali coast and on Sandwip Island.[51]

In November 1762 Governor Vansittart and Hastings tried to resolve escalating disputes between Company servants and the Nawab's officials by negotiating directly with the Nawab on the most contentious issues. Upon reaching an agreement, the Nawab immediately informed his subordinates, but the Dacca Council categorically refused to give up any of their 'rights'. Muhammad Ali Beg planned a blockade of the Lakshmipur Factory, and sent commands in particular to the 'Babupur zamindar' to render assistance.[52] In February 1763 there were several small-scale military conflicts between the British and Muhammad Ali's people at Jugdea, Lakshmipur, and Jaffer Gunge.[53] The ballad's surprise attack by Chand on the fortress of Inga may be a fictionalized memory of one or more of them.

In March 1763 with the Governor and Hastings in attendance, an expanded Council rejected the Governor's proposed agreement with the Nawab that would have subjected their private trade to a fixed duty, and ended their salt monopolies.[54] As directed by the Council's majority, Governor Vansittart then threatened Mir Qasim that the Company would 'take the law into their own hands' if Mir Qasim did not punish Muhammad Ali Beg.[55] Late in April 1763 leadership of the *nawabat* government in Dacca was erased when Company servants at Dacca on their own initiative seized Muhammad Ali Beg together with five of his officers.[56]

Events in Patna finally led to open war with the Nawab in July. The Nawab's administration of eastern Bengal 'was largely destroyed by the English occupation of Dacca city'. At the same time the Chittagong Council under Rumbold took over administration of the kingdom of Tripura and the whole *pargana* of Sandwip on the islands.[57] In October the newly-reappointed Nawab Mir Jafar complained about the Company's continued collections of revenue in Tripura and on the islands, and in a letter to Chittagong the Calcutta Board directed Company servants in Dacca and Chittagong to withdraw their collectors from the Nawab's territories.[58]

Despite British victories over Mir Qasim, Rajendra remained defiant. The Dacca Council requested permission to send Captain Grant to 'drive out and if possible to seize this man', and he finally was 'reduced' in February 1764.[59] Contrary to both versions of the ballad, Rajendra apparently remained in possession of the whole property of Babupur during his lifetime. After his death, the son of his only daughter inherited fourteen-sixteenths of the property, while by his will two-sixteenths were given to his sister's son. These descendants remained in possession of the whole property until 1793. In that year, a court decision awarded Rajchandra and his brother each half of a seven-sixteenths share. An equal seven-sixteenths share was awarded to Rajendra's daughter's son.[60]

English records depict a widespread and well-coordinated campaign of resistance to the Company's coercive use of advances, to monopoly trade in salt by Company servants, and to evasion of taxes on the private trade of Company servants. In both versions of the ballad creative interplay between public memory and historical amnesia has erased the Babupur conflict's wider political context. Company records and the ballads agree that Rajendra and his nephew Rajchandra disputed possession of the Babupur *zamindari*. They agree that Rajchandra sought assistance from the English-like 'Inga' Chaudhuri in the ballad, and from Billers and the Company according to Billers. The ballads have forgotten, however, the counter alliance between Rajendra and the Nawab's *faujdar* Muhammad Ali Beg, and Rajendra's active participation in the anti-British campaign. Moulik's version richly describes the Babupur family's internal conflict, and the destruction of local people who had allied themselves with Rajchandra. Both versions of the ballad narrate an unusual defeat of Company sepoys, but prudently disguise it by identifying Billers and the Company with 'Inga', a Muslim zamindar. Of the political context, what remained memorable in Moulik's version was the fact that the Company's government had not punished Rajendra or Chand for any of Chand's murders.

Conclusion

Ballads were culturally patterned 'symbolic practices' that represented the plurality of the social bond in eastern Bengal. 'Romantic' ballads feature stories about couples who have chosen each other in defiance of social norms or the wishes of their families, and who then are obstructed by their families. Transgressive and contested marriages introduce representations of plural social identities, and through marriages social conflict at large becomes intrafamilial, pitting parents against children and brothers against sisters. When abandoned, couples become subject to predatory attacks by men in power, and the ballads can criticize anarchic tendencies of political life. Transgressive or contested marriages may require the death of the antagonists to the marriage, or suicide or murder of the bride or groom, but regardless of their outcome 'love marriages', normalize conjugal sexual relations. Romantic ballads negotiate the social boundaries that they represent by helping audiences weigh moral sentiments that approve romantic love and individual happiness against moral sentiments that support the authority of parents, caste, class, and religious identities, and social order. Thus they represent a permeable littoral society, with individuals who could cross some boundaries of class, caste, and religion, and a social bond with multiple identities, conflicting sentiments, and inherent conflicts.

How did the 'world' of ballads intersect with the 'lived world' experienced by authors and audiences? The ballad of 'Rangamala Sundari' brings power relations into its romance, and represents threats to love that arise from the habitual use of power. It provides us with an especially rich picture of power in hierarchical social relations, and of strategies of marginal and mobile people for dealing with superiors. Memories about Rangamala Sundari suggests that conflict between Company servants and local zamindars had exacerbated conflicts along existing boundaries of wealth and power, and caste, but not along religious boundaries. Through its portrayal of fighting men (the Babupur zamindars' two strongmen, Ram and Chand Bharali, and Ramya, the Magh headman and his followers, who were armed with heavy, curved blades), the ballad reminds us that local fighters, often marginal and ethnically distinct from the majority of peasants, naturally became pitted against each other in local contests of power.

English records allow us to trace historical amnesia in the two versions of 'Rangamala Sundari'. Although based on events beginning in the 1760s, both versions have forgotten the wider context of resistance to the Company, and the coercive private trade of Company 'gentlemen' in eastern Bengal. Both versions remember an extraordinary defeat of Company sepoys. What else the two versions remember depends upon their rhetorical purposes in representing the social bond and its multiple identities and conflicts. Moulik's version criticizes the unjust and oppressive conduct of the Babupur family, Rajchandra's arrogance and his attempted change of the caste ranking of the Nar family, and Chand's violent enforcement of existing caste boundaries. In the early nineteenth century, it remembered that the Company's government had punished no one for Chand's two sets of murders that are the ballad's core. Sen's later version in contrast excludes 'concubines' from the approval of marriage bonds and sentiments. It remembers the reconciliation between the uncle and the nephew and between the Babupur Chaudhuris and Inga's family. Neither version remembers any religious motivation for Rajendra's conflict with the 'English-like' Inga Chaudhuri, but further research on other ballads that represent conflict with the Company in the 1760s is needed to clarify the motivation of the Company's Muslim opponents.[61]

After the turn of the twentieth century, some historical ballads were reshaped in a new context of Hindu and Muslim religious nationalism. In this context 'Hindu' ballads featured real abductions of Hindu women by elite Muslim men. 'Muslim' ballads countered with stories of voluntary decisions of Hindu women to marry Muslim men and to convert to Islam. Such ballads ceased to negotiate the religious boundary that they represented; instead they became proof texts supporting the superior morality of one or the other religious community. This important topic also needs further research, using ballads and versions of ballads that Sen and Moulik have not included, and focusing on the growing interface between ballads and local print culture.

Notes

1. I am grateful for the opportunity to present earlier versions of this work to the History Department of Jadavpur University, Kolkata, 2013, and to the Annual Meeting of the Association for Asian Studies, Philadelphia, 2014. I would like to thank particularly Gautam Bhadra, Tilottama Mukherjee, Indrani Chaudhuri, Ralph W. Nicholas, and Lindsey Harlan for critical comments and suggestions, and Gautam Bhadra and Prabir Mukhopadhyay for providing a copy of Moulik's edition of ballads discussed here. I also would like to thank Shaheen Akhtar, whose fine historical novel *Sokhi Rongomala* has been a great help.
2. Sen, 1923-32; Moulik, 1970-5.
3. Chakrabarty, 2004.
4. Sen, 1923-32, 2(1): xxviii-xxx.
5. Ibid.; Moulik, 1970-5, 1: x-xi.
6. Ricoeur, 2004.
7. Roy, 2011: 123.
8. Duque, 2011.
9. Mukherjee, 2006: 27-35.
10. Sen, 1923-32, 4 (1): 128, 148.
11. Ibid., 2 (1): 138-88.
12. Chatterjee, 1993: 149-51.
13. Sen, 1923-32, 3 (1): 64-106.
14. Sen was aware of three recently printed versions of the ballad, as well as a brief narrative of its events in a 'historical' Farsi account by Hamidullah Khan (ibid., 3 (1): 53-4, 57-9).
15. Ibid., 3 (1): 64-5.
16. Zbavitel, 1963: 1-31.
17. Sen, 1923-32, 1 (1): 39-80.
18. Ibid., 3 (1): 228-9.
19. Datta, 1999: 148-237; Sen, 1994: 215-28.
20. Ray, 1984.

21. Lincoln, 1989: 102.
22. Sen, 1923-32, 2 (1): 337-63; 427-54. Sen also mentioned a different, printed version of the ballad about Isha Khan, and he briefly described a ballad about a supposed family descendant named Manwar Khan Dewan (ibid.: 302, 327). Both ballads were composed in the second half of the nineteenth century by Munshi Abdul Karim of Galachipa, Maimensingh.
23. Ibid.: 302, 365-7.
24. *Deoyan Isha Khan Keccha* (Jalpaiguri: Kohinur Press, n.d.).
25. Moulik, 1970-5, 7: 178 fn., 182 fn., 196.
26. The ballad 'Firoz Khan Dewan' notes that families of elite Muslim of foreign descent would not permit their daughters to marry into the Dewan family because they did not 'observe *roja* (fast) and *namaj* (prayers) like true Muhammedans' (Sen, 1923-32, 2 (1): 443).
27. Datta, 1999: 78-87.
28. Moulik, 1970-5, 4: 196-7.
29. Sen, 1923-32, 2 (1): 391-419.
30. Ibid., 383.
31. The five printed texts are: Bachaniya Sekh, 'Saragiti'; Iyakub Saheb, 'Rangasundari'; Iyunuch Mia, 'Rangamalar Keccha'; Arasad Ali, 'Rangamalar Dighi'; and Aphchar Uddin, 'Piriter Dighi'.
32. Moulik, 1970-5, 4: 7-8.
33. The ballad imperfectly 'remembers' how the *zamindari* property was divided between the uncle and the nephew, a decision in fact reached by the Company's revenue court in 1793 (Thompson, 1919: 74-5). An example of amnesia is that the name of Rajchandra's father, the deceased zamindar, is reported as Rajkamal, and his name also is given as Babucand (Moulik 1970-5, 4: 153, 157, 149), but correctly the name is Pratapnarayan according to Company records, and according to the genealogy of the family (Thompson, 1919: 74; Sen, 1923-32, 3 (1): 233).
34. Moulik, 1970-5, 4: 157.
35. Wise, 1883: 351; Akhtar, 2010: 121, 132; Moulik, 1970-5, 4: 112. When Wise wrote, the Nars were becoming Muslims, but the ballad provides no evidence of this conversion, nor does it reveal anything about the Nars' livelihood.
36. Moulik, 1970-5, 4: 5, 87, 176, 155.
37. Ibid.: 25-8, 41-2, 176.
38. Ibid.: 54, 111, 114, 123.
39. Ibid.: 149, 160.
40. For example, *ingabanga* means Bengalis who were Angophiles or

'imitation Englishmen' (Datta and Robinson, 1995: 210). The ballad's name 'Inga', however, is spelled with long 'i' and long 'a'.

41. Akhtar, 2010: 121, 132.
42. Moulik, 1970-5, 4: 192-3.
43. Sen, 1923-32, 3 (1): 262, 276.
44. Chatterjee, 2002.
45. Sen, 1923-32, 3 (1): 287-94, 303-8.
46. Ibid.: 302, 308-9.
47. Ray, 2003: 289.
48. Ibid.: 213-301; Marshall, 1987: 84-8; Khan, 1969: 34.
49. Islam, 1978: 94-5, Billers to Vansittart, 1 July 1762; 95-6, Billers to Vansittart, 17 July 1762.
50. Ibid.: 97-8, Billers to Vansittart, 22 October 1762, and 10 January 1763. In this letter Billers writes 'the uncle Roy Chunder', but it is clear that he meant the uncle Rajendra.
51. Ibid.: 96-7, Billers to Vansittart, 14 October 1762, 98-9, Billers to Vansittart, 22 January 1762; British Library, Verelst Papers, F218/79, folio 140b, Verelst to Beaumont, 5 October 1762.
52. Ray, 2003, 284-7; Vansittart, 1766, 3: 137-9, letter from Muhammad Ali to Saiyid 'Buddul' Khan.
53. Vansittart, 1766, 2: 310-14, letter from Luckypore dated 16 February 1763; 3: 15-20, letter from the Nabob to the Governor, describing the same events.
54. Ibid., 2: 316-420, extract of the Council's consultations of 1 March 1763.
55. India, Imperial Records Department, 1911-25, 1, no. 1722, dated 1 April 1763.
56. Ibid., no. 1755, from Muhammad Salih to Muhammad Ali Beg, dated 29 April 1763; and no. 1756, from Mir Qasim to Vansittart, dated 20 April 1763.
57. Khan, 1969: 53-4.
58. British Library, India Office Records, Bengal Public Consultations, P/1/36, 10 October 1763, letter from the Nawab Mir Qasim Khan; Khan, 1969: 54-5.
59. Khan, 1969: 54; Long, 1973, no. 403, letter from Dacca, dated 10 January 1764.
60. Thompson, 1919: 74-5.
61. For example, the ballad of Shamsher Gazi; for a discussion see Sen, 1920: 136-52.

References

Archival Material

British Library. Verelst Papers, Eur. Mss. F218.

———. India Office Records. Bengal Public Consultations; Bengal Revenue Consultations.

Printed Books and Articles

Akhtar, Shaheen. 2010. *Sokhi Rongomala*. Dhaka: Prothoma Prokashan.

Chakrabarty, Dinesh. 2004. 'Romantic Archives: Literature and the Politics of Identity in Bengal', *Critical Inquiry* 30: 654-82.

Chatterjee, Indrani. 2002. *Gender, Slavery and Law in Colonial India*. New Delhi and Oxford: Oxford University Press.

Chatterjee, Partha. 1993. *The Nation and its Fragments: Colonial and Postcolonial Histories*. Princeton: Princeton University Press.

Datta, Pradip Kumar. 1999. *Carving Blocs: Communal Ideology in Early Twentieth-Century Bengal*. New Delhi and New York: Oxford University Press.

Duque, Adriano. 2011. 'Sex and the Border: Byzantine Epics and the Spanish Frontier Ballad', *The Medieval History Journal*, 14(2): 213-28.

Dutta, Krishna and Andrew Robinson. 1995. *Rabindranath Tagore: The Myriad-Minded Man*. New York: St. Martin's Press.

India, Imperial Record Department. 1911-25. *Calendar of Persian Correspondence, Being Letters, Referring Mainly to Affairs in Bengal, which Passed between some of the Company's Servants, and Indian Rulers and Notables* . . . 11 vols. Calcutta: Superintendent of Government Printing, India.

Islam, Sirajul. 1985. 'Muslim Armed Resistance to Early British Rule in Bengal', *Revolt Studies* 1(1): 7-24.

———, ed. 1978. *Bangladesh District Records, Chittagong*, vol. 1: *1760-1787*. Dacca: University of Dacca.

Khan, Abdul Majed. 1969. *The Transition in Bengal, 1756-1775*. Cambridge: Cambridge University Press.

Lincoln, Bruce. 1989. *Discourse and the Construction of Society: Comparative Studies of Myth, Ritual, and Classification*. New York: Oxford University Press.

Long, James. 1973. *Selections from Unpublished Records of Government*, 2nd edn., ed. Mahaprasad Saha, Kolkata: Firma K.L. Mukhopadhyay.

Marshall, Peter J. 1987. *The New Cambridge History of India*, II, 2. *Bengal: The British Bridgehead*. Cambridge: Cambridge University Press.

Moulik, Kshitish Chandra. 1970-5. *Pracina purbabanga gitika*. 7 vols. Kolkata: Firma K.L. Mukhopadhyay.

Mukherjee, Rila. 2006. *Strange Riches: Bengal in the Mercantile Map of South Asia*. New Delhi: Foundation Books.

Ray, Rajat Kanta. 2003. *The Felt Community: Commonality and Mentality before the Emergence of Indian Nationalism*. New Delhi: Oxford University Press.

________. 1984. *Social Conflict and Political Unrest in Bengal, 1875-1927*. New Delhi: Oxford University Press.

Ricoeur, Paul. 2004. *Memory, History, Forgetting*, tr. Kathleen Blamey and David Pellauer. Chicago: University of Chicago Press.

Roy, Tirthankar. 2011. 'Where is Bengal? Situating an Indian Region in the Early World Economy', *Past and Present*, 213(1): 115-46.

Sen, Dinesh Chandra. 1923-31. *Eastern Bengal Ballads*, 4 vols. Calcutta: University of Calcutta.

________. 1920. *Folk Literature of Bengal*. Calcutta: University of Calcutta.

Sen, Samita. 1994. 'Honour and Resistance: Gender, Community and Class in Bengal, 1920-40', in Sekhar Bandyopadhyay, Abhijit Dasgupta and Willem van Schendel, eds., *Bengal: Communities, Development and States*. New Delhi: Manohar.

Thompson, W.H. 1919. *Final Report on the Survey and Settlement Operations in the District of Noakhali, 1914-1919*. Calcutta: Bengal Secretariat Book Depot.

Vansittart, Henry. 1766. *A Narrative of the Transactions in Bengal, from the Year 1760, to the Year 1764, During the Government of Mr. Henry Vansittart*, 3 vols. London: by the author.

Wise, James. 1883. *Notes on the Races, Castes and Tribes of Eastern Bengal*. London: Harrison and Sons.

Zbavitel, Dhušan. 1963. *Bengali Folk-Ballads from Mymensingh and the Problem of their Authenticity*. Calcutta: Calcutta University Press.

6

The Story of Jayamati's Humiliation and Death

Reworking of the Indigenous Sources in Assamese Historiography of Nineteenth and Twentieth Centuries

SUDESHNA PURKAYASTHA*

The story of Jaymati is located in the power politics of the Ahom state during the political turmoil of the seventeenth century. The situation was created with the atrocities of the Ahom king Sulikpha, Lara Raja (boy king), who was instigated by the minister Laluk Sola Barphukan. He wanted either to kill or mutilate all prospective Ahom princes who would aspire to the throne in order to make his position secure. Jaymati, the wife of Gadapani, a prince of the blood royal was targeted, and the state authority found the prince missing. Jaymati was forced by the royal authority to disclose her husband's whereabouts. When the princess refused to tell the hideout of her husband, she was subject to inhuman atrocities and ultimately assassinated by the royal executioner.

The intellectual journey from the historicization of the event of Jaymati's persecution to the shaping of an institutional history forms the central theme of this paper. I have tried to focus on the reworking of the Assamese sources in the evolution of modern Assamese historiography. The paper also tries to delve into the changing dimensions of a historical phenomenon with the appropriation of multiplicity of meaning.

* I am indebted to Professor Gautam Bhadra, Dr Raziuddin Aquil and Dr Jayeeta Sharma for their comments on an earlier draft.

The episode has captured the imagination of Assamese historians since the late nineteenth century. Among the contributors on the subject Ratneshwar Mahanta is said to be the first Assamese colonial intellectual who portrayed Jaymati's event and tried to historicize it. This was followed by the writings of a galaxy of Assamese intellectuals—Padmanath Gohain Barua, Lakshminath Bezbarua, Kumudeshwar Barthakur and Hiteshwar Barbarua. Surya Kumar Bhuyan, a noted historian and a doyen of Assam history, contributed to the subject and historical narratives on Jaymati emerged as a consequence of extensive historical research. Interestingly, besides these hosts of colonial elites, Harakanta Sharma Barua, 'an Assamese gentleman of the older school who assimilated to some extent the growing influx of the western spirit'[1] made Jaymati come alive in his *Assam Buranji,* written between 1870 and 1880. The present study has selected three different narratives on Jaymati. These are Harakanta Sharma Barua's narrative on Jaymati included in his *Assam Buranji*, Kripanath Phukan's literary ballad and the rationalist professional historian Surya Kumar Bhuyan's narratives on Jaymati.

The historical validity of Jaymati's episode was not universally accepted by the Assamese elites. The accuracy of this event has been questioned by such Assamese intellectuals as Benudhar Sharma, a noted historian, a litterateur and a contemporary of Surya Kumar Bhuyan. In an article published in *Monideep,* Benudhar Sharma raised a controversy about the historical validity of the story of Jaymati Kunwari and classed it in the category of an imaginary fiction.[2] Surya Kumar Bhuyan, on the other hand, had refuted the contention and argued for the historical validity of the event of Jaymati. In the preface of Harakanta Sharma Barua's *Assam Buranji,* Bhuyan's argument has been endorsed when the editor praised Harakanta's addition of 'rational account of the self-sacrifice of Jaymati' to Kashinath Tamuli Phukan's account.[3]

The methodology of conventional history-writing relies upon the shaping of a real past that concerns itself with truth or accuracy. Recently, such notion of historicization has been questioned by historians. In the opinion of Tony Bennett, the historian's communication with the past is not direct but through some relics or 'traces' of the past. These traces are highly 'volatile' and mutable in nature which makes a difference between the 'past' and 'the writing up' of the past.[4] 'The past as constituted by its existing traces' is always appropriated textually through the sedimented layers of previous interpretations and through the reading habits and categories developed by previous or current methodological practices. 'Consequently, the status of historical knowledge is not based for its truth/accuracy on its correspondence with the past per se but on the various historicizations of it, so that historiography always "stands in for" the past, the only medium it has to affect a "historical" presence'.[5] The present study argues that the truth in history may transgress the contours of factuality and deny empiricism that claims singularity of past events; it tries to examine the historical truth under a mnemo-historical perspective.[6]

Since 1920, Assamese claim for history grew more and more pronounced and the inception of the Kamrup Anusandhan Samiti in 1912 and the Department of Historical and Antiquarian Studies (DHAS) in 1929 marked the era of collection of materials for writing the history of Assam. Surya Kumar Bhuyan was appointed as the honorary Assistant Director of DHAS. The department had taken a magnificent task of collecting handwritten *buranjis* from different quarters. The officials who were entrusted with the task of collecting the manuscripts had also transcribed them. These were used as ready materials for compilation and editing of the *buranjis*. The pre-print stage of the *buranjis* was marked by the synoptic study by the scholars which enabled them to extract the historical accuracy of the events of the Assamese past.[7] The accuracy of the episode of Jaymati as narrated in the *buranjis* needs to be mentioned in the light of these texts. It is to be noted that the event has been narrated in the *buranji* texts in a very intelligible manner. One such text has narrated the event as follows:

> . . . Dilihial Buragohain, Laithepena Bargohain, etc., went to Kaliabar to kill the enemies. Earlier at the fear of the Buraphukan Gada Kunwar had put up those two gohains at Nagachang. Ai Kunwari Deo was killed in pregnant condition. At this grief Gada Kunwar started moving around and took shelter at Banamali Bapu's Dakhinpat Sattra.[8]

Another *buranji* records: 'That day the Maharaja killed Banhagaria Gohain's two brothers at Kaliabar. Then he killed those princes whom he met. Failing to capture the Bura Raja he made his wife captive and killed her.'[9]

Jaymati's episode came to be recognized as a historical truth when Surya Kumar Bhuyan argued for the authenticity of the reports in the *buranjis*. Bhuyan wrote, 'Jaymati's story was promulgated as a legend for quite a long period. Recently, this episode has been mentioned in the handwritten Assam *buranjis*.'[10] The *buranjis* became the parameter of historical validity.

The transformation of the legend of the assassination of Jaymati into a historical event was a turning point in commemorating the Assamese past. The historic chapter of Jaymati's assassination has an emotional imprint on the Assamese mind. This passionate episode got popularized and this popularity is a part of its historicization. The episode of Jaymati became a landmark and it embarked upon an epoch-making terrain of Assamese historiography. The historical periodization took a new shape in which Jaymati's assassination was used as a milestone articulating such a framing of Assamese history writing. Bhuyan wrote, 'We are all aware of the fact that the country (Assam) witnessed a great revolution before the self sacrifice of Jaymati.'[11] This historically valid passionate story had to be transformed into a narrative that would be convenient for the modern Assamese past. For restructuring Jaymati's episode the historians needed further information on the subject than those available in the existing *buranjis*. The attempts to collect this sort of materials were made even in the late nineteenth century. From 1870 to 1880, Harakanta Sharma Barua showed the way.

Dawning of a Convenient Past

The author's preface of Harakanta Sharma Barua's *Assam Buranji* is marked by a methodology that combines the written with the oral. Barua writes,

> The history (*buranji*) of Assam, that is, the description of the kings of Indra dynasty have been scattered here and there. But these *buranjis* do not agree with each other. This has resulted in errors . . . Radhanath Barbarua and Kashinath Sharma Tamuli Phukan collected different *buranjis* from different places. Taking the abstract of all the *buranjis* they

wrote a precise book. But that book required to include many essential issues. That is why, I have taken this book and added new information from other available *buranjis* as well as reliable oral sources from the Ahom Phukans and Baruas who tell the truth and I have started to write the book.[12]

Interestingly enough, Kashinath Tamuli Phukan excluded Jaymati's assassination from his *Assam Buranji*. Harakanta tagged this event to Kashinath's account. The paragraphs from pages 148 to 157 that narrate the event of Jaymati was an addition of Harakanta himself.[13]

The commemoration of the past by Harakanta Sharma Barua tried to appropriate new meaning of the past. The meaning of the past was transformed from an event to a plot structure. Harakanta's entire narrative on Jaymati carries the beginning, middle and the end which mediates between the event and the audience. Harakanta writes:

Tungkhungia King Gobar's son Langi Gadapani, that is, Gadapani Kunwar, being a reputed strong man was being searched by the troops to take him captive. He got scared and along with his wife took shelter in the dense forest and was living in a cottage made of leaves. . . .[14]

One night at 5/6 *danda* time that Prince Gadapani was sitting with his wife in that cottage. In the meantime, Gabharu went out of the room and felt that they were surrounded by men from all sides. She told this to her husband. At first the prince could not believe it and said, "Who will come in such a dense forest and how do they come to know that we are here?" Gabharu said, "I cannot understand; probably, they have been informed by the spy that we are staying here". While communicating in such a way they heard the human voice and they came out of the cottage and found that they were surrounded by the king's men. Then the Kunwar said, "Yes, they have come to capture us, come, let us escape together". Gabharu said, "You will be caught if I accompany you. So, I will be here. Whatever happens to me, let it be happened. If they kill me, you can have ten more wives. But there will be no substitute for you.[15]

The plot structured by Harakanta is of a love story. Jaymati's love for her husband Gadapani has been prioritized and located with certain importance relative to other events. This 'hierarchy of significance',[16] as Hayden White calls it, transformed the narrative into an imagined reality that reflected the pre-colonial dominant mode of Assamese historiography. Beyond that, the distinctiveness of Harakanta Barua's narrative rests in moving the audience by the author's description of terror and atrocities on the one hand and the message of conjugal love, on the other.

In the first two paragraphs, the author has narrated the feeling of love through dialogue which is highly colloquial and dramatic in nature. The third paragraph is marked with a feeling of tension and fear that could make the reader more inquisitive on what happens at the end. Barua writes: 'In the meantime the king's men had entered the house but could not find out the prince. The prince, though driven out of the cottage for safety could not leave his wife alone and did not go far. The king's men started interrogating the princess.'

In the fourth and the last paragraph, the narrative reached its climax. The entire paragraph has described vividly the terror of brutality. With Jaymati's death the episode ended in a dramatic style as if a curtain had been swung around the stage when the performance was over. Harakanta Sharma Barua records: 'It has been said that heated iron was pressed on the princess' back. The princess started screaming. . . . The princess breathed her last suffering the inhuman atrocities.'[17]

Interestingly, the narrative of Harakanta Sharma Barua reflects an opaque presence of Surya Kumar Bhuyan. Bhuyan edited Harakanta Sharma Barua's *Assam Buranji* that was published in 1830. Therefore, the present study has used both the printed volume and the transcript of the original manuscript. The printed edition of Barua's *Assam Buranji* has been marked with the subtitles in the margin like *Gadapanir Palayan* (Gadapani's escape), *Kunwarir Patiprem* (the princess's love for her husband), *Kunwarir Hatya* (the assassination of the princess), *Satir Sasti* (the punishment of the chaste wife).[18] These captions and paragraphs have been made by Surya Kumar Bhuyan while editing the *Assam Buranji*. Interestingly, the pre-print stage of the edited volume bears the name Jaya in the caption made by the editor in the margin that was later replaced by *Kunwari* (princess) in the printed volume. The editor was on a dilemma of identifying the princess. It is to be noted that the pre-colonial *buranjis* referred to Jaymati either as *kunwari* or *gabharu* which are synonymous to princess.

Harakanta Sharma Barua also used the term *gabharu* while narrating the episode of Jaymati. Since the late nineteenth century, the name Jaymati started to feature in the writings of the Assamese colonial elites. Bhuyan as an author was no exception. Remarkably, as an editor, Bhuyan has tried to keep the tradition of the *buranjis* intact using the term *kunwari*.

In the narrative, Jaymati's image has been prefigured as *Sati* by the editor to set the ground for the shaping of a modern Assamese past. The meaning of the past was transformed from a worldly killing of a princess in a political power struggle to a mythic code. The transformation of Jaymati into *Sati* inaugurated the mission of popularization of the historic figure by the professional historian Surya Kumar Bhuyan in later years.

A Visionary Autobiography

The collection of further historical documents for narrativization of historical events took a new turn when professional historians did it through the agency of an institution. The institutionalization of historiography was materialized with the establishment of the DHAS. The event of Jaymati's assassination was required to be narrativized in order to make consistent with the modern Assamese past. Umanath Gohain, a government official, visited Dibrugarh in 1931 and collected a ballad on Jaymati from Kripanath Phukan of Tingkhang village. Kripanath Phukan belonged to the erstwhile Ahom aristocracy. He hailed from the famous Satgharia Ahom family.[19] In the early twentieth century, he was among few of the Assamese who could speak Ahom language. Obviously, Kripanath Phukan was conversant with the written prose tradition of Assam. He personally possessed a *buranji* called *Lai-Lik Buranji* (*Lai* means great and *Lik* means book). The manuscript was written in *sacipat* in Tai script and Kripanath Phukan had got it transcribed in Assamese. Interestingly, Phukan accompanied Needham, the first explorer in the north-eastern region in the nineteenth century, as an official interpreter. During this period he visited Sadiya as well as different places of Tibet and Shan states of Burma. During this visit Phukan was able to get this manuscript. It is to be noted that the manuscript contained the story of Jaymati. Interestingly enough, the literary ballad on Jaymati collected by Umanath Gohain was composed by Kripanath Phukan himself with the materials collected from the *Lai-Lik Buranji.*[20] As a native of the village Tingkhang, Phukan must have been familiar with popular Assamese balladic tradition locally called *malita/geet/pad*. Besides located in the *buranjis*, the episode of Jaymati is extensively found in Assamese bardic folk tradition.[21] Kripanath Phukan had chosen the balladic style and restructured the story of Jaymati from the memory of a written prose.

Kripanath Phukan's ballad was divided into two sections. The first section has been captioned as *Jaymatir Bilap* (lamentation of Jaymati) while the second section is named as *Shahurek Siddheshwarir Bilap* (lamentation of Siddheshwari, the mother-in-law). The first half is marked by an autobiographical mode. The historical validity of this literary ballad is not questioned. All the details have been taken as accurate. The genealogy of Jaymati's paternal side, as well as, her in-law's family has been incorporated without any factual flaws. The ballad starts with the following:

Maduri saharat
Dangar Hoi Achhinu
Bargohainr haichhilu jee,
Gadapani Kunware
Nie Tingkhangloi Chaklang biakoi di.[22]

I was brought up in town Maduri, I am Bargohain's daughter, I was given *Chaklang* marriage with the Prince Gadapani.

In the first section, Jaymati has been projected as a traditional young Assamese woman who resides in the world of love and affection within her family. Her marital status was sanctified by Ahom marriage ceremony, called *Chaklang*.

The world of love and affection was not interrupted after her marriage.

Shaahure Shahure
Anande Achinu
Nepalu akano dukh.
Madurit jenekoi
Anande achhilu,
Tenekoi bhunjilu sukh.[23]

I was staying with in-laws in happiness. I enjoyed happiness just like I enjoyed at Maduri.

The ballad of Kripanath Phukan is remarkable for a distinctive trait of lamentation that encompasses the whole work. The laments have transgressed the individual domain of Jaymati and relocate her in a larger female world where thousands of Jaymati with filial love and affection reside. Throughout the narrative, Jaymati was lamenting for her parents and all her relatives. The audience is touched by the following statement attributed to Jaymati:

Mor chenehura ai
Maribar samayat
Darishan nepalu
Bidhatai banchilu pai.[24]

God has deprived me to see my affectionate mother during the time of my death.

The laments locate Jaymati in the familial domain. In Siddheshwari's reporting Jaymati has been incarnated as a traditional Indian mother:

Lai Lechai Konwarak
Tomate arpino
Chenehat paliba ai,
Bela chai khuwaba,
Bela chai paliba,
Kshemiba sakalo day.[25]

I have given princes Lai and Lechai to you. Mother, bring them up with love and affection. Feed them in time.

Kripanath Phukan's writing also represents a distinctive vision that transcends the temporality of the material world. Phukan has imagined Jaymati with his vision of the mortal universe. In this imagined universe, the framing of a remembered past co-exist with spirituality and morality. In this part of the narrative, written in an autobiographical mode, Jaymati has been internalized by the author. The author speaks on behalf of Jaymati as well as for the audience/readers.

The second part of the poem has distinguished itself by a long dialogue of Siddheshwari Kunwari, Jaymati's mother-in-law, which encompassed the entire narrative. The interlocutor is Laithepena Bargohain, Jaymati's father, who plays the role of an audience, too.

The use of laments has decoded the telling of a love story. The author, through the laments of Jaymati and Siddheshwari, projected the qualities of love, caring, protection which configure the pangs of separation from near and dear ones. The laments expanded the world of Jaymati where conjugal love was transgressed by filial affection, sense of duty and love for her relatives.

Interestingly, the whole narrative has been worked out through a dream that was dreamt by Jaymati's mother-in-law, Siddheshwari Kunwari, twenty days before the telling of the story to Jaymati's father. She could see the future events in the dream while that vision was transformed into reality in her presence. Again, the present was transformed into past through the dialogue which was reflected on the screen of memory through the dream. In this mode of representation through the medium of dream the past has been reworked in a non-historical way if we have a conventional sense of history. 'It is essential to recognize that both factually-oriented history and the non-singular, perhaps "subjunctive" or mythic *aitihya* mode of narrating the past co-exist.'[26] In narrating the past, the author has mediated between the literal and the figurative. The dream acts as a visionary force to appropriate a new meaning of the past synthesized in a fictive as well as factual mode. In Kripanath Phukan's ballad, dream acts as a binding force to make a bridge between the literal and the figurative.

Interestingly, dreams play a significant role in the pre-colonial Assamese *buranjis*. The *buranjis* have linked up dreams with the political authority which has been represented as divine and pious through the trope of miraculous events. The *buranjis* represent a hegemonic control of royal power. State authority dominates the entire discourse. Notwithstanding their anonymity, the authors of the *buranjis* represented the Assamese past as a vehicle of state power. The *buranji* texts are marked with a peculiar form that combines the credibility of factual history as well as mythic fiction. Such mythic imagination can best be encompassed in those parts of the narratives that tell the story of the dynastic origin of the royal houses. The texts are loaded with the stories of the *Swargadeos* (gods of heaven) who owed their origin to Indra, the king of gods. (Swargadeo was the royal title of the Ahom kings of Assam). The story of the scions of God has been scattered in the motley collection of these texts. In the present study, I have used the printed texts that delineate the mythic narrative on the origin of the Ahom ruling dynasty emanating from the family of Indra. Besides the Ahom Swargadeos, the *buranjis* include all the royal houses into a single trajectory of divine ancestry. Dream has been related to the birth of a king and shown by the gods. In one of the handwritten manuscripts that form part of the edited volume of *Satsari Assam Buranji* (seven garlands of Assamese *buranji*—seven different manuscripts were collated and edited in a single volume by Surya Kumar Bhuyan) the story of the founding of the Swargadeo's dynasty runs thus:

> On that day Sengdam Raja went out for hunting. Then Indra came to his house in the guise of Sengdam Raja and made love with his consort. At night the queen dreamt that Indra was speaking to her, "I am Indra, you are now having my child in your womb. A son will be born who is my part and he will be the king.[27]

In Kashinath Tamuli Phukan's *Assam Buranji*, enlarged and re-written by Harakanta Sharma Barua, the first two chapters tell the story of the divine origin of the Ahom royal family.[28] The *Padshah Buranji*, brought to Assam from London by an eminent Assamese intellectual, Benudhar Sharma, formed part of the printed volume of *Kamrupar Buranji* and projected the story of the ancestry of the Kamrupa kings with divine roots.[29]

The stories that tell the celestial links of the royal ancestries indicate an authoritative command of the ruling power and its location in an exclusive space totally uninhabited by the common subjects. Divinity has been intensified by the visionary power of the scions of God. There was no departure from the tradition of the *buranjis* by Kripanath Phukan in remembering the Assamese past in modern times. Phukan's remembering the past rests on the tradition of the *buranji* text. He used dream as an appropriation of charismatic power by a woman (Siddheshwari Kunwari) communicating with another woman with high sense of morality (Jaymati). The metrical narrative is resonant with the general qualities of thousands of women like love, affection, sacrifice and caring in the persons of Jaymati and Siddheshwari Kunwari. This generalization has blurred the line of demarcation between ordinary women and women of blood royal with pious ancestry. The magical power of dream has been used to put royal women on a pedestal to distinguish them from women at large. It is quite obvious for an author like Kripanath Phukan who belonged to the famous Satgharia Ahom ancestry to continue the tradition. Dreams have been taken as a framing device to redefine Ahom ancestry.

Dreams are a part of the human world. Again, the reality of dreams transcends the reality of the human world. Dreams have also been taken as a mechanism to establish the truth that could transgress the worldly vision of reality. Kripanath Phukan, an untrained, unsophisticated narrator of the past was shaping a domain of historical truth that could not be questioned on the basis of the temporal notion of truth.

Professional Reconstruction

In the early twentieth century, the historical event of Jaymati attracted the attention of the professional historian Surya Kumar Bhuyan. Reconstruction of the past often involves glorification of a historical figure. The event of Jaymati's assassination acted as a marker of that suitability. Jaymati has been transformed as an icon of the glorious Assamese past.

The humiliation and death of a princess has been located in the greater Indian tradition and linked to the epic episodes of Sita and Draupadi. Interestingly, when the princess' assassination connects the local past with a larger tradition, it has, indeed, a wider significance in historiographical context. It is to be noted in this context that the exclusion of Assamese past from the Indian historiography demanded its arena to be expanded outside the geographical limits of Assam.[30] Since the first decade of the twentieth century, the task was undertaken by an institution 'Bangia Sahityanushilani Sabha (BSS)' under the guidance of Padmanath Bhattacharyya Vidyavinode and other Assamese and Bengali personalities like

Gopal Krishna Dey, Kalicharan Sen, Mahendramohan Lahiri, Hem Chandra Goswami and Dhireshacharyya.[31] Padmanath Bhattacharyya was aware of the marginalized position of Assamese history and culture. Assam's multiple language and dialects, heterogeneous culture, and history were not properly evaluated. Bhattacharyya devoted himself to introduce Assamese history and culture to the neighbouring province of Bengal. Efforts to expose Assamese history and culture to a wider public in Bengal can best be exemplified in the dissemination of the accounts of the historic episode of Jaymati. Through the efforts of the members of the BSS, the story of Jaymati was first recounted in Bengal. Gopal Krishna Dey, the first librarian of Curzon Hall (Nabin Chandra Bardoloi Hall), played a leading role in circulating this historic story.[32] Articles on Jaymati were contributed in *Nabya Bharat* and *Bharat Mahila*.[33] These were followed by the publication of a series of Bengali literary works on the historic events of Jaymati. An article on Jaymati written by Satadalbashini Biswas was published in *Bharat Mahila*.[34] Another article, entitled 'Abalar Atmadan', was published in *Anusandhan Pakshik Patra*. Narratives on Jaymati in Bengali language were also written by Priyanath Chatterjee, Purnakanta Bhattacharyya and Sarat Chandra Dhar.[35] A Bengali play (*jatra*) on Jaymati composed by Haripada Chattopadhyae was staged.[36]

With the efforts of Padmanath Bhattacharyya Vidyavinode along with other Bengali and Assamese elites, a new course of historical research had been inaugurated in Assam which was transformed by Bhuyan with a wider perspective in later years. Bhuyan was a student at Cotton College, Guwahati (1909-11), when Padmanath Bhattacharyya was teaching there. Bhuyan had the opportunity to be closely associated with Bhattacharyya. His historical research on Assam was largely influenced by the activities of Bhattacharyya and other educationists at Cotton College. Bhuyan writes:

> It may be mentioned that some of our Professors realized the necessity of apprising the wider public the great and good things of Assam embodied in its history and culture. In collaboration with some gentlemen of the town they founded the Bangiya Anushilani Sabha. Papers were read at its meetings, mostly on Assam history. It was through this Society that

the story of Princess Jaymati became popular in Bengal, leading to the compilation of a Bengali drama and a number of poems on the subject.[37]

Initially, Jaymati's story was made familiar to a handful of Assamese elites. It has been reiterated that it was first published in *Jonaki* by Ratneshwar Mahanta who collected his materials from Indeebar Barua Seristadar Dangaria.[38] The annexation of the event of Jaymati to 'the protein outlines of buranji' enabled the event to be valorized as contribution to the authentic record that was available for Assam's past.[39] Further, it has also been argued that since the latter part of the nineteenth century the elitist construction of Jaymati as a national heroine had tended to obscure the fact that the event was derived from the folk songs prevalent among women of Upper Assam.[40] Bhuyan writes, 'The Assamese elites are conversant with the name of Jaymati. But the holy episode of Sati Jaymati has not been promulgated in that way among the rural people and women of Assam who are as if the backbone of Assamese nation.'[41] In this articulation, one can notice Bhuyan's project of popularization of the historical figure that exhibits the multiple dimensions of Bhuyan's historiographical aptitude. The popularization mission undertaken in *Jaymati Upakhyan* is stamped with such markers as folk metres of *payar*, *dulari*, *chhabi*, *totay* and *lechari*, compatible with the literary taste of the subaltern social groups. Bhuyan writes:

Shese bhoila narapati Ratnadhwaj laramati,
Lara Raja tanka bole,
Ihena nripati hoia bare ashantir chhaya
Dabanal dahagun jwale.[42] (*Chhabi*)

At last the tender aged Ratnadhwaj became the king who is called Lara Raja. Due to his accession to the throne the chaotic situation has been intensified like wildfire

In folk metre called *dulari* Bhuyan writes:

Ji katha kahibon shuna sabdhane
Kunwarir parichay,
Gada Kunwarar bharya manohar
Jaymati tanka koy.[43] (*Dulari*)

Listen to the story that tells of the princess. She is known as Jaymati who is beautiful. She is the wife of Prince Gada.

The variations of metre like *payar*, *dulari*, etc., was applied to open a new dimension of history-writing. The historian has acknowledged the folk ballad style of singing publicly of a historical event. Though the written mode is always regarded as superior to the oral, Bhuyan did not like to fix history in a single mode. He deviated from categorizing history in 'a fixed and stable genre' as it happened in Western Europe.[44] Though being a rationalist historian, Bhuyan was able to prove the distinctiveness as a historian to locate the modern Assamese past in a broader arena of history-writing. Meaning of history was unravelled from the written genre to an oral tradition. Bhuyan's shift from prose to poetry in *Jaymati Upakhyan* has been an exemplar of the introduction of multiple genres in historiography. Reciting publicly is a part of oral tradition. Interestingly enough, the *buranjis* of Assam being an example of written genre share an orality. These texts were recited publicly on specific occasions. While reciting the written texts were decoded. This form of oral was not unrelated with the written. Beyond that elite orality, a subaltern orality of bardic form has occupied the concern of Bhuyan's history writing. *Jaymati Upakhyan* bears upon the relationship between the bardic form of orality and a distinct category comprising Assamese women and rural people. He wrote, 'Our girls are instinctively fond of ballads' and *Jaymati Upakhyan* 'has become very popular with our womenfolk'.[45]

Significantly, a nationalist intellectual's efforts to make Assamese women familiar with Jaymati's episode in history and women's love for ballads seem paradoxical. Jaymati's story was much more popular in folk ballads than its location in the pages of the *buranjis*. If women's preference goes with ballads, it is quite obvious that the image of Jaymati was much popular among women before the reconstruction of this historical figure in modern Assamese past. In historicizing the myth, Bhuyan followed his predecessors who wanted to popularize the image of Jaymati created by them which was different from the popular image found in folk ballads.

The unique language used in *Jaymati Upakhyan* has an appeal on the audience. The language resembles that of Assamese *puthi* by means of which religious hymns as *Keertandasham Bhagabat* as well as the marriage songs like *Bianam Ainam* were composed. Bhuyan writes:

> The language of *Jaymati Upakhyan* has been the language of old Assamese puthi, that is, the language by which the traditionally respected and beloved books of the Assamese like *Keertan Dasham Bhagabat* were composed. . . . This language was loved by the young and the old, men and women of Assam. This Assamese language, through *Bianam Ainam Kirtan Dasham Namghosha*, has entered the Assamese minds and established a permanent place in their mind like a permanent throne.[46]

It has been reiterated that in Assamese society Vaishnava literature is highly popular, appealing to all classes of Assamese people, from the elites to the subaltern. Interestingly enough, Surya Kumar Bhuyan did not like to confine his history-writing within the strict boundary of academic discipline. Bhuyan's history writing has developed a unique trend to popularize the glorious Assamese past, mainly associated with the medieval Ahom rulers, so that these could reach all classes of Assamese people. The popularizing mission of the historian has been reflected in *Jaymati Upakhyan* where the poet historian adopted a pen name 'Bhanu Nandan'. Bhuyan had first used this old style name in the poem *Madhujamini* to cope with the old language of the *puthi*.[47] *Madhujamini*, a purely literary work with poetic imagination, was written in Brajavuli language, very popular in Assamese society due to its link with the sacred theme of Krishna and Radha, the most popular icons among the Assamese. It is to be noted in this context that Brajavuli language of the poem *Madhujamini*, written in 1915, has all the traits of the romantic imagination of Vaishnava literature. The formation of words like *Madhuban*, *Madhumurati*, *Madhujamini*, *Badarabarishana*, *Hridaya-Abhilasha* bear the testimony of romantic imagination that has appeal on a very refined and enlightened readers. Deployment of such linguistic feeling in the commemoration of the past suggests the role of mediation that language has played in history with a distinct class of audience. A congenial ambience was opened for the enlightened readers of history through the mediating force of language that transgressed the oral and balladic style. Juxtaposition of this new trait with the balladic mode opened a new horizon in shaping the modern Assamese past.

Speculating Bhuyan's historiographical framework in a metrical verse, that is, *Jaymati Upakhyan*, the present study tries to delineate its linkage with the Assamese historical verse written in pre-colonial era. In this study, I would like to take one such text entitled *Kali Bharat* written by Dutiram Hazarika, a pre-colonial Assamese intellectual. It is a metrical chronicle written on Assamese past in the early nineteenth century under the orders of Jogeshwar Singha, the son of Purandar Singha. It is to be noted in this context that the manuscript of *Kali Bharat* was obtained from Assam Sahitya Sabha. It was recovered for the Sabha by Harinarayan Dutta Barua from Dutiram Hazarika's son Kamalapati Hazarika in 1926. This text along with another Assamese metrical verse written by Bishweshwar Baidyadhipa was finally compiled together and published in a printed volume of *Assamar Padya Buranji*.[48]

Dutiram Hazarika's *Kali Bharat* is remarkable for its narration of Jaymati's episode as new information regarding Jaymati's assassination has been added to our former knowledge on the subject. Dutiram's addition of the story of pregnant Jaymati's assassination along with her very young daughter was, indeed, an accretion that opens an avenue to locate more human passion in the narrative. Bhuyan has referred to *Kali Bharat* as *buranji* thereby unravelling the space of the *buranjis* from prosaic to poetic. The poetic framework has been accepted by Bhuyan as a separate genre of *buranji* literature. To quote Bhuyan, 'Collecting the royal official papers as well as the verbal information from the espionage and the commandants, the royal historians had written *buranjis* in prose form along with their composition of *buranjis* in verse'.[49] According to Bhuyan, 'These *buranjis*, written in verse, have been the main branch of Assamese *buranji* literature'.[50]

Assamese texts written on the past events in poetic form have been categorized in a distinct genre within the trajectory of the *buranji* literature. Along with the addition of facts an accretion of a different genre has been legitimized in Assamese historiography. Interestingly, the *buranjis* have accomplished the bridging of the hard facts of reality and the imagination of Vaishnava poetry. The *buranjis* were originally written as chronicles, that is, the collection of events arranged chronologically. In course of time, its form was modified and expanded with the intrusion of fictive imagination. In legitimizing fictive imagination in historiography, the medium of poetry serves as a distinct genre in history-writing. The conventional sense of history, particularly the Western model, acknowledges the medium of prose as a vehicle of factuality in historiography. Poetry ingrains emotion and imagination which inhibits the true representation of facts. Interestingly, the Assamese colonial elites of the nineteenth and early twentieth centuries restructured Jaymati's event in different prose narratives.[51] Though the narratives carried within themselves either an elaboration of the folk theme on Jaymati, quite popular in Upper Assam or the construct of an image of *sati* or selfless wife, they represented the fact through the medium of Assamese prose. While restructuring the Assamese past in early twentieth century, Bhuyan took up Jaymati to glorify the Assamese nation as well as to link Assamese culture with a pan-Indian tradition. Bhuyan's portrayal of Jaymati bears the distinctive traits that led to develop a concoction of *beeramatri*, *sati*, *birangana* and *patibrata* thereby delineating Jaymati with new meaning distinct from his predecessors.[52] The creation of a trilingual Jaymati literature (Assamese, Bengali and English) displayed recapitulation of facts, ideas and prose medium. Bhuyan's project of recreating Jaymati seeks to be represented in a different medium and language which found its expression in poetry, a supplementary device in the world of repetition.

The pre-colonial writings on the Assamese past, written either in prose or in verse, are both characterized by a religious veneration for truth. The title of Dutiram Hazarika's *Kali Bharat* literally means the epic of the Kali Age. In *Kali Bharat*, the devotional spirit of the author saw in the rise and fall of the kings, the intrigues and machinations of ministers, the secret manipulation of conspirators and assassins, the depredations and atrocities of the rapacious neighbours, a fulfilment of the prophecies regarding the *kaliyuga*, so commonly found in Vaishnava poetry.[53] The title itself is a comment on the evils of attachment to the affairs of the earth in suppression of the higher demands of man's spiritual nature.[54] It has been reiterated that the event of Jaymati claimed historical validity in the writings of the colonial elites of the nineteenth and early twentieth centuries. The episode has been a controversial one, as a few of the Assamese elites did not recognize the Jaymati episode as historical. The subject became so contentious that in the mid-twentieth century an organization was set up with the name of Jaya Anusandhan Samiti with a view to ascertaining the truth about Jaymati's event.[55] Thus, accuracy of the fact became the cornerstone of historical approach. Surya Kumar Bhuyan turned his attention to a cultural ethos where notion of truth has been founded on a universally accepted moral structure of Vaishnava poetry, which occupies an important place in Assamese cultural milieu. A remarkable trait of Assamese Vaishnava poetry has been that it revels in a world of imagination and unreality. According to Bhuyan, 'the ideas underlying the facts constitute their chief aim to permanence and universality'.[56] Moreover, Assamese past written in verse (historical poetry), categorized as a distinct genre of *padya buranji* can further be studied in its aspect as a branch of old Assamese poetry which is a direct emanation from Vaishnavism in its spirit, tone and theme. Due to this conjunction the *padya buranjis* are marked by the philosophical element as an inevitable sequence of the adoption of the poetical medium.[57] Therefore, the authors of the *padya buranjis* were more or less beyond the reach of worldly domain of truth/untruth dichotomy. Interestingly enough, the pre-colonial Assamese texts, written in prose (the *buranjis*) had been remoulded into a power structure by exalting or disgracing one's social status. Unlike these prose narratives, the authors of the historical verse were never suspected as having any interest in unjustly glorifying or maligning any personage.[58] The magnitude of such universally accepted element of truth in Assamese cultural milieu made Bhuyan inclined towards this poetic form of history-writing to justify the historical validity of Jaymati's event and set aside the controversy.

The creation of a history for the people obviously has consequences which have a bearing on the Assamese society. The commemoration of Jaymati has been acknowledged socially. Jaymati was relocated in the social arena of Assam, thereby transposing the paragon from the past to the present as a cultural icon. It connotes differently than it had been in the pages of the *buranji*. The celebration of Jaymati Day on the anniversary of her assassination on the *Sukla Ekadashi Tithi* in the month of *Chait* can be an exemplar of such popularization. The distinct connotation for Jaymati had formed an effective springboard for a new component in modern Assamese historiography too. Women of Assamese past became the new field of exploration. Since 1920, Bhuyan published the historical narratives like *Jaymati Upakhyan*, *Chaneki*, *Phuleshwari*, *An Assamese Nur Jahan*, *Garama Kunwari*—all on women in the history of Assam, hitherto unexplored. In 1934, the historic meeting at Kumar Bhashkar Barman Natya Mandir at Guwahati, organized by *Kamrup Mahila Samiti* on the occasion of Jaymati Day, was presided over by Bhuyan. His presidential address at this meeting was published in the form of a book called *Assam Jiyari* in 1935. *Assam Jiyari* is divided into two parts. In the first part, the book contains an elaborate discussion on the historical women of Kamrup, while the second section comprises a discussion on Jaymati.[59]

Importantly, commemoration of the past was not only limited to the shaping of historical narratives, but to the development of a local literature, too. Padmanath Barua and Lakshminath Bezbarua composed dramas on Jaymati, while Hiteswar Barbaruah wrote a *kavya* named *Tirutar Atmadan*. A noted criticism on Jaymati by Kumudeswar Barthakur and articles by Ratneshwar Mahanta was followed by the publication of Surya Kumar Bhuyan's article in *Jeevani Sangraha* named *Gadadhar* and poems in *Nirmali*. The vernacular literature on Jaymati was followed by the literary works in English like Bhuyan's narrative poem published in *Times of Assam* and a narrative on Jaymati by Padmanath Bhattacharyya Vidyavinode in the *East and West*, besides a booklet by M.N. Phukan.[60]

The location of an Assamese past in a larger domain of literature further accentuated the historical approach that created a greater public awareness of the Assamese past that was linked with the present. Padmavati Phukanani, an Assamese litterateur and Anandaram Dhekial Phukan's daughter says, 'Bhuyan has composed this literary piece to make the grievous mother Assam a little bit pleased through the glory of the virtuous daughter sung by men and women of Assam.'[61]

Popularity of Jaymati both within and outside Assam implies nothing but unravelling a local past to a greater world of history. The shaping of the Assamese past through a network among institutions, academic discipline and the society with a universal vision of give and take gave the local past a trans-local character. Bhuyan's shaping of a modern Assamese past shares a universal vision which can best be testified in his institutional manoeuvre. While he was the Vice-Chancellor of Gauhati University, Bhuyan had suggested in a meeting of the Faculty of Arts, held on 6 February 1958, the introduction of a postgraduate teaching course in 'Culture and Civilization of Assam', which envisaged the universal vision of the historian. Bhuyan suggested eight papers of which the first two included 'Culture and Civilization of India in the backdrop of Asian Civilization' and 'Tribes and Races of Assam in the background of their affinities with those of India, Asia and the World'.[62]

Reflection of such universal vision in a discipline like history stirred the Assamese elites to an extent. They saw in it an excellent opportunity to widen the scope of the history and culture of Assam. *Assam Tribune*, the most popular English daily from Guwahati, wrote, 'It is understood that Dr. S.K. Bhuyan has suggested the immediate opening of M.A. classes at Gauhati in an all-comprehensive subject entitled "Culture and Civilization of Assam"'. The paper also reported that the

> proposed M.A. classes are intended to create a general widespread [sic] in the study of Culture and Civilization of Assam, the preservation and promotion of which is an all accepted primary function of the Assam University. It is only by inaugurating the study of this subject that the ramification of each particular section will be determined, and an inducement will be created for filling up the deficiencies of materials. Scholars from outside will be expected to attend this course as interest in Assam's glorious past has been created all over India. The proposal appears to have received wide support from Assamese scholars and publicists.[63]

Ambikagiri Ray Chaudhury, the noted Assamese intellectual, went a step further when he welcomed the proposal in a personal letter to Bhuyan. He wrote that the introduction of such a subject would be Bhuyan's invaluable gift on behalf of DHAS to protect the Assamese nation as well as to hold Assam in high esteem.[64] Padmadhar Chaliha in his Presidential address of Assam Sahitya Sabha in 1958 had applauded the decision as an opportunity to open up Assamese culture both at home and abroad.[65]

In commemorating the story of Jaymati, Bhuyan's imagination has been captured by the masculine vigour of women as well as their glorious deeds happened again and again in the past. Bhuyan writes:

Prithibir tathya meli Chalei khantek beli
Dekhim jiliki ache Amarapurat,
Rupavati gunavati Sadhwi sati Jaymati
Jilikichhe shukra yena tarar majat.
Bisarji apon pran Satie satir man
Rakha ami dekhon tat bahu patantar,
Beeramatri shata shata Sangai pathale kata
Pranar putali priya putra senehar.[66]

The past events of the world testifies that beautiful Jaymati endowed with the virtues of chastity is, as if, shining at Amarapura just like Venus amidst the stars. Time and again chaste women sacrificed their lives and hundreds of brave mothers sent their beloved sons to wars.

The historian has referred to such female figures whose heroic deeds are being glorified in history as Raziya Sultan, Joan of Arc and Panna.[67] In this retrospection Bhuyan has questioned the singularity of a historical event. In this articulation of Jaymati's episode we can hear the resonance of the stories told many times before.

The twentieth-century Assamese historiography was resonant with Jaymati's endeavour to defend her country as well as her husband through self-sacrifice in the seventeenth century. Masculinization in Bhuyan's writings directed Jaymati to be located on the crossroads of brave mother (*beeramatri*) and a chaste woman (*sati*/controlled sexuality). Bhuyan's concept of political nation was sometimes reflected as part of the single political unit of the Indian nation state, while on other occasions the Assamese political past was shaped as a parallel political entity against Mughal domination. To Bhuyan, India under Mughal rule was a state of bondage, and his writings on the Ahom-Mughal conflict highlight the desire of Assamese independence from Mughal rule.

Interestingly, the pre-colonial *buranji* texts of Assam contain within itself the structure of an imagination creating moral anecdote. This moral leaning had a strong imprint on Bhuyan's writings. Accordingly, the rise and fall of the kingdom depended on the virtue and vice of the rulers. Significantly, the application of morality in the domain of women was a departure from this vice/virtue, piety/impiety drama to a drama of female body and the notion of *patibrata*. Bhuyan writes,

> Turbak's invasion of Assam owed its origin in the activities of a royal lady and a rescuer of Assam from this invasion was another senior royal lady. The story of the first royal lady is marked with the activities of a loose woman while the other story narrates the ideal of love and devotion for husband and martial spirit which are still today encouraging the womenfolk of Assam. The name of the first woman is Susuddhi Garama Kunwari; and the second woman's name is Mula Gabharu.[68]

Let us now turn our attention to the pre-colonial era where Jaymati's body became the target in a political turmoil of the seventeenth-century Ahom regime. As Jashodhara Bagchi wrote in a different context, 'Since the community's control over female sexuality lies at the centre of patriarchy, the female body becomes the pawn whenever there are crises in the social order'.[69] In early twentieth century, when Bhuyan restructured Jaymati's episode, he was influenced by a comprehensive patriarchal wisdom in loading female sexuality and body with the marker of 'sati'. Beyond that, Bhuyan has appropriated Jaymati's heroism with a new meaning of self-sacrifice. Bhuyan has glorified the self-sacrifice of Jaymati connoting it to be the ideal of modern Assamese women. Speaking of the background of his work *Jaymati Upakhyan* Bhuyan observes,

> The number of good Assamese books are not sufficient to offer to the Assamese women to read. This book has been written specially with the object of making Assamese women familiar with the account of Jaymati. I wish that like Sati, Savitri and Damayanti may the message of Jaymati spread the ideals of wellbeing in every house in Assam.[70]

Bhuyan's concept of *beeramatri/virangana* and *sati* have been categorized into the same group of *patibrata*. The unifying project of *patibrata* and *virangana* signify the modernity of Assamese women. To define the contours of modern Assamese women, the historian has invoked traditions derived from both history and mythology. Bhuyan's endeavour to look for the Indian classical icons like Sati, Savitri and Damayanti was explicitly to justify the cultural affinity of Assam with India's classical past. These icons have been chosen to legitimize the popular notion of good woman who can sustain the community and be the sign of Assamese nation (*jati*). Bhuyan went to the extent of personifying the Assamese nation (*jati*) with *Sati* Jaymati and strongly appealed to the contemporary Assamese women in favour of destroying the enemies of the Assamese of the present day.

The episode of Jaymati has been re-shaped with the appropriation of nationalist self by highlighting Jaymati's 'self-sacrifice'. Jaymati's assassination has been glorified to generate national spirit among the Assamese populace thereby creating Jaymati as an Assamese national icon. Unlike Mula Gabharu, who has been constructed as a virile Assamese icon to shape a heroic past of Assam against Mughal domination, Jaymati's heroic location has been traced against the deprivation experienced by Assam and the Assamese people at present. Bhuyan called for a national front to get inspired from the noble ideals of sacrifice and strong determination displayed by Jaymati. Jaymati has been marked as the cohesive force to shape a collective self of the Assamese nation.

Such Assamese nationhood has been overlapped when Bhuyan identified Jaymati with the Indian classical icons of Sati, Savitri and Damayanti and represented her as an ideal Indian woman. Interestingly, in shaping Jaymati as a marker of Assamese national identity, Bhuyan has accepted both the alternative traditions available for appropriation-classical Sanskritic culture of Aryavarta and the *buranji* manuscripts which bear the undeniable capacity of historical memory.[71] Bhuyan also made attempt to shape a popular domain in history within the scholarly professional framework. Celebration of Jaymati to establish Assamese identity was followed by the deployment of folk tradition that opened an avenue for the creation of Assamese popular history. Such popular history is intended to signal the multiple cultural sites outside the academy, among both the elite and the non-elite social groups where historical representations are generated.[72]

Notes

1. Bhuyan, ed., 1930.
2. Gogoi, 1986, p. 46.
3. Bhuyan, ed., 1930.
4. Jenkins, 1995, p. 17.
5. Ibid., p. 18.
6. The notion of mnemohistory as introduced by Jann Assmann, embraces the concept of cultural memory which implies cultural continuity through retrospection. Mnemohistory is related to the past as it is remembered. According to Assmann, the proper way of dealing with the working of cultural memory is mnemohistory. In other words, 'mnemohistory investigates the history of cultural memory'.
7. Department of Historical and Antiquarian Studies Bulletin No. 1, p. 11.
8. Bhuyan, ed., 1945, p. 12.
9. Assam Buranji from Khora Raja to Sulikpha Lara Raja, Ms 3. Record No. B3/Ms19. Department of Historical and Antiquarian Studies.
10. Bhuyan, 1920, p. 61.
11. Bhuyan, ed., 1963, p. 42.
12. Bhuyan, ed., 1963, p. 2.
13. Ibid., p. 152.
14. Ibid.
15. Ibid., pp. 53-4.
16. White, 1973, p. 6.
17. Bhuyan, ed., 1930, pp. 53-4.
18. Ibid.
19. Record No. A3/12/26, No. 12.
20. Gogoi, 1952.
21. Record No. A3/12/26, No. 12.
22. Ibid.
23. Ibid.
24. Ibid.
25. Ibid.
26. Rao, Shulman and Subrahmanyam, 2003, p. 59.
27. Bhuyan, ed., 1999, p. 31.

28. Bhuyan, ed., 1930, pp. 1-8.
29. Bhuyan, ed., 1987, p. 2.
30. Chakravarty, 2006, p. 76.
31. Ibid.
32. Ibid.; Bhuyan, 1920, p. 63.
33. Chakravarty, 2006, p. 76.
34. Ibid.
35. Bhuyan, 1920, p. 61.
36. Chattopadhyae, 1333 *bangabda*.
37. Bhuyan, 2001, p. 9.
38. Bhuyan, 1920, p. 62.
39. Sharma, 2004, p. 177.
40. Ibid., p. 178
41. Bhuyan, 1920.
42. Ibid.
43. Ibid.
44. Rao, Shulman and Subrahmanyam, 2003, p. 3.
45. Bhuyan, 1920; Personal Records A/1, vol. 7, 26 August 1928.
46. Bhuyan, 1920.
47. Ibid.
48. Bhuyan, ed., 1933.
49. Ibid.
50. Ibid.
51. Ibid.; Bhuyan, 1920, pp. 52-5; Bhuyan, 1955, p. 140.
52. Bhuyan, 1920, pp. 67-8.
53. Bhuyan, ed., 1933, p. x.
54. Ibid.
55. A2/17/3A.
56. Bhuyan, ed., 1933, pp. viii-ix.
57. Ibid.
58. Ibid.
59. Bhuyan, 1935.
60. Bhuyan, 1920.
61. Bhuyan, 1935.
62. Record No. 11-5/18, Culture and Civilization of Assam.
63. *Assam Tribune*, 30 September 1947.
64. Record No. 11-5/18 Part D.C.C.A.
65. Ibid.; Assam Sahitya Sabha, Tinsukia, 1958.
66. Bhuyan, 1951; *Nirmali*, p. 15.
67. Ibid., pp. 16-17.
68. Bhuyan, 1951; *Buranjir Bani*, p. 52.

69. Bagchi, 1997, p. 77; Bhuyan, 1920.
70. Bhuyan, 1920; Deshpande, 2007, p. 215.
71. Aquil and Chatterjee, eds., 2008, p. 14.
72. Deshpande, 2007, p. 215.

References

Archival Material

Assam Buranji from Khora Raja to Sulikpha Lara Raja from Ms. 53 obtained from Sj Sarat Chandra Goswami. Copied by Sj Basudev Misra, Dt. 11 April 1932, pp. 1-153. Record No. B3/Ms. 19. Department of Historical and Antiquarian Studies, Guwahati.

Assam Tribune. Guwahati, 30 September 1947.

A2/17/3A Jaya Anusandhan Samiti's letter to the Editor, *Dainik Assom*, dt. 20 May 1948. Department of Historical and Antiquarian Studies, Guwahati.

A3/12/26-No. 12. *Jaymatir Bishaye Natun Katha*. Guwahati: Department of Historical and Antiquarian Studies.

Department of Historical and Antiquarian Studies Bulletin No. 1, p. 11.

Personal Records A/1 Vol. 7. From S.K. Bhuyan to Miss E. Vickland. 26 August 1928. Guwahati: Department of Historical and Antiquarian Studies.

Record No. 11-5/18. Culture and Civilization of Assam. Department of Historical and Antiquarian Studies, Guwahati.

Record No. 11-5/18 Part D.C.C.A. Padmadhar Chaliha, *Sabhapatir Bhashan*. Assam Sahitya Sabha, 16th session, Tinsukia, 1958. Department of Historical and Antiquarian Studies, Guwahati.

Printed Books and Articles

Aquil, Raziuddin and Partha Chatterjee, eds. 2008. *History in the Vernacular.* Ranikhet: Permanent Black.

Bagchi, Jashodhara. 1997. 'Female Sexuality and Community in Epar Ganga Opar Ganga', in Meenakshi Thapan, ed., *Embodiment: Essays on Gender and Identity*. New Delhi: Oxford University Press.

Buragohain, Hem. 2004. 'Janageetar Buranjit Jaymatic Bichari', in Dayananda Bargohain, ed. *Khwam Rap*. Sibsagar.

Bhuyan, Surya Kumar. 1920. *Jaymati Upakhyan*. Guwahati: Pragjyotish Granthashala.

________. 1935. *Assam Jiyari*. Guwahati: Kamrup Mahila Samiti.

________. 1933. *Assamar Padya Buranji*. Guwahati: Department of Historical and Antiquarian Studies.

________. 1955. *Buranjir Bani*. Guwahati: Pragjyotish Granthashala.

________. 1951. *Nirmali*. Guwahati: Pragjyotish Granthashala.

________, ed. 1930. *Assam Buranji*. Harakanta Sharma Barua. Guwahati: Department of Historical and Antiquarian Studies.

________, ed. 1999. *Satsari Assam Buranji*. 3rd edn. Guwahati: Department of Historical and Antiquarian Studies.

________, ed. 1945. *Assam Buranji*, collected from Sukumar Mahanta's Family. Guwahati: Department of Historical and Antiquarian Studies.

Bhuyan, Surya Kumar. ed. 1963. *Tungkhungia Buranji (Assamese)*. Guwahati: Department of Historical and Antiquarian Studies.

Chakravarty, Prashanta. 2005. 'Padmanath Vidyavinod: Guwahatir Bangia Sahitya Sanskriti O Samakal'. *Phoenix*, vol. 1. Guwahati.

Chattopadhyae, Haripada. *Rani Jaymati* (historical drama staged at the jatra of Mathuranath Saha and Neelkanta Das). Calcutta: 1333 *bang-abda*.

Deshpande, Prachi. 2007. *Creative Pasts: History, Memory and Identity in Western India*. Ranikhet: Permanent Black.

Dube, Ishita Banerjee. 2001. 'Reading Time: Texts and Pasts in Colonial Eastern India'. *Studies in History*. 19: 1. n.s.

Gogoi, Hari Chandra, *Jerengat Mahasati Jeevanit Ebhimukhi*. Guwahati: Bhuyan Family Library.

Gogoi, Lila. 1986. *The Buranjis: The Historical Literature of Assam*. New Delhi: Omson Publication.

Guha, Ranajit. 1988. *Indian Historiography of India: A 19th Century Agenda and Its Implication*. Kolkata: K.P. Bagchi and Company.

Jenkins, Keith. 1995. *On What is History*. London: Routledge.

Rao, Narayan V., David Shulman and Sanjay Subramaniam, 2003. *Textures of Time: Writing History in South India, 1600-1800*. New Delhi: Permanent Black.

Sharma, Jayeeta. 2004. 'Heroes of Our Time', in John Zavos, ed., *The Politics of Cultural Mobilization in India*. New Delhi: Oxford University Press.

Srinivasan, Ramya. 2007. *The Many Lives of a Rajput Queen: Heroic Pasts in India c. 1500-1900*. Ranikhet: Permanent Black.

White, Hayden. 1973. *Metahistory*. Baltimore: Johns Hopkins University.

7

Retelling Medieval History for Twentieth-century Readers

Encounter of a Hindu Prince and a Sufi Master in Khwaja Hasan Nizami's Nizami Bansuri

Mikko Viitamäki

Introduction

Nizami Bansuri is a creative retelling of medieval history for twentieth-century readers. The work was authored by a Sufi shaikh and prolific author, Khwaja Hasan Nizami in 1941 and it narrates the life story of the celebrated Sultanate Sufi, Khwaja Nizam-ud-Din Auliya (d. 1325). The work is based on the allegedly contemporary diary of Nizam-ud-Din's Hindu disciple, Prince Hardev, and it is this narrative framework that makes *Nizami Bansuri* unique among the numerous accounts of the master's life. Nowhere else is the theme of being a Hindu disciple in a Sufi brotherhood given such an extensive treatment.

For the purposes of this chapter, it has been impossible to trace the origins of Hardev's diary. This effort is further complicated by the fact that Hardev's diary is fully amalgamated with Khwaja Hasan Nizami's footnotes, insertions and appendices so that *Nizami Bansuri* is essentially a new literary work, not a mere translation. For this reason, it is more fruitful to turn the attention from speculating about the historicity of Hardev's diary to analysing *Nizami Bansuri* in relation to its writing context. I argue that the text should be read as a twentieth-century handbook of a Sufi disciple. The text is not a transparent account of medieval events, but an effort to shape the present in a dialogue with the past. The issues a Sufi disciple is likely to encounter in twentieth-century India are discussed through projecting them to the formative early history of the Chishti-Nizami brotherhood.

The central theme of *Nizami Bansuri*, a Hindu disciple's encounter with a Sufi master, closely relates to a question tackled by most historians studying the Sultanate period: what was the role of Sufis in the spread of Islam in India and what was their perception of Hindus. The answers to this question have varied greatly from assuming that Islam offered an egalitarian alternative to the strict caste system, to an attempt to portray Sufis as zealous missionaries who did not hesitate to take up arms when needed.[1]

The conclusions of the recent studies seem to lie somewhere between these extremities. According to Carl W. Ernst, the Sufis were no doubt pleased to see people convert, but asserting that missionary activity was their main occupation is untenable.[2] Most medieval texts show a marked indifference towards the Hindu environment. In his study of the Sufi literature produced in the fourteenth- and fifteenth-century Khuldabad, Ernst has noted that most conversion stories feature literary characters rather than actual people encountered by the authors.[3] This lack of material in contemporary sources has led several scholars to turn to wider historical and social circumstances in their attempt to explain conversion to Islam. Richard Eaton, for example, has linked the conversion in Punjab and Bengal to the spread of agriculture and sedentary lifestyle.[4] In the case of vernacular poems written in the medieval Deccan, he has argued that although these texts were written for Sufi adepts, they may have unintentionally helped to further the Islamization of the socially unprivileged Hindus who were exposed to them in the Sufi hospices and shrines.[5] Thus, the conversions seem to have happened as a by-product of social changes.

It will be interesting to relate Hardev's narrative found in *Nizami Bansuri* to this background. However, it should be remembered that the text is essentially a twentieth-century representation of medieval history. For this reason, it will be more intriguing to analyse how a Hindu disciple's entry to a Muslim Sufi brotherhood is envisioned by a modern Sufi author. The focus of scholars studying the interaction of religions in the modern period has shifted from conversion to shared religious spaces and the tension between fluid and clearly defined religious and communal identities. Several anthropologists and ethnographers have documented the attendance of Hindus at the rituals of Sufi shrines.[6] However, Hindu participation in Sufi brotherhoods has attracted less attention. Although the requirements of Sufi discipleship vary from one tradition to another, becoming a member of a Sufi brotherhood by taking an oath of allegiance (*bai'at*) usually requires a greater degree of commitment than visiting the shrines. Discipleship normally entails some kind of a practical regime of repeating litanies (*aurad*) and religious formulas for remembrance of God (*zikr*) even when conversion to Islam is not required. A rare study to discuss this thematic is Thomas Dahnhardt's exploration of a sub-branch of the Naqshbandi-Mujaddidi order in Hindu environment.[7] If *Nizami Bansuri* is indeed to be read as a prescriptive handbook for Sufi disciples, as I argue, it provides an interesting instance of conceptualizing the presence of Hindu disciples in a modern Sufi environment through a historical projection.

I begin by briefly discussing the Sufi career and literary oeuvre of the author, Khwaja Hasan Nizami. I touch on the possible origins of Hardev's diary, but argue that they are extraneous to the discussion pertaining to the text as a twentieth-century Sufi handbook. I continue by summing up the main narrative line of Hardev's diary and then proceed to discuss the writing process of the book. In the course of reworking Hardev's story into *Nizami Bansuri*, the author has transformed the linear narrative into a multifaceted entirety that not only moves on various levels of the text, but also involves various agendas and discourses. I conclude by examining different ways of reading the text in the context of twentieth-century Indian Sufism.

The Author and His Literary Oeuvre

Khwaja Hasan Nizami was born in 1878 into a family of hereditary custodians of the shrine of Khwaja Nizam-ud-Din Auliya in Delhi. Orphaned at an early age, he spent his youth in impoverished conditions. Yet he became an influential figure in twentieth-century

Muslim India: a versatile author, an activist campaigning against the Arya Samaj, an outspoken supporter of the Sufi practices condemned by Muslim reformists and a spiritual guide to numerous disciples. His training took place in the traditional environment of his home and the Sufi hospice (*khanqah*) of Pir Mihr Ali Shah (d. 1937) in Golra as well as in the reformist *madrasa* of Deoband. As a Sufi shaikh he combined classical Sufism and traditionalist religious learning with progressive modernism. This helped to endear him to Indian Muslims, who were in favour of modern education and secularism but at the same time unwilling to reject Sufism.[8]

Nizami was a prolific author. In the foreword to *Nizami Bansuri* written in 1941, fourteen years before passing away in 1955, he claims to have written about 200 books in addition to newspaper articles and other short pieces.[9] The appraisal of his works by the literary critics has varied greatly: some have lauded his flowing, accessible prose while others have accused him of publishing books written by his associates and disciples as his own.[10] Whatever the critics' opinions on the literary merit of his writing, the books were Nizami's primary means of effectively engaging in discussions on various topics relevant to contemporary Indian Muslims. The books were also an important medium to communicate with the disciples who, according to his own estimation, numbered hundreds of thousands and were spread throughout the Indian subcontinent.

The topics the author discusses in his works include modern applications of *shari'a*,[11] Sufi practice,[12] and current political issues.[13] He also translated the Koran into Urdu and Hindi[14] and claimed to have introduced the diary as a genre of Indian literature. He wrote diaries to document the events of his life in India,[15] as well as his journeys to Afghanistan[16] and the Middle East.[17] His best-known works are his autobiography,[18] the 12 historical books describing the events and aftermath of the 1857 uprising[19] and the topic of this paper, *Nizami Bansuri*.[20]

The peculiar title of the book, *Nizami Bansuri* (The Bamboo Flute of Nizam [-ud-Din] or The Nizami [Brotherhood] Bamboo Flute), alludes to the Sufi master Nizam-ud-Din and to the flute-playing god Krishna, who are part of a mystical experience of the protagonist, Prince Hardev. *Nizami Bansuri* is a reworked

Urdu translation of a Persian text called *Chihal Roza* (Forty Days) that is supposed to be a fourteenth-century diary of a Hindu prince Hardev, describing his experiences with Nizam-ud-Din in Delhi. Nizami relates how he came across this book in Bharatpur where it had ended up after Suraj Mal Jat had ransacked the shrine of Nizam-ud-Din during Muhammad Shah Rangila's (r. 1719-48) reign. Studying the book, he discovered it could help him fulfil a long-cherished dream: writing a comprehensive life story of Nizam-ud-Din that would cover his teachings (like the *malfuzat* genre), historical context (like the *tazkiras* and dynastic histories) and, simultaneously, address modern concerns. He had the text copied and set to work in 1941.[21] A second, enlarged edition was published in 1945 and the book has been in print since, the sixth edition being published in 2009. *Nizami Bansuri* is also among the author's few books that have been transliterated into Devanagari script in an attempt to reach Hindi speaking audiences.[22]

Nizami Bansuri documents the life of Hardev in Delhi before he entered the limelight of history as Ahmad Ayaz Khwaja-yi Jahan. According to *Nizami Bansuri*, Hardev received the name Ahmad Ayaz when he was initiated into the Chishti-Nizami brotherhood by Nizam-ud-Din whereas the sobriquet Khwaja-yi Jahan (Master of the World) was earned in the service of the sultans.[23] Historical chronicles like *Tarikh-i Firuz-shahi* and *Tarikh-i Firishta* record Ahmad Ayaz's actions as the commander of the army in Gujarat and, later on, as the prime minister of Muhammad ibn Tughluq (r. 1325-51). They also give a detailed account of his attempted rebellion against the new monarch Firuz Shah Tughluq (r. 1351-88), and his subsequent killing.[24]

The events covered in *Nizami Bansuri* take place between Hardev's arrival from Deogir to Delhi in 1297 and the death of Nizam-ud-Din in 1325. The subsequent events that include Hardev's political career as Ahmad Ayaz are only briefly summarized in the footnotes. It is unclear how Ahmad Ayaz has become identified with the converted Hindu prince of *Chihal Roza*. Barani even mentions Ahmad Ayaz's father who is not a member of Deogiri aristocracy but Ala-ud-Din Ayaz, the chief of police at the Siri fort built by Ala-ud-Din Khalji (r. 1296-1316).[25] Furthermore, considering Barani's attitude towards converted Muslims whose emergence in the Delhi Sultanate he considered 'as a perverse burlesque of the society',[26] it is unlikely that he would not have commented on the background of Ahmad Ayaz had he originally been a Hindu. It is also telling that the fourteenth-century *Siyar-ul-Auliya*,[27] the earliest biography of Nizam-ud-Din and his followers, mentions neither Hardev nor Ahmad Ayaz.[28]

However, there is no reason to challenge Nizami's claim that *Nizami Bansuri* is based on a text called *Chihal Roza* in the light of the literary strategy used in most of his books. The author rarely writes purely fictional text. Instead, he takes historical or contemporary events as a starting point and then embellishes them with Sufi meaning and dramatizing literary touch.[29] What remains unclear is the provenance of *Chihal Roza* and the reason for Ahmad Ayaz's identification with Hardev. If Nizami's account on how the text ended up in Bharatpur is correct, the answer may lie in the largely unexplored literary production of the hereditary guardians of the Nizam-ud-Din shrine. These works include practice manuals, poetry, as well as *tazkiras* incorporating material not found in the earlier works like *Siyar-ul-Auliya*.[30]

The speculations about the provenance of Hardev's story are further frustrated by the fact that it is practically impossible to tell the voice of Nizami apart from that of Hardev. In the process of writing *Nizami Bansuri*, the author reworks the original so thoroughly that the book becomes essentially a literary product of his own. For this reason, *Nizami Bansuri* is best analysed as a twentieth-century text. From the point of view of this chapter, questions about the origins of *Chihal Roza* and the historicity of Hardev's narrative are irrelevant. It is more rewarding to inquire what the author wanted to communicate to his twentieth-century readers by this retelling of medieval history.

The Story of Hardev

Hardev's diary begins in 1295 with a description of the future sultan, Ala-ud-Din Khalji's attack on Deogir. This time, the ruler of Deogir, Ramdev, was able to save his territories from annexation by paying a ransom and promising to pay tribute to the Sultan. However, the growing might of the Delhi Sultanate encouraged him to have a few princes—Hardev among them—tutored in Persian language in order to better communicate with the enemy, if the need arose.[31]

After two years, Ala-ud-Din ascended to the throne in Delhi and sent Amir Hasan Sijzi (d. 1336) as his emissary to Deogir to ensure the continuation of paying the tribute. Amir Hasan happened to be also a close disciple of Nizam-ud-Din who would record the discussions of his master in a work titled *Fawa'id-ul-Fu'ad*. During his sojourn in Deogir, Amir Hasan used to tell stories about Nizam-ud-Din and thus he kindled a desire to personally meet the Sufi master in Hardev's heart. Obtaining permission from his parents, Hardev travelled to Delhi with the returning delegation.[32]

In Delhi, the narrative revolves around Hardev's meetings with Nizam-ud-Din and his disciples. During their first encounter, the prince was warmly welcomed and offered vegetarian food in Nizam-ud-Din's common kitchen (*langar*). Moreover, the food was served from separate places in accordance with the Hindu custom. This provoked protests from certain foreign Muslim travellers, who were, however, silenced by Koranic quotations.[33] Over the following months, Hardev visited Nizam-ud-Din on a regular basis and had long discussions with him and his disciples. He attended the assemblies of the master, during the course of which the participants discussed religious topics and experienced mystical states induced by music and poetry. Over the years, Hardev became a close associate of Nizam-ud-Din, so much so that he was regularly invited to meet the master along with his dearest disciples Amir Khusrau (died 1325) and Sayyid Muhammad Imam, a grandson of Baba Farid-ud-Din Ganj-shakar (d. 1266) living in Delhi.

In Hardev's view, Nizam-ud-Din was a paragon of virtue: truthful, free from scheming and false pretensions. He was a person who saw everyone as equal regardless of his background.[34] But he was also a spiritual stalwart capable of performing miracles (*karamat, kharq-i adat*). The miracles are essential to the narrative, since they feed Hardev's fascination and pull him closer to Nizam-ud-Din. The first miracle Hardev witnessed took place soon after he had arrived in Delhi. He had just met Nizam-ud-Din for the first time and was wandering around the bazaars of the capital city, marvelling at the goods available for purchase. In a shop trading arms, he encountered a vendor who criticized Nizam-ud-Din's practice of *sama'* and how he allowed the disciples to prostrate in front of himself. After a heated argument, Hardev succeeded in persuading the vendor to visit Nizam-ud-Din's hospice (*jama'at-khana*). There, Nizam-ud-Din explicated the vendor these controversial topics before being even asked about them. The vendor repented and became his disciple.[35]

Nizam-ud-Din is also routinely seen managing the affairs of the inhabitants of Delhi. Sometimes the episodes touch only few individuals like in the following story. One day, Nizam-ud-Din received two trays of pearls as a gift from the Sultan. Instead of distributing them to everyone present in the assembly, as was his habit, he gave them to three vagrant mendicants. When Hardev followed these men outside the *jama'at-khana*, he found out that they were in reality his relatives evicted from Deogir after Ala-ud-Din's campaign. Their wanderings had brought them to Delhi, where they had donned the garb of Muslim mendicants in order to secure the generosity of people. The pearls they were given were originally looted from Deogir by Ala-ud-Din and were now returned to their rightful owners. By way of selling the pearls, Hardev's relatives were able to give up their peripatetic lifestyle and establish themselves as cloth merchants.[36]

At other times, Nizam-ud-Din is portrayed as a king-maker. He foretold Muhammad ibn Tughluq's ascension to the throne when he was visiting the *jama'at-khana* incognito, and he bestowed the crown of the Deccan upon an Iranian prince in the form of a piece of bread.[37] On another occasion, Nizam-ud-Din emerges as the virtual protector of Delhi. When the Mongols were about to attack in 1303, Ala-ud-Din Khalji's army was engaged in laying a siege to Chittor. Under these conditions, repelling the invaders was left to Nizam-ud-Din. He begun by a prayer (*du'a*) and then became absorbed in his thoughts. Nizami's description of the anxious anticipation of his disciples, who do not dare to disturb the master, makes the passage one of the most impressive in *Nizami Bansuri* and an excellent example of the author's ability to dramatize his narrative. After some time, Nizam-ud-Din stood up from his seat as if to respect someone's arrival to the assembly. When this was repeated seven times, he turned to his disciples and explained that he had noticed a dog on the street. This dog had reminded him of another dog that used to live in Ajodhan during Baba Farid's lifetime. Nizam-ud-Din interpreted this as an assurance that his prayer would be answered, and he set to saving the city and its inhabitants. He did this by sending to the Mongol chief Targhin a handkerchief he had used for drying his face after ritual ablution. When Targhin placed it respectfully on his eyes, he saw a plot that was spun in his homeland to usurp the power. In order to foil the attempted coup, the Mongol chief turned on his heels and left Delhi unscathed.[38]

Stories of miracles are not limited to fascinated observation, but Hardev acquires personal experience of them as well. Once, he carried out the practice of staying ritually pure for 40 consecutive days and thus achieved the ability to see hidden realms like the hearts of people and objects hidden in the ground.[39] In addition, Nizam-ud-Din taught him, Amir Khusrau and Sayyid Muhammad Imam the art of *ilm-i jafr* by which one could foretell consequences of actions through the application of certain calculations.[40]

Not all extraordinary events Hardev encounters are connected with miracles, but they also include what could be termed mystical experiences. The climax of *Nizami Bansuri* is an episode from which the book derives its title. Once, an eminent deputy (*khalifa*) of Nizam-ud-Din, Nasir-ud-Din Mahmud (d. 1356), presented a *ghazal* to his master. The main topic of this *ghazal* was *wahdat-ul-wujud*, 'oneness of existence'. The core *wujudi* concept that only God really exists while all other being is contingent upon that existence was first discussed by the Spanish-born Ibn 'Arabi (d. 1240) and it subsequently spread throughout the Islamic world.[41] In the beginning of the assembly described by Hardev, Nasir-ud-Din's recitation of the *ghazal* alternated with Nizam-ud-Din's comments. Soon, however, those present were moved to tears. Hardev's interested observation of the course of events turned into an uncontrollable mystical state when Nizam-ud-Din looked into his eyes. Hardev started to shake and eventually lost his self-control and began to dance. The assembly stood up in order to share in his state and musically gifted Sayyid Muhammad Imam begun singing the phrase *contains nothing but love* from Nasir-ud-Din's *ghazal*. Nizam-ud-Din was crying and in his tears Hardev beheld various visions: he saw Deogir, his parents and finally an image (*murti*) of Krishna playing the bamboo flute (*bansuri*). The sound of the flute merged with Sayyid Muhammad's singing. Suddenly, Hardev was inside Nizam-ud-Din's tear, dancing with Krishna, and the entire universe was repeating the phrase *contains nothing but love* in unison. In the end, Hardev lost consciousness and when he came to, the assembly had dispersed.[42] Interestingly, Hardev's experience that involved both Nizam-ud-Din and Krishna is not deemed to require a commentary by the author but is left to stand as it is.

Despite encountering Krishna in Nizam-ud-Din's tear and notwithstanding the lack of pressure to become a Muslim, Hardev converted in the due course. When he inquired about converting from Nizam-ud-Din, the latter answered that the right faith was more important than repeating certain formulaic words. Nizam-ud-Din then went on to ask, if Hardev believed God to be one, Muhammad to be his last prophet and if he would refrain from worshipping idols. When he answered in the affirmative, Nizam-ud-Din noted: 'See, you are already a Muslim'.[43] When the formal conversion later takes place, it is described as a simple, almost commonplace occurrence and it does not feature among the high points of the narrative. Subsequently, Hardev was also initiated into the Chishti-Nizami brotherhood and given the name Ahmad Ayaz by Nizam-ud-Din.[44]

Towards the end of the diary, political events are given more attention and Hardev's ties with the court become firmer. Sultan Qutb-ud-Din Mubarak Shah's antagonism to Nizam-ud-Din is described in detail as is his assassination and the ensuing turmoil.[45] Although Qutb-ud-Din's successor Ghiyas-ud-Din was just and righteous in comparison with his predecessor, his black-and-white understanding of *shari'a* made him suspicious of Nizam-ud-Din. This culminated in summoning Nizam-ud-Din to the royal court to defend the practice of *sama'*.[46] And when Ghiyas-ud-Din was on his campaign in Bengal, he sent letters to his viceregent in Delhi demanding Nizam-ud-Din to leave the city before his return. Although the disciples were growing anxious, Nizam-ud-Din calmly responded to the letters with *hunuz dehli dur ast* (Delhi is still far) and, eventually, Ghiyas-ud-Din never reached the city but died in an accident on his way back. Nizam-ud-Din passed away soon after. Hardev's narrative ends with the building of a dome on Nizam-ud-Din's tomb and Hardev's marriage with the daughter of the new Sultan, Muhammad ibn Tughluq, marking his rise to power.[47]

From *Chihal Roza* to *Nizami Bansuri*

Nizami Bansuri is not a mere translation of *Chihal Roza*. Nizami has also edited, commented upon on, elaborated, annotated and added appendices to the text. The main narrative summarized above includes only those parts of Hardev's diary that discuss Nizam-ud-Din while the remaining portions have been omitted.[48] Since the diary was written over a period of twenty-eight years and hence fragmentary, it had to be reworked into a consistent narrative. So the author filled in the gaps concerning Nizam-ud-Din's life with material derived from the three collections of the master's discussions,[49] the comprehensive biography *Siyar-ul-Auliya* as well as from the works of the Sultanate historians.[50] In addition to the literary sources, the author seems to have drawn from the oral tradition connected with the Nizam-ud-Din shrine. Consequently, the narrative is interspersed with lengthy passages discussing the historical context of the events, Nizam-ud-Din's life before Hardev's arrival in Delhi and Nizam-ud-Din's predecessors. These sections are normally integrated into the narrative as extensive responses by Nizam-ud-Din or one of his disciples to Hardev's inquiries.[51]

The main body of the text is further augmented with copious notes in which Nizami discusses some historical discrepancies or comments on the contemporary relevance of the events described. In addition to the annotated narrative running for 363 pages, *Nizami Bansuri* includes a two-hundred-page appendix that covers the lives of the important disciples of Nizam-ud-Din as well as the history of the shrine where he is entombed.

Although the author included historical background information into *Nizami Bansuri* in the hope of reaching also those without particular interest in Sufism,[52] the core readership of the text has probably always consisted of the disciples of his Sufi lineage. The main function of the text seems to be instructing Sufi disciples through a spiritually nourishing narrative that reads like a historical novel and is both entertaining and educative. *Nizami Bansuri* is a fine specimen of Nizami's literary style. He eschews florid parlance and refrains from using complicated Arabic and Persian vocabulary in favour of lucid and accessible Urdu expressions. His narration is straightforward, almost colloquial, and the rhythm of his writing is akin to spoken language.

The inclusion of footnotes and appendices as well as lengthy passages from other literary and oral sources into the text brings the author's voice forcibly into the work. Through these elaborations, he enters into a dialogue with the past and succeeds in making the medieval events highly relevant to twentieth-century Sufi disciples. Nizam-ud-Din's Sufi practices that were contested by religious scholars in the fourteenth century were also a subject of the criticism of the Deobandis, Tablighi Jamaat and Ahl-i Hadis since the late nineteenth century. The warm welcome of Hardev into the circle of Nizam-ud-Din challenged the idea of clearly defined religious boundaries that had gained currency in twentieth-century India. The passages boldly defending the most controversial Sufi practices and the exploration of similarities between Islam and Hinduism resonate more strongly with the writing context of the book than with the medieval period.

Relationship of Islam and Hinduism is largely discussed in the beginning of Hardev's narrative, when he has freshly arrived in Delhi and strives to conceptualize the phenomena he is encountering in Nizam-ud-Din's *jama'at-khana*. His lengthy discussions with Nizam-ud-Din's disciples cover the life story of Krishna and an explanation of the key teachings of Hindu faith which the author calls Hindu *aqida* by a term borrowed from Islamic theology.[53] When Hardev and his companions compare Hindu and Muslim concepts, the statements often follow the pattern 'in Islam there is a concept *x* which corresponds to the Hindu concept *y*'. This rhetoric presupposes a single reality which different religions describe with varying terms. Parallels are drawn between *muraqaba* and *samadhi* as well as between the Islamic idea of God's essence (*zat*) and qualities (*sifat*) and the concepts of *nirgun* and *sagun*.[54]

This discourse is linked with the author's attempt to portray Nizam-ud-Din as an ideal human being for the needs of all humanity. The notion resonates with the distinctly modern portrayal of South Asian Sufis as benefactors of mankind. This rhetoric is not limited to concrete acts of charity such as feeding the people, but it permeates also the spiritual phenomena. As was mentioned above, Hardev encountered Krishna during the mystical experience induced by Nizam-ud-Din's glance. Sufism is also portrayed as open to non-Muslims. For example, Hardev's parents do not convert, even if they are initiated by Nizam-ud-Din.

Many of Nizam-ud-Din's miracles discussed above recall the manifestations of yogic *siddhis*, but this parallel is never drawn by the author. On the other hand, other similarities with Hindu ascetics require a comment, namely Nizam-ud-Din's celibacy and his apparent vegetarianism. These topics are introduced into *Nizami Bansuri* through a foreigner who argues that Nizam-ud-Din resembles the Hindu ascetics to a great extent. The criticism is countered by explaining that Nizam-ud-Din was afraid that having a family would distract him from the worship of God and thus considered it better not to marry. The question of vegetarianism is left open by noting that all one could say on the matter is that no-one has ever seen him eating meat.[55] In this manner, Nizami strikes a delicate balance in his portrayal of Nizam-ud-Din. He is a spiritual teacher who appeals to people across the religious boundaries, but is simultaneously an exemplary Muslim distinct from Hindu ascetics.

Discussions on controversial practices focus on prostrating in front of the Sufi master[56] and listening to *sama'*. These are mainly dealt within the main narrative[57] whereas a more extensive and nuanced debate on miracles takes place in both Hardev's story and in the author's notes. In his study of Islamic religiosities in nineteenth- and early-twentieth century Bombay, Nile Green demonstrates that the miraculous powers of Sufi saints continued to fascinate in the modernizing industrial city in spite of the rise of secular modernism and Islamic reform. In Green's study, however, the consumers of miracle stories appear different from those advocating modernist and reformist projects.[58] *Nizami Bansuri*, on the other hand, illustrates that in the case of Nizami, the forceful advocation of miracles was not incompatible with his generally modernist, progressive outlook.[59]

According to Nizami, the miracles of Sufis are instances where a human being uses the knowledge of the hidden realm (*ilm-i ghaib*).[60] The question of miracles has immense theological significance, since one of the main contestations of reformist Islamic movements was that only God could know the hidden whereas the Sufis acknowledged that God could make this knowledge available to the prophets and saints. However, Nizami's interest in miracles is not limited to defining a theological stand; he made concrete use of them in his campaign against the Shuddhi movement of Arya Samaj designed to reconvert Muslims into Hinduism. He describes the foiling of Swami Shraddhanand's attempts to reconvert a group of Muslim Rajputs in 1925 in a footnote. The Rajputs stipulated that a miracle should be produced by the Muslims or otherwise they would convert. And so Nizami challenged Swami Shraddhanand to perform four miracles: make a withered tree green, bring water into a dry well, make a cow push the Koran down from a stone instead of the Vedas and spend forty days in a locked house with him without food or water. Swami Shraddhanand declined the challenge and the Rajputs remained Muslims. Later the same year, the author successfully resorted to similar tactics in Burma, where Lala Lajpat Rai was intending to reconvert local Muslims. Nizami notes drily that his activities were decried as un-Islamic by certain Muslim clerics even though they were solely intended to prevent losing Muslims to Arya Samaj.[61]

Conclusion

If *Chihal Roza* was indeed written in the fourteenth century, it would easily be the most detailed account of a Hindu disciple's experiences in the Sultanate Sufi scene. However, it is safe to state only that the text was probably written some time between the mid-fourteenth century and the first half of the eighteenth century, provided the author's account of its looting from the Nizam-ud-Din shrine is correct. However, the existence of such a text indicates that the question of Hindus entering a Sufi brotherhood was considered significant enough to merit an extended discussion. Khwaja Hasan Nizami's choice to base his major work on Hardev's account in the twentieth-century India indicates the continued relevance of the topic.

Nizami Bansuri is layered to the extreme. The text proceeds in the main narrative, in the passages inserted into it from other textual sources and oral traditions as well as in the extensive footnotes and appendices. Numerous agendas and discourses penetrate these textual layers to such an extent that to discuss them all in depth would be impossible here. However, Hardev's experiences remain in the focus throughout the book.

The welcome Hardev is extended by Nizam-ud-Din and his disciples is pronouncedly warm. His Hindu background is taken into consideration whenever food is served and he is given certain Sufi practices to follow when he asks for them. He has open-minded discussions comparing the teachings of the two religions with Nizam-ud-Din's disciples. He is not pressurized to convert to Islam and during his most forceful mystical experience, he sees his beloved deity Krishna in the tear of Nizam-ud-Din. When Hardev eventually converts to Islam, the incident appears as something commonplace, even trivial.

Interestingly, the description of Hardev's experience is not so different from the recent conclusions of historians studying the relationship of Sufis and the Hindu environment during the Sultanate period. The Sufis of *Nizami Bansuri* are neither zealous missionaries nor liberators of the Hindus oppressed by the caste. They are showed as clearly conscious of their identity as Muslims, and although sensitive to the pain of human beings in general, their focus is none the less in the practice of Sufism. Hindus are welcomed to the Sufi circle and their occasional conversion to Islam is greeted with joy. Bearing in mind that *Nizami Bansuri* was written in the twentieth century when various religious groups were increasingly engaging in missionary work, the lack of triumphalism over Hardev's conversion in *Nizami Bansuri* is striking. This attitude is also in marked contrast with the author's exultant description of his anti-Arya Samaj campaign elsewhere in the text.

In respect to the genre, *Nizami Bansuri* is a Sufi disciple's handbook rather than a historical account dealing with religious themes. It teaches rather than describes. It is a cornucopia of information about the formative history of the Chishti-Nizami brotherhood and the Nizam-ud-Din shrine, where the disciples would gather during the annual festivities. It includes arguments that a twentieth-century disciple could utilize on encountering the reformist criticism of Sufi practices like *sama*ʿ and prostrating in front of the shaikh. By the means of Hardev's narrative, the book prescribes the proper etiquette towards Hindu disciples, some of whom may convert like Hardev, while others remain Hindus like Hardev's parents.

When *Nizami Bansuri* is read against its writing context rather than in relation to the medieval period, it is tempting to see it as an attempt to establish a place for Muslims in the increasingly Hindu nation space of India. In retrospect, it is easy to see how deep the communal divide has grown since the partition in 1947. No doubt, the two-nation theory was already taking root and the demand for a separate state for Muslims had been voiced in 1941, when the writing of the book began. Yet I doubt the author foresaw the course the events would take over the following years. Furthermore, it was probably inconceivable to him that the state of Hyderabad, a stronghold of South Asian Muslim culture and home to a great number of his disciples, would cease to exist in 1948.

For this reason, I argue that Hardev's story in *Nizami Bansuri* is not a bid to ease the integration of Muslims into the Hindu nation space, but a legitimation of continued incorporation of Hindu disciples into a Muslim Sufi brotherhood in the era of rising communal tensions. By introducing Hardev among the key characters of the formative period of the Chishti-Nizami brotherhood, Nizami creates a space for Hindu disciples in his own circle by using the historical projection to hallow his undertaking.

Integration of Hindu disciples into a predominately Muslim Sufi brotherhood necessitates an identity that has the potential to transcend the religious boundaries. In *Nizami Bansuri*, this identity is based on the disciples' relationship with the Sufi master. The allegiance and affection towards Nizamuddin shared by Hardev and other disciples is portrayed so powerfully that it makes even the question of a person's religious background secondary. This relationship is in *Nizami Bansuri* the glue that has the potential to bind disciples hailing from different backgrounds together.

Nizami Bansuri is unusual among other religious biographies in that it resists succumbing to archetypal and flat descriptions of characters with set qualities. In part no doubt owing to the influence of contemporary novels, I believe it to be also a reflection of the author's dynamism as a Sufi master and his resistance to standardized versions of Sufism in favour of the more personal approach in, for example, prescribing different sets of practices for different disciples. Undertaking of this effort in *Nizami Bansuri* by a Sufi master, whose countless disciples were scattered over vast geographical areas, indicates the author's conviction that retelling medieval history could be an effective way to address contemporary issues.

Notes

1. For a criticism of the 'liberation' theory, see Aquil, 2004. For a discussion of the 'missionary' theory, see Ernst, 2004: 157-68.
2. Ernst, 2004: 157.
3. Ibid.: 162-4.
4. See Eaton, 1982 and 2006 for Punjab and Bengal, respectively.
5. See Eaton, 1974.
6. See, e.g. Bellamy, 2011; Pinto, 2004 and Sikand, 2004.
7. See Dahnhardt, 2002.
8. For more information on Nizami, see Hermansen, 2001 and Ernst & Lawrence, 2002: 113-18. For his 'official' biography, see Vahidi, 1957, and for a discussion of his literary activities, see Deobandi, 2007 and Bakhsh, 2012.
9. Nizami, 2009a: 9.
10. See Hermansen, 2001: 328-9 and Ernst & Lawrence, 2002: 115-16.
11. On taxation, see Nizami, 1917.
12. See Nizami, 2006 for a lengthy discussion on *Hizb al-Bahr*, the celebrated prayer composed by Abu'l-Hasan ash-Shadhili (d. 1258).
13. He usually debated these in the pages of the Urdu newspapers *Sufi*, *Munadi* and *Zamindar*.
14. See Nizami, 2007a and 2007b, respectively.
15. See Nizami, 2012.
16. See Nizami, 1933.

17. See Nizami, 2009b. For a discussion on the Middle East travelogue, see Viitamäki, 2013.
18. See Nizami, 1922.
19. See Nizami, 2008.
20. It is interesting to note that, contrary to the common practice of his contemporaries professing literary ambitions, Nizami concentrated almost exclusively on writing prose instead of poetry.
21. Nizami, 2009a: 11.
22. An attempt to determine the audience a printed book reached in mid-twentieth-century India remains incomplete, if the fact that books were often read aloud to the illiterate is overlooked. The author acknowledges the practice by invoking blessings for both the readers and hearers in the beginning of *Nizami Bansuri* (Nizami, 2009a: 3).
23. Nizami, 2009a: 291.
24. See Barani, 2005: 481, 491, 509, 520, 539-48 and Firishta, 1967: 449, 470, 475-6, 483-6. For Nizami's more lenient interpretation of Ahmad Ayaz's rebellion, see Nizami, 2009a: 53-4.
25. Barani, 2005: 278.
26. Aquil, 2004: 218. For a detailed discussion on Barani's attitude towards Hindus and converted Muslims, see Aquil, 2009: 48-75.
27. al-Kirmānī 1885.
28. Both Barani (2005: 389) and Firishta (1967: 416) as well as Amir Khusrau (1949: 191-202) mention a certain Harpal Dev who rose against the Sultan Qutb-ud-Din Mubarak Shah (r. 1316-20) in Deogir. He was soon defeated and Deogir was forced to pay heavy tribute to the Sultan. In his account of the events in *Nuh Sipihr*, Khusrau occasionally portrays Hindus in favourable light, yet commonalities between Harpal Dev and Hardev do not go beyond the similarity of the name and the connection with Deogir. It is thus difficult to conceive Harpal Dev as an inspiration for Hardev's character. For a discussion of Turk and Hindu in *Nuh Sipihr*, see Gabbay, 2010: 66-85.
29. Nizami's Sufi interpretation of the abdication of Edward VIII in 1936 is a fascinating specimen of a work where this literary strategy is utilized. See Nizami, 1937.
30. See, for example, *Matlub-ut-Talibin* (Bulaq, 1899) written during the reign of Muhammad Shah 'Rangila' by Khwaja Muhammad Bulaq. The work was translated into Urdu as *Shavahid-i Nizami* by Ghulam Nizamuddin in 1899.

31. Nizami, 2009a: 16-19.
32. Ibid.: 23, 26.
33. Ibid.: 28-9.
34. Ibid.: 31.
35. Ibid.: 40-1.
36. Ibid.: 94-5, 174.
37. Ibid.: 320, 322.
38. Ibid.: 89-94.
39. Ibid.: 195-6.
40. Ibid.: 298.
41. This passage of *Nizami Bansuri* is somewhat anachronistic, since *wujudi* metaphysics reached India only during the decades following Nizam-ud-Din's death. For an overview of Indian *wujudi* literature, see Chittick, 1992.
42. Nizami, 2009a: 81-3.
43. Ibid.: 192.
44. Ibid.: 209, 291.
45. Ibid.: 238, 248, 288-90.
46. Ibid.: 302-14.
47. Ibid.: 341, 350, 362.
48. Ibid.: 363.
49. I.e. *Fawa'id al-Fu'ad* by Amir Hasan Sijzi as well as *Afzal-ul-Fawa'id* and *Rahat-ul-Muhibbin*, both attributed to Amir Khusrau.
50. Nizami, 2009a: 12, 15.
51. See, e.g. Nizami, 2009a: 19-23, 57-68 and 101-48.
52. Nizami, 2009a: 15.
53. Ibid.: 76-8.
54. Ibid.: 75.
55. Ibid.: 347-8, 351.
56. Nizami has also written a separate treatise on the difference between the prostration of respect (*sajda-yi ta'zim*) in front of a Sufi master and the prostration of worship (*sajda-yi ibadat*) reserved for God. See Nizami, 2005.
57. See, e.g. Nizami, 2009a: 302-14, 324-5, 329-32.
58. See Green, 2011, especially 49-89.
59. For a discussion of Nizami's progressive Sufi modernism in the context of his 1911 tour to Middle East, see Viitamäki, 2013.
60. Nizami, 2009a: 200.
61. Ibid.: 201-4.

References

Aquil, Raziuddin. 2004. 'Scholars, Sufis and Sultans: Some Aspects of Religion and Politics in the Delhi Sultanate', *Indian Historical Review*, 31(1-2): 210-20.

________. 2009. *In the Name of Allah: Understanding Islam and Indian History.* New Delhi: Penguin Viking.

Bakhsh, Maula. 2012. *Khwaja Hasan Nizami ki Nasr. Saqafati La'iha-yi Amal.* Delhi: Arshia Publications.

Barani, Ziyauddin. 2005. *Tarikh-i Firuz-shahi.* Sir Syed Ahmad Khan, ed. Aligarh: Sir Syed Academy.

Bellamy, Carla. 2011. *The Powerful Ephemeral: Everyday Healing in an Ambiguously Islamic Place.* Ranikhet: Permanent Black.

Bulaq, Khwaja Muhammad. 1899. *Shavahid-i Nizami Mashhur ba-Matlub-ut-Talibin.* tr. Zamin Ali, Delhi: Matba'-i Jan-i Jahan.

Chittick, William C. 1992. 'Notes on Ibn al-'Arabi's Influence in the Subcontinent', *The Muslim World*, 82 (3-4): 218-41.

Dahnhardt, Thomas. 2002. *Change and Continuity in Indian Sūfīsm: A Naqshbandi-Mujaddidī Branch in the Hindu Environment.* New Delhi: D.K. Printworld.

Deobandi, Majid. 2007. *Khwaja Hasan Nizami: Ek Tahqiqi Mutali'a.* Delhi: Anjum Book Depot.

Eaton, Richard M. 1974. 'Sufi Folk Literature and the Expansion of Indian Islam', *History of Religions*, 14(2): 117-27.

________. 1982. 'The Political and Religious Authority of the Shrine of Bābā Farīd', in Barbara Metcalf, ed., *Moral Conduct and Authority: The Place of Adab in South Asian Islam*, pp. 333-56. Berkeley: University of California Press.

________. 2006 [1993]. *The Rise of Islam and the Bengal Frontier 1204-1760.* New Delhi: Oxford University Press.

Ernst, Carl W. 2004 [1992]. *Eternal Garden: Mysticism, History, and Politics at a South Asian Sufi Center.* New Delhi: Oxford University Press.

Ernst, Carl W. and Bruce B. Lawrence. 2002. *Sufi Martyrs of Love: The Chishti Order in South Asia and Beyond.* New York: Palgrave Macmillan.

Firishta, Muhammad Qasim. 1967. *Tarikh-i Firishta*, vol. I, ed. Muhammad Reza Nasiri. Teheran: Anjuman-i Asar o Mafakhir-i Firangi.

Gabbay, Alyssa. 2010. *Islamic Tolerance: Amir Khusraw and Pluralism.* New York: Routledge.

Green, Nile. 2011. *Bombay Islam: The Religious Economy of the West Indian Ocean, 1840-1915*. New York: Cambridge University Press.

Hermansen, Marcia. 2001. 'Common Themes, Uncommon Contexts: The Sufi Movements of Hazrat Inayat Khan and Khwaja Hasan Nizami', in Pirzade Zia Inayat Khan, ed., *A Pearl in Wine: Essays on the Life, Music and Sufism of Hazrat Inayat Khan*, pp. 322-53. New Lebanon: Omega Publications.

Khusrau, Amir. 1949. *The Nuh Sipihr of Amir Khusrau (Islamic Research Association Series, No. 12)*. Ed. Mohammad Wahid Mirza. Calcutta: Oxford University Press.

al-Kirmani, Muhammad Mubarak al-Alawi Amir Khvurd. 1885. *Siyar-ul-Auliya*. Delhi: Matba'-i Muhibb.

Nizami, Khwaja Hasan. 1917. *Khuda'i Inkum Taiks*. Delhi: n.p.

________. 1922. *Ap-biti*. Delhi: Halqa-e Mashaikh Book Depot.

________. 1933. *Qadim o Jadid Afghanistan ke Do Safarname: Ek Har [sic] Majasti Ghazi Muhammad Badshah Tajdar-i Afghnistan ka, Dusra Musavvir-i Fitrat Khwaja Hasan Nizami Dihlavi ka*. Delhi: Halqa-e Mashaikh Book Depot.

________. 1937. *A Modern Gulistan for Modern Man: Ex-King Edward's Diary, "The Sufi's Secret of Real Happiness"*. Delhi: Munadi.

________. 2005 [*c.* 1970]. *Murshid ko Sajda-yi Ta'zim*. New Delhi: Khwaja Hasan Sani Nizami.

________. 2006 [1952]. *A'mal-i Hizb al-Bahr*. New Delhi: Khwaja Hasan Sani Nizami.

________. 2007a. *Tartili Tarjuma-yi Qur'an Majid (Urdu)*. New Delhi: Khwaja Hasan Sani Nizami.

________. 2007b. *Tartili Tarjuma-e Qur'an Majid (Hindi)*. New Delhi: Khwaja Hasan Sani Nizami.

________. 2008. *1857. Shams-ul-Ulama Hazrat Khwaja Hasan Nizami ki Barah Qadim Yadgar Kitaben*. New Delhi: Khwaja Hasan Sani Nizami.

________. 2009a [1945]. *Nizami Bansuri*. New Delhi: Khwaja Hasan Sani Nizami.

________. 2009b [1913]. *Safarnama: Hijaz, Misr, Sham, Filastin o Lubnan*. New Delhi: Khwaja Hasan Sani Nizami.

________. 2012 [1932]. *Tarikhi Roznamcha: 1931*. New Delhi: Khwaja Hasan Sani Nizami.

Pinto, Desiderio. 2004 [1989]. 'The Mystery of the Nizamuddin Dargah: The Accounts of Pilgrims', in Christian W. Troll, ed., *Muslim Shrines in India: Their Character, History and Significance*, pp. 112-24. New Delhi: Oxford University Press.

Sikand, Yoginder. 2004. 'Shared Hindu-Muslim Shrines in Karnataka: Challenges to Liminality', in Imtiaz Ahmad and Helmut Reifeld, eds., *Lived Islam in South Asia. Adaptation, Accommodation and Conflict*, pp. 166-86. New Delhi: Social Science Press.

Vahidi, Mulla. 1957. *Savanih-i Umri Imam-ul-Masha'ikh Shams-ul-Ulama Musavvir-i Fitrat Hazrat Khwaja Sayyid Hasan Nizami Dihlavi*. Delhi: Munadi.

Viitamäki, Mikko. 2013. 'Modern Conveyances, Traditional Destinations: Khvāja Hasan Nizami's Tour to the Middle East in 1911', in Sylvia Akar, Jaakko Hämeen-Anttila and Inka Nokso-Koivisto, eds., *Travelling through Time: Essays in Honour of Kaj Öhrnberg* (Studia Orientalia 114), Helsinki: Finnish Oriental Society, pp. 213-32.

Contributors

RAZIUDDIN AQUIL is Associate Professor in the Department of History, University of Delhi. He has extensively published on Islamic religious movements, literary and historical traditions, comparative historiography, and political culture in medieval and early modern India. His books include *Sufism, Culture, and Politics: Afghans and Islam in Medieval North India* (OUP); *In the Name of Allah: Understanding Islam and Indian History* (Penguin-Viking), and (co-edited) *History in the Vernacular* (Permanent Black).

MATTHEW CLARK is a freelance lecturer, researcher and musician (Mahabongo). Since 2004, he has been affiliated to the School of Oriental and African Studies (SOAS), University of London, as a Postgraduate Research Associate. His publications include *The Daśanāmī-Saṃnyāsīs: The Integration of Ascetic Lineages into an Order* (E.J. Brill) and (co-edited) *Creating a Dialogue: Text Belief and Personal Identity (Proceedings of the Valmiki Studies Workshop)*, (SOAS).

DAVID L. CURLEY is Professor Emeritus in the Department of Liberal Studies, Western Washington University. He received a PhD in modern South Asian History from the University of Chicago under the direction of Bernard S. Cohen, where he also studied Bengali and Bengali literature with Edward C. Dimock, Jr. and Clinton B. Seeley. He has published a collection of interdisciplinary essays on social history and literary criticism: *Poetry and History: Bengali Mangal-kabya and Social Change in Precolonial Bengal* (Chronicle), as well as other, more recent essays on this topic. His current research is on changing identities and moral sentiments before and after the British conquest in Bengal.

SCOTT KUGLE is a research scholar in comparative religion and Islamic culture. He serves as Associate Professor at Emory University (USA) in the Department of Middle Eastern and South Asian Studies. He has conducted research in India, Pakistan, Morocco and the Netherlands, and has lived and taught in Hyderabad, India. His research focuses on Sufism, on devotional poetry and music, and on gender. He has published six books and many articles. His forthcoming book is about gender and spirituality with regard to Urdu poetry written in the late eighteenth and early nineteenth centuries in the Deccan region (focusing on the poets Siraj Awrangabadi and Mahlaqa Bai Chanda).

MRIDULA JHA teaches history at PGDAV College (Evening), University of Delhi. She holds a PhD degree from Jamia Millia Islamia on 'Dara Shikuh: A Study of his Life and Works'. She has co-edited *Beesvi Shatabdi Mein Vishwa Itihaas ke Pramukh Mudde* and *Vishwa Itihaas ke Pramukh Mudde: Badalte Aayam* for the Directorate of Hindi Medium, University of Delhi. She is currently working on a monograph on Dara Shikuh.

SUDESHNA PURKAYASTHA is Associate Professor in the Department of History, Assam University, Silchar. Her research interests include modern Indian economic history and questions of Assamese historiography. She is the author of *Indigenous Industries of Assam, 1870-1925* (K.P. Bagchi).

SANDHYA SHARMA teaches History at Vivekananda College, University of Delhi. She holds a PhD degree from Jawaharlal Nehru University, New Delhi. She has been exploring Braj Bhasha poetry for studying society and culture in Medieval India, and is the author of *Literature, Culture and History in Mughal North India, 1550-1800* (Primus).

MIKKO VIITAMÄKI is completing his doctoral studies at the University of Helsinki. His dissertation analyses the usages of poetry in South Asian Sufi practice with special reference to *qawwali* music. His other research interests include Sufism in colonial and post-colonial periods and the popularization of Ibn 'Arabi's thoughts in the Indian subcontinent. He also teaches courses on Islam with an emphasis on South Asia at the University of Helsinki. He has published articles on Sufi poetry and Sufism in modern India in *Studia Orientalia*, *Oriente Moderno*, and in other edited volumes.

Index